ROBERT LAIDLAW

MAN
FOR OUR
TIME

March 2000

Castle Publishing Ltd
PO Box 68-800 Newton,
Auckland, New Zealand
Phone +64-9-378 4052
Fax +64-9-376 3855

ISBN 0-9582124-0-6

Printed in New Zealand
by Wentforth Print
Cover design by Jeff Hagan

ROBERT LAIDLAW

MAN FOR OUR TIME

IAN HUNTER

CASTLE PUBLISHING
AUCKLAND
NEW ZEALAND

FOREWORD

BY

DAVID LEVENE

"Call me Bob, David." With those words one of the princes of the Auckland business community welcomed me into the Auckland Rotary Club. Thus did Robert Laidlaw make it easy for me – then a very young man and a newcomer to such exalted company, replete with what would be known today as the city's movers and shakers – to enter into the club and become part of it. I have always remembered him with affection for that.

But Robert Laidlaw had had a memorable effect on my life long before then – from my childhood, in fact. Back then my mother would take me into the city and we would go to the Farmers to have lunch in the cafeteria – invariably pie and potatoes – then I would be allowed to play on the tricycles and pedal cars in the children's play area. There were the odd trikes in our neighbourhood – we were relatively poor – but no one had a pedal car, and to play on them at Farmers was really something.

As I grew older my parents would give my cousin and me sixpence each and we would ride into town on the tram for a penny, have our pie and potatoes at Farmers for fourpence, and have a penny left to get home again. But the food wasn't nearly as attractive as the time we spent in the play area, devised by Robert Laidlaw to make shopping easier for parents, mothers particularly. Those memories are treasured, even today.

When I began work with my father and uncle in our little paint shop in Karangahape Rd, I used to think about Farmers and dream that perhaps one day I might be involved in a vast enterprise like that. And, of course, they had a paint and wallpaper department which I used to visit regularly, looking at what the competition was up to. I doubt, though, that they saw me as competition.

So, as was the case for tens and tens of thousands of other Aucklanders, Robert Laidlaw and the business he founded and developed had a not insignificant influence on my life. He commanded immense respect in all areas of the Auckland community – and further afield, as well. I never heard an ill word spoken of him and if any further testimony were needed to his qualities as a gentleman, it is to be found in the children he helped to bring up – very fine people.

David Levene

FROM THE LAIDLAW FAMILY

We have been delighted to act as sounding boards for Ian Hunter as he has meticulously researched this absorbing account of the life of the innovative entrepreneur and open-hearted Christian who was our father. And we have been intrigued to learn a number of things about him that we didn't know.

There is probably no more precious gift a father can give to his children than the knowledge that they have not only his love but his respect. And that is what our Dad gave us. Never did he talk down to us, nor did he belittle our ideas. We always felt we could discuss anything with him and that our opinions counted. Even when, with his incisive and logical mind, he noted weaknesses in our arguments, they were always gently and kindly pointed out.

Dad's warm personality and his caring consideration for his family are still fresh in our memories. Dad's ready sense of humour and his delight in tackling new projects made life with him a constant and exciting adventure. He was an early example of the "can do" man who was never daunted by the apparent difficulty of a task. Whether it was building a stone wall, dismantling and reassembling a gearbox, preparing a speech to deliver to an audience of 3000 or persuading a bank manager to lend him a fortune on the sole security of his word.

While there is no doubt that at work he was a high achiever, at home – be it Auckland or Taupo – he took time to amuse a four-year-old Lillian (and anyone else who was listening) with the world travels and exciting adventures of an imaginary "Poppy Porpoise," who travelled the world with a little girl on her back.

And he would even find time to spend several hours each Saturday morning teaching 13-year-old Lincoln to paint with oils. What more could you ask of a father? We were indeed fortunate to be his children and we hope that as you, the reader, get to know him through this book, some of what made Robert Laidlaw the man he was, will rub off on you, too.

ACKNOWLEDGMENTS

I wish to convey my deep thanks to many people and organisations who have helped with the research and production of this book. First and foremost my wife, Debra, whose unstinting support for this book from inception to completion was amazing. She heard more than any other person "I'll be finished in three weeks," and still managed a smile every time. Secondly, my grandmother, Eve Hunter, whose generous support and commitment meant this book could be a reality. Her tireless sacrifice for future generations leaves us all richer.

Lincoln and Lillian Laidlaw tirelessly answered my many questions, and their thoughtful comments added so much to the final work.

Librarians and staff at the following institutions were of great assistance in sourcing material and gaining access to collections. The University of Auckland Library, The Auckland Institute Library (War Memorial Museum) who hold the Farmers archives. Also the library of the Bible College of New Zealand and in particular archivist Christine Tetley. Historian David Billing carried out investigations in the South Island at both the Hocken Library and the archives of Otago Boys High School.

The Auckland Public Library, New Zealand Herald Library and the Library of the Assembly Bible School were also very useful. To Campbell Fountain who assisted with Treasury archives I express my thanks. Thanks also to the Farmers Trading Company in Auckland for granting access to the Hobson Street Store, and to Rob Clarke and Wyn Christian for their assistance.

Special mention goes to the late Rawdon Busfield, whom I

had the privilege to interview just days before his death. Thanks too to Wayne Walden of the present day Farmers Trading Company for greeting the project with such enthusiasm.

I gratefully acknowledge too the support of the Historical Branch of the Internal Affairs Department (NZ), whose award in history was a great help in the research and writing of this work.

I extend my sincere thanks to Blyth Harper who gladly joined my panel of editors and provided willing 'translations'of Robert's handwriting on numerous occasions.

Thanks also to Garth George and Stewart Hillman whose editorial expertise polished the finished product considerably, and to John Massam of Challenge Communications who caught the vision.

To the many friends and colleagues of Robert Laidlaw in various capacities who gave their time and memories I am very grateful. In no special order: Frances Yeoman, Marjorie Bardsley, Ken Hunt, Gilbert Hicks, John Massam, Les Rushbrook, Ruth and Griff Harvey, Alan Mason, Trevor Bond, Fred King, Wyn Christian, the late Joe Setters, Grace Laurie-Walker, David Stewart, Tom and Marjorie Haughey, David Burt, David and Deane Liddle.

It is popular sometimes for biographers to critically analyse the events and activities of their subject. In writing this book I have chosen not to do so. What you have here is the essential story. All the recorded text in the book came from tape recordings, transcripts or other documentary records.

This project is the culmination of seven years of research and writing, even so, the more I find out about Robert Laidlaw the more I am astounded at the expanse of his accomplishments, and of the thousands, possibly millions of people his life affected in some way or another. I am convinced I could spend the rest of my days and still there would be more people to talk to, more instances to record. But it has to end somewhere, so I end this acknowledgment with an apology. To those who knew him personally; maybe as a child playing at the Farmers Trading Company, or a soldier on the battlefields of Europe, or a businessman in need of advice, to the many whose precious memory is not recorded here I ask your forgiveness. But I trust you will join with me in hoping the recollections and the story recorded here, will encourage and inspire yet another generation, as he has already done for you.

Ian Hunter
Auckland
May 1999

*To Debra
with all my love*

CONTENTS

Early on Monday morning Robert turned the corner from Queen Street into Fort Street and made his way quickly along the pavement. A dark three piece suit of English manufacture hung elegantly on his frame and on his head a black bowler hat – the very height of fashion. Jack hastened along behind his brother who strode through the early morning crowd with characteristic resolve. The traffic in Fort Street was continuous. Dozens of drays pulled by obedient Clydesdales made their way back and forth. Some were bound for the ports to uplift their first cargoes, others were already discharging into the cavernous loading docks pocketed in the grey buildings. It was clearly downtown Auckland, yet it could have easily been the back streets of Chicago. The sounds of commerce were international.

Robert looked up. His target lay straight ahead and nestled in amongst the three and four-storeyed giants was his small two-storeyed shop. He paused momentarily. Four years of planning and preparation had gone into this day – an entire life's saving. It was one of those moments that come but once in a lifetime and he knew it. Whatever happened from this day forward his life would never be the same again. He crossed the street and in his pocket his hand found the key. He opened the door and there at his feet lay a small pile of letters. A brief smile crossed his lips – he was in business.

✤ ✤ ✤ ✤ ✤ ✤

1

NEW ZEALAND BOUND

Scotland 1885

"You must use what you have to get what you want. You must start from where you are to get to any destination. You can carry with you only what you have."[1]

Robert Laidlaw, 1915.

The road between Peebles and Dalry was never easy. Sitting upright in a tightly buttoned tunic, a young Scotsman spurred the horses on for the last few miles. His face looked tired, his eyes partly shadowed by the peak of his driving hat, his large brown moustache covered his lips. Huddled closely by his side, his young wife sat awkwardly on the wooden seat. She too tried to show some interest but by now she was worn out. Her long brown hair so neatly tied up at the beginning of the trip had fallen loosely round her face. With one hand she clasped the seat as they lurched along, the other rested gently on her stomach. Her dark flowing dress only partly concealed her obvious discomfort. She was in the latter stages of pregnancy, and although this was meant to be a holiday she wondered if they had left it too late.

At last they neared the cottage. They had come here several times before, and its tiled roof and plastered sides spoke of a welcome meal and fresh sheets. As the summer's day came to a close the young couple, Robert and Jessie Laidlaw, unpacked their belongings and settled themselves into their new surroundings. Their journey of several days had brought them to the town of Dalry on the west coast of Scotland. It was a pleasant spot, not too far from the sea and nestled in grassy hill country. A picturesque place, it had become a popular holiday retreat and the young couple had looked forward for some time to this break away from the pressures of the family business.[2]

As the days passed it became clear that the birth of their first child was not far away. Jessie's discomfort increased and she went into labour. On September 8 1885, at 3.30 pm, she gave birth to a son. Robert looked down into the infant's face. His first-born and a boy as well. He felt a surge of emotion as he touched the little fingers and arms. The birth had gone well and the newborn was a picture of health. He had big blue eyes and a thick matt of dark brown hair.

Finding a name for him was easy and Robert proudly announced that the child would be named after himself, Robert. It was something of a family tradition. He had been named likewise by his father, and his grandfather before him. The infant's full name, Robert Alexander Crookston Laidlaw, was quickly shortened by his adoring parents and he became affectionately known as 'Bertie.'

With little Bertie in tow the family returned to Peebles, the small village where they lived, about 90 miles inland. This time the journey was sweetened as Jessie cradled the child in her arms, arriving home to a tumultuous welcome. The entire extended family lived in and around the district and all came to see this new little Laidlaw.

They were a popular family and worked a large woollen mill in the nearby town of Hawick. Grandfather Laidlaw owned the mill and under his watchful eye it had grown into a successful business. Ten hours a day, six days a week its expansive rooms filled with the sounds of knitting machines constantly working away. His sons all took charge of different parts of the operation and Robert, who was the traveller for the firm, sold their wares travelling up to Edinburgh and across to Glasgow. The business had gone from strength to strength.

Not long into the new year Grandfather Laidlaw called his sons together. He had been thinking for some time of stepping down and letting one of his sons take his place at the head of the business. The old Scotsman announced the obvious and, as tradition would have it, passed the business on to James, his eldest. Robert was not completely surprised but it still came as a shock. He had not expected it so soon. The family firm had suited him well, especially as he and Jessie now had Bertie. Yet he had the same passion for business as his father, and had no desire to make his brother rich. There seemed to be little left for him in Hawick, and with the family inheritance decided he began to consider his options further afield.

By the mid-1880s, colonial expansion was well under way and many Scots had already travelled as far as New Zealand. The woollen trade in particular was proving popular in the new colony, and some who had ventured out earlier were already returning home looking for skilled workers to staff their growing factories. Robert and Jessie had heard such stories and decided it worth the risk. They packed up what possessions they owned, as well as some hand-operated knitting machines from the factory, and journeyed south to catch a boat for New Zealand.

On October 23 1886, when Bertie was barely 13 months old, a small cluster of family members huddled together at the Plymouth docks on the Cornish coast. It seemed a world away from their peaceful Scottish home of Hawick. The masts of the steamers and schooners stretched skyward and rows of oceangoing ships lined the famous port. Parties of sailors, dock workers and traders all seemed to be moving in unison as endless crates and cargo bustled round the busy wharves. Jessie clutched little Bertie even closer. Next to her stood her mother, Grandma Crookston, and two other relatives, Auntie Annie and cousin Alice.[3] Their booking had been a last-minute affair. Jessie had desperately wanted her mother to travel with them, not sure if she might ever see her again. It had taken some convincing but eventually she had elected to come, and altogether they made a party of six.

Before them lay their impressive transportation, the R.M.S. *Aorangi*, a direct mail steamer of the New Zealand Shipping Company line. She was a new ship, only three years old, and her white sides with a single row of tiny symmetrical portholes glistened in the sun. Atop her decks were a maze of intricate railings. In the middle of her three masts a large black funnel whispered the first signs of travel. Steamers of her size were a relatively new innovation and had started to make the crossings between the Mother Country and New Zealand in record time, despite their large cargoes. Fully laden, the *Aorangi* carried over 300 passengers as well as 2500 tons of cargo.

She pulled out of the docks at 2 pm and headed south. The family watched as Land's End disappeared into the distance, then with the other passengers settled into the relative comfort of the steamer's saloons and dining areas. It was a turbulent introduction to sea travel. A strong head gale and high seas made the passage through the North Atlantic less than pleasant until the Bay of Biscay when at last the weather moderated. They reached Madeira on October 27 before heading down the African coast. Fresh trade winds and head seas again made progress irksome until they reached Capetown 16 days later.

After taking on board supplies and cargo the *Aorangi* pulled out that evening to begin the journey across the Southern Ocean. At last they found fine weather and with gentle breezes the many deck amusements could finally be put to good use. At night, with an irresistible charm, the southern sky lured eager admirers onto the ship's broad decks.

The time passed quickly. Three weeks later, as the morning sun broke, they caught their first glimpse of New Zealand's shores. Within a few hours Captain Turpin and his crew had negotiated Dunedin Harbour and at 8.15 am on the morning of Thursday, December 2, the *Aorangi* drew up to the George Street pier, 39 days after they'd left England. Passengers and crew were in good health and the Laidlaws disembarked, ready for life in their new land.[4]

Dunedin was a logical choice, a growing city of 40,000 people near the bottom of the South Island of New Zealand. It had rapidly developed into the centre of commerce for the new colony. A variety of manufacturing industries had sprung up and were producing textiles and other goods for the local area. Since the early 1880s the colony had been in the throes of a sharp recession but the effects on Dunedin were mixed. Some sectors like farming had been badly affected, but the woollen industry seemed to be in good shape. The nearby Mosgiel Woollen Mills had just undergone a major expansion programme and electric lighting had been installed in their new brick factory.[5]

Robert had some savings from home, but rather than buy property he chose to put whatever money he had into business and rented a small house in Maitland Street on the town belt. He could easily have applied for a job at the local mills but had not travelled 12,000 miles to work for somebody else. Instead he set himself the task of earning a living from the knitting machines he had brought with him from the factory back home.

It quickly became a family affair, and with local wool Grandma Crookston and Jessie knitted socks on the machines as Bertie played at their feet on the stone kitchen floor. Robert then sold their wares in the streets to goldminers heading off to the Otago fields.

Business was difficult, however, and his enthusiasm for the new colony waned. Six weeks after they arrived he returned home one afternoon completely disheartened, having sold nothing. Angrily he pushed open the door to their small house.

"We are going to pack up and get back to the old country at once."

Jessie and her mother sat at the table stunned at the prospect.

"I can earn a living there, but not in this place."

His spirit was nearly broken and Jessie didn't know what to say. She had watched her husband's anguish at the bleak trade in the city's streets. It was Grandma Crookston who spoke up. She was smaller than her daughter but having travelled to the other side of the globe was not about to pack up and head home again.

"I am not going," she declared. Robert moved uneasily on his feet, the outburst had taken him by surprise. "Six weeks," she continued, "is not a fair test of how things might turn out, Robert Laidlaw." He had no option. The Laidlaws were staying – and stay they did.

It was not long, however, before Grandma Crookston's words proved correct and trade turned for the better. Selling woollen socks made in the kitchen grew into an entire hosiery factory. Robert busied himself with his business activities and Bertie was reared under the watchful eye of his grandmother, while his mother attended to the affairs of the household. Over the next few years further newborns were added to the fold. First was a sister, Minnie, and then in 1889 a brother, Arthur, and in 1892 another brother, John. Their youngest child, Queenie, was born in 1897.

They were a Christian family and had attended a local

Brethren church in Scotland. When they arrived in Dunedin they joined a fellowship meeting in Dunedin's Farley Hall in the centre of town, and while Robert did not wait long to throw his energies into business, neither did he delay when it came to Christian activities.[6]

Not long after settling he hired a tent and held his own open-air meeting in one of Dunedin's suburbs. Often on late nights he would venture in to the city with several other men from the church and preach in High Street. It was a busy life and Bertie and the other children were taught the Bible by their grandmother in a home where there was no gambling, no cards and no dancing.

When Bertie turned five he started attending Dunedin's Kensington primary school not far from their home. A busy and frisky little boy, he showed early on the characteristic Laidlaw nerve. Once while walking along the High Street with his mother they strolled past a chocolate factory. The beautiful smell wafting through the air proved too much, and attired in a handsome blue sailor suit he ran over and peered through a grate into the lower levels of the building.

Inside he saw two men hard at work making the enticing treats. Bertie's attentions annoyed one of the men who, grabbing a nearby jug of water, hurled it up through the grating and soaked him. He didn't run to his mother or cry, simply turned around and walked to the street a few feet away. Taking his cap off he bent down, filled it full of stones and went back for the attack, flinging it at his unsuspecting victims below!

At the end of January 1894, three months after his eighth birthday, he was enrolled at High Street Primary school with his sister Minnie and cousin Alice, where they completed their primary education. His younger brothers Arthur and Jack followed in successive years. By now the family's business activities in Dunedin had prospered significantly and in 1896, at the age of 37, Robert moved his family out of their Maitland Street home and over to the more progressive district of St Clair, leasing a house in Forbury Rd. He also sold his woollen factory and with the proceeds joined forces with another Scot, John Gray, buying the Dunedin firm of Johnston's Hardware. The pair aptly renamed their fledgling business, Laidlaw & Gray.

Bertie, now 11, began working outside school hours in the new family firm as a cash boy. It was a good job for him. He had lots of energy and loved being with his father in the business. The salesmen took the order from the customer, and Bertie took it from the salesmen to the central cash desk, returning with change and receipt. Trade was brisk and soon Laidlaw & Gray opened another branch in Timaru, not far up the coast.

His schooling progressed quickly and he did well at school, if not a little distracted by the interests of business. Finishing Standard 6 in August of 1899 he went on to the private Otago Boys High School – a daily two-mile cycle for him across Dunedin. Already it had been quite a year with the move to a new school and his 14th birthday, as well as the prestigious Dunedin Exhibition. Thousands had flocked to see the imposing displays and spectacular entertainments. Bertie too had made his mark. One of his loves was painting, and he had spent many long hours practising his technique and painting scenes from the coast as well as copying the works of other artists. One of these he had entered into the Exhibition, and won the Under 17-year-old category for artists with a painting of a South Island fiord. It was quite a triumph.

Not all his pursuits were so passive and as much as any lad he enjoyed the thrill of hunting. He mastered firearms quite early and was allowed to hunt by himself in the hills surrounding Dunedin. One afternoon he and another local lad, Jack, shouldered their rifles and headed off to see what they could shoot. Coming to a densely wooded valley they split up and Jack ventured up one spur while he went up the other. After walking about a mile, he began to feel very alone in the quiet of the dense bush. Looking over to the other side he tried to spot his companion but there was no sign of him.

Suddenly, without warning, an awful thought came upon him, one he'd had before as a youngster in the dead of night. His grandmother had taught him about Christ's second coming and now it seemed it had happened. Jack had been taken and left him behind. He yelled at the top of his voice across the valley and waited for Jack's voice but there was no reply. He yelled again but again no answer.

Running headlong through the bush he called out Jack's name over and over but still there was no reply. Worn out, he fell to the ground, now certain that he was alone.[7] He had gone to church every Sunday with his family but he hadn't become a Christian and now it was too late; nothing but judgment awaited him. His whirling mind was interrupted by a cracking sound in the trees. As the undergrowth parted Jack's friendly face appeared and Bertie's fears fell away. In the joy of the moment he also put aside his thoughts of God.

For the next two years he attended Otago Boys High and not being adept at languages took a commercial course studying bookkeeping and commercial practice. In the summer months he played cricket for the junior team as well as trying out his skill as a swimmer at the school's inaugural swimming tournament in May 1901. In the backstroke race he managed to get through to the second heat but wasn't fast enough to score a place in the finals. Yet his real love was obviously business and not school.

He found hardware exciting. He wasn't so much interested in building, but loved machinery. Passionate about how it worked, he would consume any reading material he could on engineering and mechanics. Often he would pull a piece of equipment apart just to find out how it worked. Never did he fear that he couldn't put it back together. His logic was simple: if someone had put it together in the first place then he could always put it back together again.

One object of his mechanical attentions was his bicycle and like many others he enjoyed riding the well-developed roads and pathways around Dunedin. One day while out cycling he came across a young man several years older than himself riding a rather peculiar looking bike constructed with a bamboo frame. The bamboo frame wasn't entirely uncommon, but instead of pedalling round and round it was being pedalled up and down in straight vertical strides.

This fascinated him and eagerly he rode up and introduced himself. After some discussion about this new invention they set off together for a ride in the country. Bertie was determined to have a go to see how it worked, so when they had gone far enough out of town he suggested they swap bikes for the journey home. He quickly found the pedalling up and down motion considerably more difficult than it looked and watched somewhat disappointedly as his new companion cycled off into the distance. It was a long journey back to town and he was pleased at last to be reunited with his own cycle before the young inventor and he parted company.[8]

2

A SEED IS PLANTED

1902-1907

"Many times the reading of a book has made the fortune of a man – has decided his way in life."[1]

R.W. Emerson

Bertie carefully pulled the vest around his shoulders and slipped his arms into the neatly pressed woollen jacket. He paused for a moment in front of the mirror. He was unmistakably a Laidlaw. The soft oval face with characteristic chin, his prominent straight nose dividing clear, soothing blue eyes. His cheeks were still slightly chubby and although he had grown taller and more athletic he still had a boyish look about him.

He reached the top button on his vest. The heavily starched shirt collar dug into his neck and he loosened his tie just slightly. Parting his hair he brushed it firmly over to the left with just enough hair cream to hold it in place. His black felt hat lay on the dresser and he picked it up, shouldered his satchel and made for the front door. He was now 16, bubbling with energy, occasionally witty, at times a little headstrong. It was common practice for children to leave school at 16 and he was no exception, convincing his father to let him leave at the end of the third term in 1901 after his birthday to work in the family business. His first full-time job in the firm was as a junior clerk and as such was employed at the rate of seven shillings and sixpence, for 54 hours work per week.

Nor as a family member was he allowed any special privileges and he received no extra pay for overtime.[2] His mother watched as her young son strode down the street to meet the tram. By now the family had also dropped the name Bertie. He disliked it, and introduced himself, like his father, as 'Robert Laidlaw.'

Early in the year he visited Christchurch and one afternoon he and a few friends went out for a spot of sailing off Brighton. The four were enjoying the relative calm of the day's outing when suddenly the weather changed for the worse. The light breeze swept up into a strong offshore wind as grey rain clouds assembled in the distance. Within minutes the calm waters were transformed into an angry squall.

They were stuck in a difficult predicament. Either they could stay where they were and try to ride out the storm, or attempt to head back to the shore. By now neither was a good option. If they stayed out they risked being blown down the coast or, worse, further off shore. If they headed back towards land they would certainly be flipped by the large waves now crashing on the beach. Before long the choice was made for them as the tide moved them towards the beach. Within seconds of reaching the first line of breakers their boat was flipped like a coin and its occupants hurled into the water.

Three of the party were thrown clear but Robert was not so fortunate. He remained trapped in the boat, and as the craft turned another wave crashed on top of it and it sank straight to the bottom jamming hard on the sea floor. He was now a prisoner of the sea. Slightly dazed with shock in the darkness he could see nothing, and his hands splashed in the water seeping in round the edges of the boat. Frantically he edged himself to one side and grabbed hold of the seat trying to lift the boat up, but it snapped off in his hands.

"Remain calm," he told himself under his breath. He tried working his fingers under the edge of the hull but it was no use. It was stuck firmly in the sand.

On the surface his companions had regrouped. Realising that both he and the boat were missing one of the men dived down to find him. Within seconds he found the boat, and squeezing his fingers under one side pushed off the bottom with all his strength. The boat lifted up and Robert popped out and up to safety. It was 60 seconds he did not wish to remember in a hurry. Surprisingly, the experience didn't leave him with a fear of water but he never went sailing again. His future boating expeditions would always be in motorised craft. The incident also prompted him to think again about Christ and the eternal life that he'd heard so much about while growing up. Perhaps he should do something about it? That October he was to get his chance.

In 1902 two well-known American evangelists, Dr Reuben A. Torrey (preacher), and Charles Alexander (song leader), were on a worldwide crusade. They had visited Japan, China and India and arrived in New Zealand fresh from successful revival meetings in Melbourne where crowds of up to 50,000 gathered each night.[3] After further meetings in Sydney they crossed the Tasman and held a 10-day mission in Christchurch where at one meeting alone 10,000 were turned away unable to get in.

As they travelled the country by train hundreds flocked to railway platforms to see them. So many, in fact, that railway authorities saw their opportunity and began charging platform entrance fees – much to the disgust of normal passengers who now had to pay extra just to get to their train.

The pair arrived in Dunedin on Thursday, September 18,

after leaving Christchurch that morning by express. By now Dunedin was a city of 47,000, and large crowds were again expected. The two biggest buildings in the city were Garrison Hall, which could hold 2000, and just over the road First Church Presbyterian. Robert didn't attend the first meetings but his interest was kindled by the announcement at the first Friday night meeting that there was to be a half night of prayer that evening. Real revival had broken out in Melbourne, and the Dunedin crowd were anxiously waiting for Torrey to perform something special for them, too.

This concerned the preacher who declared to his audience, "I want to tell you that we need a fresh movement of the Spirit everywhere we go. I am going to call you now to a half night of prayer tonight at the YMCA." Robert had never been to a half night of prayer before. So perhaps out of youthful curiosity more than anything else he went along to see what 'religious few' might turn up to such an occasion. He was as surprised as those organising the meeting to find the hall packed, and 500 people blocking the street waiting to get into a building that seated only 250.

After a brief song the meeting was about to start when there was some movement in the middle of the hall. Out in the audience a man stood up. He was a well-known lawyer in the city and all heads turned to see what was going on. "Mr Speaker," he said clearing his throat, "let me say this first. I believe God," his voice gaining momentum, "is just as willing to bless us here in Dunedin as he did in Melbourne. As there's nothing wrong with God, the fault must be in us. I am a Christian lawyer in the city and I used to be a keen soul-winner. However, it is near on a year since I spoke to anyone in my office about their soul. Confessing my guilt, I pledge to God to start afresh on Monday morning."

The hall sat frozen in an astonished hush. Robert wondered

what would happen next when another man on the other side of the hall stood up.

"I haven't gathered my family for prayer and the reading of God's Word in three years. I too confess my guilt and pledge to begin again."

He sat down and then around the hall, like shots going off, men stood up one after the other. Robert had never seen anything like it. Grown men standing confessing their sins and consecrating themselves afresh to God and His work. The meeting didn't stop till midnight. There was no gathering planned for the following day, so he was as anxious as many others who had attended Friday night to see what would happen next. They would have their chance on Sunday afternoon, September 21.

The service on Sunday was for men only and was scheduled to begin at 3 o'clock. By 2.45 every seat in the house was taken. He was among those fortunate enough to get in before the doors were shut. There was an expectant buzz inside the hall as men spoke of the Friday night prayer meeting and what might happen next. The excitement was interrupted by a loud banging. Several hundred had gathered outside the hall and were now angrily trying to kick in the thick oak doors and force an entry. This was like no other religious meeting Dunedin had ever experienced before.[4]

Safe inside the building the audience was a cross-section of Dunedin's male population. It was evenly split between young and old, professional and manual worker. Row upon row of faces watched as Dr Torrey mounted the stage to address his audience. His topic for the afternoon was 'Fools in God's sight', and he didn't waste any time coming to the point.

"Any man who makes light of sin is a fool," he barked. "What is sin? Sin is rebellion against God. God is infinite wisdom, infinite power, infinite holiness, and infinite love.

Every act of sin is an act of rebellion against infinite wisdom, holiness, power and love."

"Sin puts out the eyes of the soul," he continued. "How many men are so blinded by sin that they cannot see the difference between purity and impurity ... Sin robs a man of peace ... Sin robs a man of joy ... Sin brings inevitable suffering." Torrey carried on for half an hour. He concluded with a direct challenge to those present.

"Look to Christ," he said, "and him crucified, and in his strength come out and fight against sin."

Robert sat there almost numb. What Torrey had said gripped his heart. He had not experienced a joy or a peace like Torrey spoke of and felt the guilt of sin in his life. Many of his own friends had not come to the meetings. This was not a direction they wanted to head in. They seemed to do whatever they pleased with no outward sense of guilt or remorse but he knew this was not right. He knew they had no deep peace but he wanted it.

He felt God touching his heart and looked around. No one in the building moved. All eyes faced the front. Torrey looked back down at his audience. An anger welled within the evangelist and he exploded.

"No-one," he shouted thumping the pulpit, "I cannot believe it? This is an experience I have not had anywhere. In Sydney there were 70 men who got up on this line of thought. Are you all Christian men? Have you all broken with sin before you came here?"

Silence fell in the auditorium. The men of Dunedin sat glued to their seats and no one moved a muscle. Torrey clasped the rostrum and leaned into his audience. His voice dropped but his words lacked none of their force.

"Scotsmen were not afraid to stand up in the days of the covenanters," he exclaimed, "and I do not see why Scotsmen should be ashamed of their convictions now."

That last barb hit a raw nerve. The Scots were undeniably proud of the Scottish covenanters who had broken with the English church. Some uneasy shufflings could be heard in the hall and Robert was one of them. His heart began to race. He tried to ignore it but it wouldn't go away. He knew he should step forward. Why wouldn't someone else go first?

Just then there was a noise in the gallery and a man stood up and began to push his way to the front. All eyes in the building seemed to fix on the burly Scotsman as he awkwardly made his way through the crowd. Robert followed the man's movements until his eyes fixed on a familiar face in the crowd. It was his old schoolmaster Barney Campbell. He froze. There was no way he could go up to the front now. If Campbell saw him he'd think Robert was just making a fool of himself. Half a dozen more men moved to take up Torrey's invitation, but Robert was not among them. The possible embarrassment chilled him to the bone and he kept his seat.

That evening as Robert made his way home for tea he mused over the afternoon's events. He did not feel happy with his decision. The embarrassment would have been momentary, but the guilt was lasting longer. Inside he felt terrible. He wished he'd gone up the front. If only he'd never seen Barney Campbell. There were two meetings scheduled for later that night. He didn't have time to go to the first, but he would go to the second.

He downed his dinner quickly and walked back into town. There were crowds of people everywhere. Something strange was gripping the city. As he arrived at the hall the first meeting had just finished and people were being led out a side entrance. The large doors of the Garrison Hall were finally swung open and the crowd surged ahead. Three and a half minutes later every seat in the house was filled. Again there were hundreds left outside unable to gain admission. The city was alive. The eyes of Dunedin had turned to what was happening here.

Torrey mounted the stage and took as his subject 'God.' He addressed the certainty of divine existence in the face of evolution. "All that science has done," he said, "is to prove that higher forms of life have succeeded lower forms of life. But it does not prove that the higher grew out of the lower." He turned then to the brevity of life. "I exhort you," said Torrey, "to be prepared sooner or later to meet God, and make yourselves ready to go into His presence." With memories of Brighton's near drowning playing on his mind, and today's already forfeited opportunity, Robert left his seat and moved quickly to the front.

He stood in front of the preacher. Torrey looked deeply into his eyes and smiled. He rested a hand gently on Robert's shoulder and prayed. As Torrey led him in prayer he felt a shiver go down his spine. He opened his heart to God confessing his sinfulness, and his acceptance of Jesus Christ as Saviour and Lord. He was not alone. Among the 50 men and women who made a confession of faith that night were his two sisters. It was a decision that would radically affect every part of his entire life. He was now 17 years old.

The following morning when he reached the Rattray Street premises of Laidlaw & Gray in the centre of the city's commercial district there were about a dozen fellow employees waiting to be let in to start the day. When he saw senior salesman Don McIvor arrive with the key he announced with all the courage he could muster, "I came to Christ at the mission last night Mac."

Don looked kindly at the young Christian and gripped his hand firmly: "Robert," he said, "I'm delighted to hear it."

As the shackles of fear fell off, he related to all those standing by the story of what had happened at the mission last night and his conversion. At the Garrison Hall four days later, during the Thursday midday meeting for businessmen, Robert mounted the stage and testified before 1000 of the city's merchants of his conversion and acceptance of Christ.

In the weeks that followed Dunedin was turned upsidedown. Shops closed at midday so their staffs could attend the lunchtime meetings. Passengers on trams to and from the city at night would spontaneously break into song and start singing hymns from the mission hymnbook. The Garrison Hall was filled to capacity every night with overflow meetings at First Church to cater for those who could not get in – often another thousand people. Four meetings were held every day and there were special meetings for businessmen, children, and each night a separate meeting for women with a follow-on meeting for men. The local newspaper began a separate column dedicated entirely to the mission.

"In order to accommodate the thousands of people desirous of attending the revival services in the Garrison Hall the missioners decided to run two meetings last evening and tonight instead of one. The result was to show more clearly that the building has yet to be built in this city that will accommodate the people in times when they are stirred up with religious enthusiasm.

"The women's service was announced to begin at quarter to seven. About an hour before that time people were making their way to the hall and shortly after 6 o'clock the seats were all taken up. When filled from end to end, stage included, Garrison Hall is estimated to hold nearly 2000 people. As the building was packed twice last night, it would be a fair estimate to put down the attendance for the four services for the day at 7000."[5]

Often 300-400 people would miss out altogether and be left waiting outside. Once the crowd of latecomers became so incensed that a party of workers had to be retained to stop them from breaking their way into the hall. The demand to see the evangelists grew and grew, and on Thursday, September 25 the Tramways Committee of the City Council passed a special resolution that no trams would run on Sundays so that the tram drivers and their families could attend the meetings. The drivers were even issued priority tickets so they might be certain of seats. When Torrey and song leader Alexander finally left Dunedin on Tuesday, September 30, 1902 the crowd at the railway station was so large that Alexander himself had to climb into his carriage through the window.

Robert with two friends gathered a group of about 15 other young Christians. They called themselves 'Daniel's Band' after the Bible hero and took the popular mission chorus as their motto.

Dare to be a Daniel,
Dare to stand alone,
Dare to have a purpose firm,
And dare to make it known.

The group began to hold their own meeting every Monday night. Every week it followed a similar routine. After dinner they met in one of Dunedin's main streets at 7.30 pm and began to sing songs and preach to those who gathered around. About 8.30 pm they shifted the meeting to a local hall where they would pray till midnight.

Robert's life had changed. His priorities and friends had changed overnight, yet he still had the same thirst for business. A year later, after his 18th birthday (September 1903), he was given a book that was to greatly influence his thinking. Simply entitled *God in Business* it was a collection of letters from businessmen all over the world testifying to the different ways in which God had worked in their businesses. It included letters from bankers, stockbrokers, newspapermen and ministers – even such well known figures as George Muller, D.L. Moody and William Colgate. The book spoke of a worldwide movement of men who had covenanted with God to give increasing percentages of their incomes to God and had then seen God bless them as they were faithful in this. After much thought he decided to do the same and began dutifully giving a tenth of his income to the local church he and his family attended. In his diary he made the following entry: 'Feb. 1st 1904. Age eighteen and a half, wages £1 per week. I have decided to start giving one tenth to the Lord.'[6]

1904 was a year of excitement and change. His father imported a motorcar and in doing so became the first car-owner in Dunedin, and only the sixth in the whole of New Zealand. The crate arrived at the premises of Laidlaw & Gray and was opened with much excitement on the pavement in front of the shop. They were, of course, faced with a dilemma, for although opening the box and putting the thing together wasn't a difficult task for the machine-minded Laidlaws, no one knew how to drive it.

"I'll do it," volunteered Robert and after reading the instructions he put some petrol in and started it up. Several nervous starts later he was soon under way and over the next few days drove the tiller-steered 1903 Darracq around the horse-filled streets of Dunedin.

The Darracq had no roof and the following weekend the family decided to head out down the coast for a picnic in the little car. It was a beautifully clear summer's day and Robert, by now complete with driving goggles, drove the eager revellers to the beach. After an afternoon in the sun they packed up their things and clambered back on board for the journey home. Robert's father had been watching his son's actions intensely. He sat next to him in the passenger seat and up till now had not driven the car himself. Half way home he plucked up courage: "That looks easy Robert. I'll drive it from here."

Robert pulled over and nervously swapped seats with his father. After a hesitant start he soon had the car moving along the rough Otago road and with surprising ease edged up the next hill and over the top. Downhill the car's speed began to increase rapidly and up until now slowing down had not been a consideration. In desperation he called out to Robert over the engine noise, "Quick son, how do I stop it."

It was too late. He lost control and the car scuttled off the road into a ditch tossing its occupants into the waiting gorse bushes. When the dust settled the party surveyed its damage.

Despite some scratches and bruises everybody seemed all right. It was clearly the car that had suffered the most. It lay like a toppled statue in two broken halves on the roadside. The body, which was made of wood, had pulled away entirely from the chassis. On closer inspection it was not a complete disaster. Putting matchsticks in the torn holes Robert and his father screwed the two halves back together and they continued on their journey home. This time, however, with Robert at the wheel. His father purchased many more cars in his lifetime but did not take to driving, and Robert assumed the chief motoring responsibilities in the family.[7]

He turned 19 in September that year and his life took an abrupt turn when his father offered his entire interest in the successful hardware business to his younger partner, John Gray.[8] Gray accepted and bought Robert's father out for a handsome sum after which his father and mother left for an extended holiday in Europe and America early in 1905.[9]

The news was not so good for Robert however. Not that he wasn't pleased for his father, for he was, but what of his future? Like his father 20 years earlier it was obvious that he too was to have no part in the family inheritance and would have to make his own way in life.

He didn't leave the firm but continued his employment at Laidlaw & Gray and was by now an accomplished salesman in his own right earning extremely good wages. A few weeks after his father left the country, John Gray summoned Robert into his office with a proposition.

"Robert," he said with some pleasure, "William Bright, who has been our senior wholesale traveller in Otago and Southland, is leaving and I want you to take over his territory." Robert didn't know what to say. What an opportunity. He was still only 19 years old and was being offered the job of senior wholesale traveller. Had his father been around, he would perhaps not have been offered such a job and would certainly not have been allowed to take it up.[10]

Excited at the prospect, he cut himself short when he suddenly had a sobering thought. Travellers were renowned for their drinking exploits and entertaining their customers with liquor. He didn't drink. In fact he was a total abstainer. How on earth could he do such a job when drinking was so much a part of the job description? He baulked at the thought of being the only non-drinker in the field. Looking up he replied somewhat sheepishly to Mr Gray.

"Thank you sir, but as you know I am a total abstainer, and it would be too difficult a task for me to handle."

Gray was also a Christian, and saw that perhaps his young salesman needed to think through the offer a little more deeply. He also did not want to lose the chance to put one of his best people in the field.

"Go and pray about it lad and come back in three days and give me your answer."

"Umm, yes sir," stammered Robert, and left the room a little bewildered by his boss's offer. He relished the opportunity to be a traveller, and Gray had given him a second chance.

He went immediately and hunted down his old friend Don McIvor and another Christian man in the business whom he trusted. His father was not there and he needed some older advice. In turn he told each of them his situation and of Gray's offer and asked them to pray for guidance as to what to say to the request. He also forbade each man to talk to the other about what they might think. By the third day he felt strongly that his earlier reply had been a cowardly response. He hadn't a strong reason for not exposing himself to other travellers as a non-drinker. He was simply afraid of the ridicule he was bound to face from them and customers alike. As he leafed through the Bible that morning before going to work he stumbled on a verse in the book of Isaiah that he had underlined on a previous occasion.

"I will go before you and level the mountains; I will break down gates of bronze and cut through bars of iron."[11]

He felt a rush of excitement. What a promise from God! What a promise for a hardware salesman breaking brass gates into pieces. Surely nothing would be able to stand in his way now. God was behind him accepting Mr Gray's offer. He still had to discuss it again with his two friends and was impatient to hear what they had to say. Arriving at work early he sought out Don McIvor first. Don's words couldn't have been more direct:

"I have prayed about a good many things in my Christian life Robert," he said solemnly, "but I have never prayed about any–thing I am so sure of as this. You should accept Mr Gray's offer."

He trusted Don and greeted his words enthusiastically. It was added confirmation to what he'd read that morning. Stumbling round the corner he met the second friend whom he'd also asked to pray.

"Have you had a chance to pray about what we discussed?" he asked eagerly.

"I have," said the friend, "and I have to tell you Robert, I have prayed about many things, but I have never prayed about ..."

"Stop," said Robert, "You've been talking to Don McIvor, haven't you.."

"No I have not," protested the friend, a little annoyed to be so rudely interrupted in midstream.

"But you're saying exactly what Don said to me," clamoured Robert, "You must have spoken to him."

"Well I haven't," said the friend, "I haven't discussed this with Don at all. I can't help it if I'm using the same words as he did."

And with that the friend continued with what he'd intended to say.

"I have prayed about many things Robert, but I have never prayed about anything that I am so sure of as this. You are to take Mr Gray's job."

Robert thanked him kindly for his help and apologised for his abruptness. The two parted and Robert went on his way a little humbler in his disposition and a little wiser in the ways of God. Returning to Mr Gray he thanked him and accepted his offer of senior traveller, now confident it was the Lord's will for him to do so.

A few days later, after word had got out in the shop that he was going to replace Bill Bright, he was stopped in the street by the man in person. Bright had resigned to start up business on his own and was more than a little perturbed that such an important job as his was going to somebody so rash and unsuitable as the young Laidlaw.

"Laidlaw," hollered Bright.

Instantly he recognised Bright's voice and turned to face his adversary as the portly figure sauntered towards him.

"I hear you're going out on my territory as a total abstainer," he said with a scowl.

The shop gossip was working well and all Robert could

muster was a feeble, "Yes."

"Well," said Bright puffing up his chest, "you'll never do it, son, you'll never do it." He was only warming up and launched into the attack.

"For instance," he said pointing his finger accusingly, "when you call on Nathaniel Bates the blacksmith in Waireo, he won't wait for you to invite him, he will simply walk across the road into the pub and order a round of drinks. And you will have to pay for them. What are you going to do then, eh? Tell Bates you're not paying for the drinks. Ha Ha Ha."

Bright didn't wait for a reply; he laughed himself furiously into the distance. Robert hadn't known what to say and was glad in a way he hadn't been given the chance. At least he had some time up his sleeve to think about what he was going to do.

A few days later he bought himself a season rail ticket and headed off on his rounds as senior wholesale traveller for Laidlaw & Gray calling on builders, storekeepers and blacksmiths in the Southland and Otago region.

Two and a half weeks later he came face to face with the ominous Nathaniel Bates. No amount of worrying could have prepared him for the situation. He had hoped to find Bates in at least a congenial mood so he might be able to explain his position before the inevitable dash to the local pub. He had brought with him a selection of finely crafted pocket-knives which so far had proved very popular with his customers instead of the usual liquor, but he didn't even get the chance to offer one. He heard Bates long before he actually saw him.

Bates was in his small blacksmith's shop single-handedly trying to shoe a Clydesdale draught stallion. It was a meeting of two stubborn minds. The massive horse was shoed only once a year so was not used to it, nor did it like it. It kicked viciously back and forth. Bates had its legs roped to the rafters but even the tight ropes only slightly dampened the angry horse's temper.

When Robert set eyes on him Bates looked almost as big as the horse. He was a large man, probably about 50. His eyes were almost hidden, set in a thickly bearded face that had not seen a razor for many years. Sweat and grime mixed in glistening black beads all over his body and his bulk flexed as the horse kicked back and forth. Bates cursed over and over again. Robert was sure the whole of Waireo must be able to hear his thunderous oaths as he battled it out with the stallion. He called out a suitable greeting and said he would wait till the shoeing was finished.

Bates struggled with the horse, grabbed its leg even tighter and brought the hot shoe up into position, the steam billowing in his face. He swore violently after his efforts revealed the shoe was no longer the right shape. The stallion gave a relieved bolt and Bates and he parted company. The blacksmith muttered under his breath as he walked over to the furnace, not even raising his head to the new onlooker.

Grasping the bellows he barked at Robert as the furnace received its due punishment for the misfitting shoe.

"I don't hear you swearing young fellow," he said as the flames leapt into life.

"No, Mr Bates," he said, "I don't swear. I find I can get along fairly well with the King's English, but you certainly have some provocation this afternoon."

Bates didn't reply. His eyes were fixed somewhere in the red hot coals. As he drew the smoking shoe out of the furnace he said inquiringly: "Don't you smoke, young fellow?"

"No Mr. Bates, I don't smoke," he said nervously.

Bates slammed the shoe down on the anvil. Robert was not put off.

"You are old enough to be my father Mr Bates. Don't you

think it is rather hard on me to pick out all my faults the first time I call on you? You ask me if I swear and I say, no I don't swear. You ask me if I smoke, and I say no I don't smoke. In a minute you will ask me if I drink, and I will say "No," Mr. Bates, "I don't drink."

Bates was motionless. In his left hand he held the red-hot shoe, in his right hand the hammer, poised above his head ready to come crashing down. Slowly he lowered the hammer, bringing it to rest. He turned and looked at Robert eye to eye for the first time. With a faint smile he placed his large sweaty hand on Robert's nervous shoulder and gave it a good grasp.

"Stick to it laddie, stick to it."

Robert's heart was pounding. In his mind he heard the reassuring words: "I will go before you and will level the mountains, I will break down the gates of bronze and cut through bars of iron." God's promise had come true, and over the next two years while Robert worked as senior traveller, Bates was always pleased to see him and every time gave him a large order.

His journeying around the Southland-Otago area was in relative style. The roads were good and extensive rail links meant travelling could be done in comfort. While away from home he stayed in the many fine hotels and country pubs dotted around the region. Since he didn't drink he had few close friends among the travellers; however he did have some companions and one was fellow commercial traveller, Jack White. Occasionally on the trains they would bump into each other and they would always spend some time together.

During 1905 while travelling from Owaka to Balclutha, he saw Jack's friendly face approaching him in the carriage. Jack was holding a thin package which he handed to his friend as he sat down.

"Here," he said, "I've been holding on to this for you for

sometime now. It was given to me and I thought you'd be interested."

Robert opened the wrapping not quite sure what he'd find. It was a magazine. He turned over to the front cover. "*System The Magazine of Business*," he said under his breath. "Building a Business Machine ... Great Initiatives of Business."

It looked too good to be true. He thanked his friend profusely and began to leaf carefully through the pages. A quick fingering down the contents showed him that this was definitely the magazine for him, – 'Stories of Travelling Salesman, The Managers of Tomorrow, The Organisation of a Retail Store.'

When the train arrived at Balclutha an hour and a quarter later he asked Jack if he could post it on to him since he was headed south and Jack was going north.

"No," said Jack, "you keep it."

Robert thanked his friend and happily went on his way with his new treasure tucked under his arm. He read it from cover to cover. He knew the hardware business well but organising things to the extent described in this magazine was new to him. Business as far as he had known was more art than method and he never dreamt of the kind of thinking and organisation that was being used here, with the results in profitability plain to see. It appealed directly to his mechanical mind. *System* described how to run the different parts of an organisation, how to control stock, write business letters, the practice of scientific selling, how to maximise sales and use card index systems. He immediately sent for 12 back issues and a year's subscription.[12]

By now he was an avid reader and in the evening, instead of socialising in the bar with the other the travellers, he patronised the hotel reading rooms. *System* became his travelling companion and he began to amass notes on the different techniques being used in the magazines and even put some of the suggestions into practice with his own customers. The country stores he visited rarely kept any kind of stock inventory and often did not know what they were out of when he arrived. The common sales technique was merely to fill the storekeepers' requirements, but much of the buying they did was based on guesswork or educated hunches.

System encouraged Robert to apply scientific methods to his selling. Many of the merchants he dealt with did not have good stock control and would often run out of more popular items. Following the magazine's directions, he analysed what his most popular items were, compiling lists of frequently selling goods and the preferable inventory levels. This he carried with him and presented to his different customers. The combination of suggestive selling and scientific method raised his sales dramatically and improved his standing with his customers, who found their own stock levels and sales improved. They began to rely exclusively on his use of inventory controls. Not only did it increase his sales commission, it vastly improved his knowledge of retail selling.

Many hotels he stayed in subscribed to overseas magazines and British farming journals were popular as well as titles like *Scientific American*. He read them with great interest, not only the technical articles and editorial copy but especially the advertisements.

His father had great skill with English and wrote catchy advertisements for Laidlaw & Gray that both enticed and complimented the customer. He inherited the same skill and spent many hours studying and critiquing the various magazines he read. The advertisements always appeared at the back so he could remove them without affecting any of the articles. Over time he put together his own file of clippings, building up a strong copy sense.

One night as he was relaxing in the reading room of a country hotel and rummaging through the usual pile of literature he came across a book that was entirely new. Picking it up for a closer look he found it was not a magazine at all, but rather a mail order catalogue from American mail order giant Montgomery Ward. He had heard of them but had never seen a catalogue. They had been in business since 1872 and were the oldest mail order firm in the world doing a business of $10 million a year. He pored over the pages. It wasn't only the advertisements that fascinated him, it was the brilliance of the idea.

Here was the power of advertising combined with postal delivery knocking out the huge retail margins. He knew retail stocks as well as wholesale prices. Many of the items stocked by Laidlaw & Gray were either from Britain or America, but the prices in Ward's catalogue were far more competitive than anything they were offering. He sat up most of the night reading and absorbing every detail. By the next morning he had amassed a small folder of notes and immediately sent a letter to America requesting an up-to-date catalogue. Ward's catalogue and *System* became his constant travelling companions over the next two years.[13]

Something deep began to stir inside him. He began to see the possibilities for a business like Montgomery Ward's mail order operation in New Zealand; a business he could set up and run; a business like no other in operation he knew, scientifically organised, precisely engineered, thoroughly planned.

System was giving him the kinds of skills needed to run such an operation, but there was so much more he needed to learn. In the December 1905 issue of the magazine he was particularly challenged. A few pages inside he came to one of the feature articles, 'Great Initiatives of Business – Wholesaling by Mail.'

It was the first article he had seen on the launch and development of a mail order business, the story of George, Charles and Edward Butler, three brothers who, with a background in sales but no capital, started a small mail order operation from a 50 x 20ft room in the back streets of Boston.

They sold small popular lines that they knew moved quickly and their idea was an instant success. The business grew until Butler Brothers became the largest wholesale mail order business in the world, with sales in the millions each year. Perhaps he, too, could start a similar venture.

In the advertisement section he came across a book by Arthur E. Swett, entitled *Principles of the Mail Order Business*. He sent for it immediately and read it thoroughly. It was an absolute goldmine. It showed him how to write advertisements that would pull people in, how to develop systems for filling orders promptly, how to keep all his records by a card index system, how much money to spend on advertising and how to write follow-up letters to customers.

It gave plentiful examples of all of these techniques as well as citing the stories of actual mail order businesses in manufacturing, retailing and wholesaling and the mistakes to avoid along the way. *System* and Montgomery Ward had given him the vision; now the details were starting to fall in place and his enthusiasm was growing by the day.[14]

He also saw advertised in *System* courses by a young American management consultant, A.F. Sheldon, entitled 'The Science of Salesmanship.' Robert wrote personally to Sheldon in Chicago and took his course of study by correspondence. Sheldon taught him not only about scientific selling but also how to build a large, successful business. He taught him about leadership, about organisation and departments, about the importance of training and executive development, about motivation.

During this time his success as a travelling salesman also continued to grow. In 1905 when he was appointed senior traveller his wage had doubled. Believing that it was God who was blessing him in his work, a year later he altered the covenant he made to the Lord in his diary about giving:

"February 12th 1906. Before money gets a grip of my heart, by the grace of God I enter into the following pledge with my Lord that: I will give 10% of all I earn up to £500 per annum.

"If the Lord blesses me with £1000 per annum, I will give 15% of all I earn.

"If the Lord blesses me with £1500 per annum I will give 20% of all I earn.

"If the Lord blesses me with £2000 per annum I will give 25% of all I earn.

"The Lord help me to keep this promise for Christ's sake, Who gave all for me."

These were not small amounts and he knew it. Two thousand pounds per year was 20 times the wage of an accountant and four or five times the value of a house.[15] The stories he had read of God's providence to businessmen in the book *God in Business* he hadn't forgotten.

Circumstances in Dunedin, however, soon began to change. When his mother and father returned from their overseas trip in 1906, they had moved north to Auckland leasing a large house in Herne Bay on Clifton Rd called 'The Grange.' Robert stayed on to work in Dunedin but trade at Laidlaw & Gray soon became difficult. Mr Gray, while a sound businessman, had exhausted nearly all his working capital buying out Robert's father. Hardware was not a seasonal business but payments from farmers owing money fluctuated as crops allowed. Carrying these debts placed large demands on the capital resources of the owner. The business previously had this kind of cash but Mr Gray by himself did not. He eventually ran out of money and the business went into liquidation. In 1907, at the age of 21, Robert left the familiar sights and sounds of Dunedin for good and journeyed north to join his family in Auckland.

3

AUCKLAND CALLS

1907-1909

"Nowhere is the goal of him who follows the route of anywhere.
The man who aims at nothing in particular hits his mark. No
friendly wind is going to pilot your business ship into the
port of profit. You must map out the course of your entire
business voyage before you lift the anchor of initiative or set
the sail of action."[1]

System, 1905.

Auckland in 1907 had become an important city in the colony. The port serviced the north and central regions of the North Island and an increasing range of trading, commercial and manufacturing enterprises had set up operations. By now it was New Zealand's largest city and boasted a population of 80,000 spread widely over its hilly suburbs. There was a distinct gap between the upper and lower classes. The working-class suburbs consisted of mostly wooden single-storey dwellings, quite different from the gracious two and three-storeyed mansions of the more established suburbs, which could be up to 10 times the price of their poorer relations.

His mother and father were by now well settled in their new home. Upon moving north Robert's father had started a new business called Laidlaw Brothers in Symonds Street selling drapery and other soft goods. Already he had opened another branch in nearby Karangahape Rd.

A brother from Scotland, Gordon, had also moved out to New Zealand and was assisting him in this new venture, and like his previous business in Dunedin this too was prospering. Their homestead 'The Grange' was a large, white, two-storey wooden property on spacious grounds and housed all the family comfortably. Robert's youngest brother Jack was now attending Kings College, his middle brother Arthur had finished school and was working in the family drapery firm. His sisters Minnie and Queenie both helped mother at home.

The family had also settled into a new church. His father's reputation as a Christian worker and businessman was known in Auckland Brethren circles and he and the family began attending Auckland's newest Brethren church, Howe Street Gospel Hall in the city. A cream wooden building adjacent to Auckland Girls Grammar School, its main auditorium seated 300 and it was attended by several of Auckland's notable businessmen as well as worshippers from the surrounding district.

Auckland initially proved something of a challenge for Robert. In June of 1907 he began to work for Wingate & Co hardware merchants located in lower Queen Street, the hub of Auckland's commercial district. He took up a similar position to that he had held at Laidlaw & Gray as a hardware traveller, although this time at the weekly wage of £2/10/0. Transport in the Auckland region was quite different from Otago as roads and railways were far more advanced in Dunedin than in Auckland, and for the commercial traveller this presented special problems. Whereas back home he'd been able to secure a year's rail pass and spend his travelling hours in the refined comfort of a passenger car and his nights in country hotels, the terrain around Auckland was much rougher.

Wingates assigned the new traveller a large territory. He

got the far-flung outposts from Whangarei to the far north, the Bay of Plenty from Tauranga to Opotiki, and on the East Coast from Gisborne to Port Awanui. His mode of transportation changed too. His comfy rail pass became a horse and saddle and remained so for the next 18 months –18 months of negotiating roads that were dustbowls in summer and muddy bogs in winter. More than once he spent the night sleeping under a haystack.

Remaining out of touch for days at a time he began each run by taking the coastal steamer from Auckland to the furthermost wharf. There he would hire horses and begin his trek back towards home, calling on builders and country stores. Each trip might be five to six days in length. He travelled light, taking with him only two small saddlebags. One held his price and order books, the other his personal belongings – pyjamas, a shirt, handkerchiefs and shaving gear.

His attire changed too and now he looked more like a trooper than a salesman. Gone were his much-loved suits and bowler hats. Now it was riding breeches and leggings with an oilskin strapped across his saddle. Often in winter he would be soaked to the skin, not so much by the driving rain but the many rivers and streams he had to ford along the way. On one trip alone he crossed the same river 13 times as the trail twisted and turned on itself.

Planning for his new business enterprise was now well under way and it was obvious that it would be Auckland where he would set up his activities. The family had no inclination to move south again and in some ways Auckland would be better suited to a mail order business than Dunedin. His potential customers, the farmers and country folk outside the main city, were quite isolated. They had no quick and easy access to large shopping areas and were mostly at the mercy of the high retail prices charged by the handful of country stores. It was a breeding ground for a mail order firm and almost exactly the same kind of conditions that Montgomery Ward had faced when setting up its American operations about 40 years earlier.

Robert got plenty of opportunity to meet and talk to his future customers as he travelled the long roads and horse tracks of the North Island. Whereas his job in Dunedin had seen him travelling with fellow salesmen on trains, this time his travelling companions were largely farmers.

He spent many long hours riding with them on their way to saleyards or to and from towns. He engaged his riding partners directly, asking them about the potential of a mail order business. He wanted to know whether such a thing would appeal to them. What would they buy? Would they pay cash? Would a catalogue with all the illustrations and everything clearly set out be useful to them? Their reply was always the same – a firm "yes!"

Interestingly enough, he always got the opposite response when he returned home to Auckland. The businessmen with whom he discussed the idea told him it would be an utter failure. They confidently believed that what suited America wouldn't work in New Zealand and, above everything else, the farmer would never pay cash for his goods. Even if he wanted to, he wouldn't have the money to do so because of his seasonal income. Robert thought it over carefully. He could see the reasons behind the arguments but he trusted the farmers more than the businessmen. He knew from reading *System* that Montgomery Ward had encountered the same kind of opposition and he, like Ward, remained undaunted and even more determined to put his ideas into practice.

By the end of 1908 his success as a salesman was well known. His wage at Wingates had doubled again and he was now earning the substantial sum of £4 per week.[2] It was little surprise that by the end of 1908 he had saved £280. He could have used the money to purchase a house mortgage free, or at least put down a substantial deposit on one in Auckland's better suburbs, but he didn't. He made a decision that surprised many and in December, 18 months after he started, tendered his resignation.

He had thought constantly about starting the mail order business and his planning and investigations were well advanced. As a Christian he also felt it important to seek God's guidance on the matter, and after much prayer felt it was definitely God's will for him to launch out on his own. His mother was behind his initiative and gave him a small upstairs room in their homestead where he could work undisturbed.

His father, however, took the opposite view. He had proudly watched his son progress as a salesman and was horrified to learn he was giving it all away to pursue such a foolhardy venture. Like others, his father believed it would be an utter failure. How ever hard he tried he could not dissuade his son and in January 1909, Robert began work on the catalogue that would be the flagship of the mail order business.

From talking to farmers while riding the trails he knew how crucial it was to get the catalogue just right – informative, catchy, and most importantly, well illustrated. This was something that would take time. He had saved the money to produce the catalogue and go into business, but there was no way he could afford to pay for someone else to put it all together. He would have to do that himself and over the next few months his artistic skills found new outlets.

He had already thought much about the business operation and how the different parts of the business would function. He had decided what kind of goods to stock, and knew from his travels which coastal ports to use and the location of railway terminals. From his constant reading of Montgomery Ward's catalogue he knew how to set out a mail order catalogue, and from his many hours in hotel reading rooms he had cultivated an eye for advertising. Everything he had prepared for over the last four years was coming together.

Largely copying the layout of Ward's catalogue he went a step further, and using every inch of space put catchy slogans at the top and bottom of each page like 'We sell from catalogue only,' and 'save traveller's expenses,' and 'satisfaction or your money back always' and 'wide-awake people buy our beds' and 'where quality counts Laidlaw Leeds.'[3]

From the American business magazine *System* and Swett's *Principles of the Mail Order Business* he had learnt much about how such an operation needed to run. Not only the nuts and bolts issues like inventory control and sales, but he devised a sophisticated management accounting system so that when his business eventually did get under way, he knew exactly where his money was coming from and what efforts were returning what amounts of revenue.

He had also written to America and received two letter-writing books, large, bound volumes that taught the person using them how to write business letters in a variety of situations, and how to construct form letters for such things as credit inquiries, discounts, complaints, returned goods and special offers. As the months of 1909 ticked by he called on merchants, manufacturers and warehousemen across Auckland.

He was a 'night owl' and enjoyed the peace and tranquillity of the night hours, finding them his most productive times. To some he lived a very disciplined life and to produce the catalogue followed a strict schedule. After the evening meal each day he headed upstairs to his room to begin work around 7 pm. Arranging the material he had collected during the day, he wrote advertisements and carefully drew illustrations for items if the merchant was unable to supply him with drawings. He also prayed and wrote notes in his Bible late into the night. Every detail of the business and its operation he committed to the Lord in prayer for His blessing and guidance. At 5 am he finally went to bed just before the rest of the family started to wake for the day.

At 11.30 the following day he got up and after lunching with his mother and father put on a suit and tie and set off to visit the wholesale warehouses and indenters dotted in the back streets of Auckland. Many of these were at the bottom of town in the narrow streets around the port and central post office. The ridicule he had received from friends and family he also received from the commercial community. He was now 23, yet he still looked more like 18. He had lost his boyish fat but his smooth, clean-shaven face, slim frame and neatly combed hair gave the appearance of an even younger man.

Incredibly, none of the wholesale houses he visited turned him away. After some discussion they readily agreed prices and terms of trade, but few thought they would ever see him again. Word even got around town to the bigger merchants of what he was up to, but none attempted to stop him or hinder his activities; none believed the madcap venture would succeed.

As the months passed he amassed a list of over 2000 items for the first catalogue. They covered everything from groceries to beds to bicycles, hardware, lace goods, drapery, crockery, paint, stoves and furniture. He also arranged to have his own brand of tea produced under the label 'Rival.' To do all this in itself was a massive undertaking, but it was only the beginning. He now had to put a price on all of these items. He knew the prices for which he could buy all his goods, and from working for Wingates knew what price the country stores in the Auckland region charged for many of the goods. Those he didn't know he quickly found out by visiting the necessary retailers. However, one major part of the equation was still missing: what would his expenses be?

From *System* he estimated his working expenses as a per-centage of total sales knowing that they should be around 10%. But he did not know accurately what they might be until he was up and running. His dilemma was that he needed to sell at a price that was not only lower than the country stores, but still lower than the stores once a freight cost had been added from Auckland, since his customers would pay their own freight. For each item he estimated what the freight cost would be from the freight schedules he obtained from the Railways, Post Office and shipping companies. This amount he deducted from the ruling price in the country on each item or line, and after considering his estimated working expenses deducted still more from the price so as to be competitive.

At best it was a calculated guess. Two things would stand in his favour. First, he knew the country stores charged far more than his retail price plus freight. They had a monopoly in their respective areas and exploited it to the fullest. Secondly, he intended to use the same weapon as Montgomery Ward and other mail order houses – loss leaders.

He already knew which items these would be, not taking any risk on goods that might prove unpopular. From constructing inventory lists for his country customers he knew what the most popular items were: watches, denim trousers, plain iron beds, boots, bicycles and tea. These he would price well below retail if not at cost, and these would be the hooks that would bring the customers in.

There was still one question that remained. He was a new firm and as such an unknown quantity, yet was asking people to send cash in advance to someone they had never met, nor even heard of. He needed a 'cast iron' character reference so wrote to the previous Under Secretary of Justice, C.J.A. Haselden. Haselden, like the Laidlaws, was a Brethren and had retired to Auckland from Wellington, now living in Remuera. Robert had met him briefly before and although he knew that his agreeing was a long shot, he was more than a little surprised when he received an affirmative reply in the post not long afterwards with the following for publication ...

"To whom it may concern,

You need have no misgivings about sending your cash in advance to Messrs. Laidlaw Leeds and Co., Mail Order Merchants, Auckland, as, from intimate knowledge, I know them to be an honourable and financial firm. I further believe they will carry out in every detail their written guarantee to refund your money in full if you are not more than satisfied with their wonderful value."[4]

The guarantee that Haselden referred to Robert had written and shown him. No other firm in the country had ever done anything like it before. He boldly placed it on the first page of the catalogue above Haselden's letter. It read:

"This is to certify that you may return within one month of having received them, any part, or all, of the goods received from us, if you, after examination, are not more than satisfied with the value or quality of same, or if for any other reason you would rather have your money back. If such goods are returned in the same good order and condition as we shipped them, we agree to refund in full the money you paid for the goods as well as what you paid in freight, and in addition we will pay the freight back so that you will not have lost a single farthing in the transaction."[5]

In the first few pages of the catalogue he laid out the advantages of the mail order method for customers and the disadvantages for his competitors – the country stores and city retailers who sent travellers into the country. He was never disrespectful but always direct. He made it quite clear to his competitors from the start that his intention was to build the biggest mail order business in the Southern Hemisphere and that they had no hope trying to compete with him.

"Mr Retailer: Though we have referred many times to the injustice of your high prices, we do not mean that you are not honest in your charges. It is the big expenses that are added to your goods before and after you get them that make up the difference.

"Whether you admit it or not, the old expensive way of doing business is doomed. Thinking people everywhere are demanding 20 shillings worth of goods for 20 shillings worth of silver. We have set out to build the greatest direct supply mail order business in the Southern Hemisphere. You need not fear unfair competition, no trickery or misrepresentation will be used; our policy, 'stern, old-fashioned, unfailing honesty,' will govern all our business transactions. We will win by giving men and women in your district quality goods at prices far below what they can get at your store.

"We will not ask orders from one of your customers unless we can save them money. They know what you charge; they have our prices in this book; they are the judges; we will stand by their decision. Our business is founded on sound, solid principles. We cut out the big selling expenses and supply our customers direct from our catalogue."[6]

To his prospective customers a few pages later he laid out his position in even more detail: "Dear Friend," he said, "Were we to send you a £10 note it would not be as valuable a gift as this catalogue, because by using this book continually you will save far more than £10.

"If you buy from a traveller representing any Auckland firm, remember he gets 12½% commission to pay his wages and expenses; or in their words 2/6 is added to every £1 of goods you buy to pay the traveller. If you buy from a firm which gives credit, 5% or 1 shilling in the pound is added to allow expenses. Even if you send your order with cash, direct by mail to these firms, as they have one price to all, you still have to pay the same high rates.

"Here are the reasons why our quality can be high and yet our prices so low: We have no Travellers, Agents or Salesmen at all; we serve no one on our premises; we sell direct from catalogue only. We have no bad debts because we never break our rule of cash with every order; we do this for our customers' protection. We do no city trade, but deal exclusively with the out-of-town buyer; therefore we need no retail shops so save all high rents.

"Send your order today, and make us prove in a practical way that we put all these savings into quality, price, value and service, and when we have convinced you, for our mutual benefit, be a Laidlaw Leeds buyer for all and everything you ever need."[7]

Bringing the catalogue together like this had been an exciting time but personally they had been lonely months. He had spent many solitary hours in the small room on the top floor of Clifton Rd. His friends did not share his vision for the new business and, like the wholesalers, their comments bordered on ridicule. There were only two supporters who never left his side: one was his mother, the other his brother Jack.

Jack was his younger brother by six years, a little taller and of much stronger build. They had always got on well together and were good friends as much as they were brothers. They shared many of the same passions. Both had a love of speed and enjoyed motoring around together in their father's car, and both loved the thrill of business. In a move which annoyed their father but pleased their mother, Jack left his position at Messrs Smith & Caughey and joined Robert as he was finishing work on the catalogue.[8]

By August Robert had nearly everything in place. He had not only produced the proofs for a detailed 118-page catalogue, but also the initial letter inviting farmers to apply for a catalogue, a price book, and three follow up letters if the first failed to get the desired response. He had also found and rented suitable premises, in Fort Street, downtown Auckland.[9] It was a small two-storeyed building nestled among rows of larger warehouses in the busy downtown street. Its plain white plastered frontage did nothing to enhance its appearance and two arched windows stood either side of the front door.

Inside there was just a single open room, 20ft by 30ft, and in the far corner a plain brick fireplace for some warmth. On the other wall a single set of narrow stairs led up to the second floor landing that would serve as their offices. Here a row of three smaller windows faced down into the street. Everything about the building spoke of functionality not beauty, but it was affordable, and it was somewhere to begin.

In many ways the Fort Street location was an ideal choice for a mail order business. All the essential services were within easy walking distance. The Post Office was in Fort Street, the railway station was only a couple of minutes walk, and over the tracks towards the port was the Northern Steamship office. Even his bank, the Bank of New Zealand, was only a short walk up Queen Street. Everything was at his disposal for the quick and efficient movement of goods.

All that remained was to organise the printing of the catalogue. He was called on at Fort Street by Mr Seabrook, a sales representative of the Brett Printing and Publishing Company located just down the road. Seabrook was not endowed with optimism when he saw the operation. Greeted by Jack he was shown in to Robert who by now was almost buried by stacks of paper and piles of printing blocks. Seabrook found it hard to imagine how such an enterprise could make any money. His faith was even more stretched when Robert showed him a mock-up of the first catalogue and asked for a quote for printing 5000.

Such a run was unheard of; what's more the folly was going to cost a massive £125 – an entire year's wages. However hard Seabrook tried to dissuade him Robert could not be deterred and with price, quantity and delivery agreed Seabrook left, hoping that, if nothing else, he might recoup his initial investment from the venture.

The catalogues were duly printed and delivered. The building was small to begin with and by now things were getting rather crowded. Jack and he got down to work. In the middle of the building's facade Robert erected a large sign about 15ft long by 3ft high and on it painted the words 'Laidlaw Leeds.' It was not his first choice of name. He had thought of calling the business Robt. Laidlaw Jnr., but this didn't create the kind of impression he was looking for.

Wanting something with a little more punch, and with complete faith that the business would some day be the market leader, his next choice was rather obvious – 'Laidlaw Leads.' Yet even this did not sit easily with him. He preferred it over 'Robt. Laidlaw Jnr.' but worried it might seem a little egotistical. Liking the catchy alliteration of L's, in the end he settled on something that delivered the same effect, but with a little more modesty – 'Laidlaw Leeds.'

Jack and he had already worked out who would be the recipients of the first catalogues. They had searched through North Island postal directories and selected a number of names from each region. Together they amassed a list of several thousand names and addresses. Robert intended to send only about half the catalogues initially and hold back the rest until word of mouth created a demand.

Nor was he going to risk such a large investment on those who might not even want them, so his introduction to his future customers was not in fact the catalogue but rather a letter. Using the list of names he and Jack mailed out hundreds of letters to selected people telling them of the mail order business. A reply card was enclosed and the person was invited, if they were interested, to fill in the card and post it back to Laidlaw Leeds. They in turn would receive a catalogue free.

Nearly all those who were sent the original invitations replied positively. Robert and Jack were soon furiously busy addressing and sending out catalogues into the country and mailed the first batch in late September. It was now Friday, September 28, 1909. The following Monday would be the day of reckoning for the young Laidlaws and they prepared for work.

Our Guarantee

Absolute Satisfaction in Every Transaction or Money Back and Freight Both Ways.

No Exceptions

LAIDLAW LEEDS.

THE GENERAL INDEX is on the Coloured Pages in the centre of this Catalog.

Our Financial Position. Bankers: Bank of New Zealand, Auckland, where you may obtain a Bank Reference if you wish, and the following reference which speaks for itself, from Mr. C. J. Haselden, J.P., late Permanent Head of Justice Department, New Zealand. The original may be seen at our Warehouse, Auckland.

Financial Reference

TO WHOM IT MAY CONCERN.

You need have no misgivings about sending your cash in advance to Messrs. Laidlaw Leeds, Merchants, Auckland, as from intimate knowledge I know them to be an honourable and financial firm.

I further believe they will carry out in every detail their written guarantee to refund your money in full if you are not more than satisfied with their wonderful value.

Yours very faithfully,

⟨Sgd.⟩ C. J. A. Haselden, J.P.,

Late Permanent Head of
Justice Department, New Zealand Govt.

See illustration below for actual size.

S1020.

Our "Rival" Ball-Bearing Machine
£4 19s.

Turn back and read Page 113 for full description.

THE SHUTTLE is absolutely self-threading, built on the best reciprocating principle, which has revolutionised sewing machines in the past few years, as this style of shuttle has only half the friction of the old-fashioned machines. The needles are self-setting. of the latest flat shank type, so that you cannot possibly put it in wrongly, even if you tried. The Bobbin Winder is automatic, and fills the Bobbin quickly and evenly.

MATERIAL.—Is all selected and specially tempered for the purpose. After 40 years' experience we contend that our manufacturers know the steel and the right temper to best stand hard usage.

THE WEARING PARTS are all hardened and ground to fit. Simple adjustment is provided at all bearing points to compensate for wear in after years.

THE CABINET WORK is of the finest Golden Oak, hand rubbed, of the latest swell front design, with carved drawers. The table is built up and veneered, and the centre drawer extends the full width of the stand. The machine, when closed, makes a handsome piece of furniture, and may be used as a side table or reading desk.

LAIDLAW, LEEDS & CO.

SUPPLIERS OF EVERYTHING IN THE WIDE WORLD.

MAIL ORDER MERCHANTS,
FORT ST.
AUCKLAND.

CATALOGUE

1910. 1910.

IT SPEAKS FOR ITSELF.

OUR GUARANTEE~
SATISFACTION,
OR YOUR MONEY BACK;
OUR MOTTO~
STERN OLD-FASHIONED UNFAILING HONESTY.

QUALITY

PRICE

THERE'S MONEY IN IT FOR YOU.

4

THE BIRTH OF LAIDLAW LEEDS

1909-1911

"Someone has said 'Opportunity knocks at a man's door but once.' I say emphatically this is not true. Opportunity is everywhere around us. She is beckoning us continually if we only had eyes to see. Some men expect opportunity not only to knock at their door but to knock the door down, come in and lead them gently out. No – opportunity is not a nurse ... No bar or padlock stands between you and the opportunity you seek. Its door is always open and you can pass in whenever you will, if you can show the passport of competency. Success has its price – you can pay it if you will. But ability is the only coin that passes current in its purchase." [1]

Robert Laidlaw, 1912.

Early on Monday morning Robert turned the corner from Queen Street into Fort Street and made his way quickly along the pavement. His dark English three-piece suit moved elegantly with him as he made his way along the pavement. Behind him, Jack struggled to keep up. His older brother always walked at more of a quick trot and the early morning crowds were making his passage difficult. The street was already filled with drays and carts making their way back and forth. The wharves had discharged their first cargoes of the morning and Fort Street was a common thoroughfare.

Robert looked up. His destination lay straight ahead. In

among the brick and plaster three and four-storey warehouses was a row of two-storey shops. His was one of them. Hardly noticing the bustling street he looked across at the freshly painted sign that hung on the wall. It was a dream fulfilled. Four years of planning and preparation had gone into this day and an entire life's saving. What ever happened from this day forward his life would never be the same again. He crossed the street and took the key out of his pocket. Opening the door he couldn't help but notice the small pile of letters that lay at his feet. A brief smile crossed his lips – he was in business.

Bending down he quickly picked the top one off the pile, his first customer requesting a roll of wire netting. Leaving Jack to deal with the rest he made for the wholesalers to pick it up. Finding them just a few streets away he approached the warehouse manager directly and requested the netting. A few minutes lapsed and a slightly embarrassed looking assistant reappeared minus the netting. They were out of stock of that particular grade. Robert didn't waste any time but purchased a thicker gauge netting at a higher price. Taking it back to Jack it was quickly despatched to the customer. The first transaction had been at a loss, but the customer was won for life and they were under way.

Soon the orders started rolling in. In October he did £380 of business averaging eight to 10 orders a day. Each order might in itself be for a dozen or more goods all of which had to be fetched from a variety of different wholesalers, manufacturers and importers around the city, brought back to Fort Street, packed, then despatched to either the port, train station or post office.[2] It was quite an exercise in logistics. As Robert carried no stock, it meant fresh trips all over the city each day, and on top of that they also had many more requests for catalogues which he and Jack hastily despatched.

In November the business almost doubled. There were still many more requests for catalogues and things got even busier. Then in December sales jumped to £850 for the month.

There were easily 20 to 30 orders a day which meant several hundred goods, everything from saddles to dresses to groceries and furniture were going in and out of their little Fort Street premises, and Robert quickly worked out the routines of the business.

During the day he and Jack collected and despatched goods paid the necessary accounts and made the daily trip up Queen Street to the Bank of New Zealand. After the doors shut they wrote up orders from 6 to 10 pm then started the correspondence, continuing until it was finished. Regularly this would not be completed until 2 o'clock in the morning and most days they worked from 8 am till midnight.

Paperwork was a substantial part of their work in the early months. Robert kept a card index file on all the customers who had received catalogues, over 2500 and growing by the day. Those who had received catalogues but had not yet requested orders were sent typed letters politely informing them that they had requested the catalogue, and when would their order be forthcoming? For those who had not replied to this he still had a further two follow-up letters.[3] Letter number three always produced the desired response.

The pace of work was relentless and the business didn't stop growing. Their all-time record for work began one Monday morning at 7.30 am. They worked all through the day and night and the following Tuesday till 6 pm without a break. Then he and Jack started again at 8 am Wednesday morning and worked again all day and night until 6 o'clock on Thursday evening. They had worked 68 and a half hours over four days with only eight hours sleep. While this record was never broken, more than once the work was so great that they worked through the night till early the next morning, motored home in their father's car for a bath and some breakfast at 7am, then returned to start another day.

This kind of routine continued well into the first six months of the business and the two brothers worked six days a week every week. On Saturday night they stopped work at midnight. On Sunday they attended Howe Street Gospel Hall with the rest of the family and enjoyed a day of rest. Robert and Jack spent many hours in each other's company. They grew closer than ever. He had asked a lot of his younger brother and Jack had more than met the challenge. Neither considered it a burden; business was their passion.

Eight weeks after starting business Robert made his first staff appointment. A boy was needed to help run around, pick up and deliver goods. He wrote a quick ad and placed it in the morning paper: 'Wanted, a young man with grocery experience – apply 62 Fort Street at once.'[4] His advertisement drew the immediate attention of a Mrs McAneny and she called in to see him. It was an industrious yet unspectacular sight. There was no executive desk to be seen and a large assortment of goods and packaging were lying in piles all over the room. Naturally she inquired as to why her son should leave his current place of employment for this. Robert was not put off.

"Your son's prospects," he said, "will be much brighter at Laidlaw Leeds than Smeetons where he is employed. They only sell a small range of goods, whereas Laidlaw Leeds intends to sell merchandise of every kind. Your boy will get a general knowledge of business that would be impossible where he is now."

Sensing something of the determination of the young man in front of her and the amount of business that was already taking place Mrs McAneny agreed, and young Frank duly became the first employee of Laidlaw Leeds.

By December it was also obvious that their premises were no longer suitable. Much time and effort was being spent picking up goods around the city, often from the same warehouse several times a week. It was clear what the more popular items were, but his Fort Street location did not have any space for storage. He started looking for new premises that would enable him to carry stock but his search proved fruitless. He could not find anything the right size or so close as they were to all the necessary shipping points.

One late December morning a man walked in off the street unannounced. Finding Robert working furiously he approached him directly.

"I hear you are looking for premises."

Robert looked up. He did not know the man and his outburst had taken him by surprise.

"Yes."

"I represent the NZ Express Company," continued the well-dressed gentleman, "and we are just leaving our premises in Commerce Street around the corner from here. Would you like to come and have a look?"

Would he what! Immediately he left what he was doing and hastily followed the man out of the shop. An Express Company's premises might be just the thing for a busy mail order warehouse that needed to get goods out in a hurry.

When he arrived in Commerce Street he was more than pleased. It was exactly what he was looking for, a large two-storey building with ample facilities for moving and despatching goods. There was a basement, a cart dock, a loading platform as well as a hydraulic lift for transporting goods between floors. It seemed ideal and he inquired the terms of the lease. The rent was £5/10/0 a week with 10 months still to run with a further right of renewal for two years. This was more than agreeable and he accepted on the spot.

Overall the new building had 5000 sq ft of floor space as opposed to their 1200, more than four times the size of Fort Street. In January he closed down for a week and the infant business of Laidlaw Leeds changed premises. Sales dropped slightly with the traditional holiday season but this enabled them to organise their substantial new building. In February business picked up again, quite enough to justify the move.

It had been a busy five months with some impressive achievements. His cash up front with orders policy meant the business had no outstanding debtors. Further staff had been added, including an accountant to handle the increasing amount of bookwork. The move to larger premises and the associated refitting and buying of stocks meant that what profit Robert could have realised he reinvested into stock and premises. Quite understandably, by the end of February he had only £16 of his original capital left.[5]

It was a business on the move and he was not the only one who sensed it. His new accountant, David Robertson, after the February accounts were written up came to see him and cheekily offered to buy the business. Robert graciously declined, knowing too well that this was only the beginning. He was right, for in March it happened – sales exceeded the £1000 mark. The long hours were well rewarded and the move to the new building more than justified. In July business doubled again, as sales went over the £2000 mark, and in August £3000 came within their sights.[6] It was a 700% increase on their first month of trading only 10 months previously.

September came, it was his birthday, yet he hardly had time to celebrate. The past 12 months had been at a phenomenal pace and were showing no signs of slowing down. He turned 25 and sitting down in the little room in the Grange at Clifton Rd opened his diary and looked at what he had written four years ago. While still working in Dunedin he had made a promise to God to increase his giving as his own earnings increased. He had pledged to give 10% of all he earned up to £500, 15% if he earned £1000, 20% if £1500 a year and 25% if the Lord blessed him with over £2000 a year.

When he'd written this, such amounts almost seemed incredible and he knew it. Even now £2000 was still 10 year's wages. He looked across at his own bank balance and thought of how many people had ridiculed him when he left his £200-a-year job nearly two years ago. It had been a difficult decision, but he had given it much thought and prayer. Now more than ever he believed God had blessed his move. His faith was strong but the blessing he was experiencing at Laidlaw Leeds was already more than he imagined. His greatest expectations had far been exceeded.

Picking up his pen he made a new entry in his notebook ...

"Sept. 1910, aged 25. I have decided to change the above graduated scale and start now giving 50% of all my earnings."

Incredibly, too, he had already outgrown his new premises. When he had moved in he was doing sales of almost £1000 a month, now the business was doing three times that and showing no signs of slowing down. He again went looking for a larger building and found what he was looking for back in his old hunting ground at 51 Fort Street, over the road from the original store.

There a wealthy widow had built two large four-storey warehouses next to each other but they had lain empty the whole time he and Jack had been there. Clearly visible from the upper storey of their first shop, to think that they might be theirs 12 months later would have seemed a pipedream. Now he wondered if only one of the warehouses would be enough.

He decided to lease just one at a rate of £600 a year, and moved premises in late September, opening officially on October 1 1910. It was a memorable moment for the two brothers. The business was exactly one year old and they no longer stood alone. Robert's staff now numbered 122. He had spent the past three months, aside from organising new premises, hiring staff and all his other duties, personally preparing the second catalogue. It was over one and a half times the size of the first at 178 pages. He had had 5000 copies of his first catalogue printed; this time he ordered 14,000. For his first 12 months in business he had total sales of £16,862 and aside from his wages reaped a net profit of approximately £1000.[7]

In the second catalogue he kept up his same distinctive personal style of communication:

"Yes – gladly we share our success with you," he said to his customers, "by giving you still lower prices, and thank you whole-heartedly for the support you have given us during the past year, which has forced us to open our big, new four-storey building in Fort Street, where we'll make you right welcome when next in Auckland. Just feel when you write that it is not a soulless, hard business company, but to men who personally appreciate your every order, and are intensely interested in seeing that it is carried out just as you wish.

"It is not your money that counts. We try to infuse into our business dealings with you, that personal interest which makes ordinary commercial transactions a source of true pleasure. If ever you receive anything from us which is not all we said it was, on no account keep it, we will look on it as a special favour if you write us, as it is our desire that not one word in our catalogue should misrepresent.

"Our ambition is to have a great company of staunch, loyal customers who, from experience, have learned to trust us altogether – our catalogue, our advertisements, our letters. We thank you sincerely for your orders in the past, and we will appreciate your whole-hearted support in the future. May we expect it? Yours very truly, Robt. A. Laidlaw."[8]

The claims he made about his prices were not unfounded. Retailers complained bitterly all over the district, some came to see him personally, and one country newspaper even refused to publish his advertisements for fear it would ruin trade in the surrounding area. Everywhere it went his catalogue quickly became the ruling price guide for the district.

In defence of the low pricing he stated: "Our conviction is, that the farmers are the true wealth-producers of the Province, and that method of trading which eliminates unnecessary expense and leaves most money in the hands of the farmer is the method that will increase the productiveness of the land, and thus the prosperity of the Province." [9]

In the second catalogue he also launched the Laidlaw Leeds Co-operative Workers' League, the first in a series of marketing initiatives. With the aim of increasing sales and his customer base the idea was simple. Customers could join the league and through their own sales and those of friends they encouraged to buy from him, be eligible for prizes.

All a customer had to do to join was send in their name and address and in turn they received a set of stickers which they affixed to their and their friend's orders. Every two months Robert tallied up the amount of business done by each member and awarded a prize to whomever had put through the most. His trump card was the staggering amount of money he offered in prizes – £900 worth. Such an amount was unheard of. An English piano worth £44 was the first prize, second a home organ, third a bicycle, and 50 other prizes of gold watches, English silverware, saddles and jewellery. There was also an annual award of £150 cash – a year's wages. His intention in forming the league was to double business. The result in November alone proved its worth; sales tripled.

This pushed his month-old premises to the limit. The son

of the owner of his new warehouse wrote to him offering the second warehouse, which was still vacant, another 16,500 sq ft. He was interested but a little hesitant and seeking God's guidance on the matter in prayer he felt that he should wait until the new year to make sure the spectacular increases were not just the rush before Christmas. January sales dropped to £3909 but were still nearly twice what he was doing when he had moved in. He waited no longer and wrote back accepting the son's offer.

He received a quick but surprising reply saying that the building had in fact been already let and was now no longer available. Immediately Robert went round to see the son only to be informed that the son had in fact leased the premises himself from his mother because the lease on his business had been shortened to three years. Robert was not put off. He convinced the son to stay where he was for another three years and let him have the other warehouse for that time.

The new building required substantial alterations. The despatch department had become terribly congested, so the ground floor of the additional building was radically altered to allow for an additional two cart docks instead of one. Aside from that, some 40,000 feet of kauri timber was used to make purpose-built shelving in varying sizes to carry stocks.[10]

Each warehouse had a hydraulic lift that could lift one ton of goods at a time from the ground to the fourth floor, but already it was clear that other improvements were necessary for efficiency. He had two chutes installed to carry goods from the various floors directly down to the despatch department on the ground floor. In addition he had 13 telephones installed with seven direct lines to the central exchange. He also purchased a Burroughs automatic adding machine which he had seen advertised in *System*, and used it to total up the figures each day. It took four men to open the mail every morning and 20 typists worked non-stop in the correspondence department. The new premises added an extra 18,500 sq ft, the combined floor space of the two warehouses now 35,000 sq ft.

Carrying stock meant that he also had to have a very effective way of keeping track of exactly what was on hand and where it had come from. Following similar examples in *System* magazine he devised a card index inventory system that allowed him to not only monitor stock levels and reordering but also told him the source of each item he had in stock.

If he went short of an item and had to purchase it locally it was invariably more expensive and this was information he wanted to know. The degree of office mechanisation and the energy with which he incorporated the latest processes to aid efficiency had never been seen in New Zealand business; he was 40 years ahead of his time.[11]

All these additions meant increased staff and even then he was only just keeping pace with the growth of the business. Sales were climbing £2000 a month and in May he did more sales in one month than the entire first 10 months of business put together. In August the unthinkable happened and the business nearly doubled in size again when sales rocketed to £18,278. Total sales for the second year of business to September 1911 were £95,749 – five and a half times those of the first year. Robert made a net profit of approximately £6000, enough to buy 12 homes.

As more and more staff were added the business took on another dimension. In the new buildings he created departments and appointed managers over the various sections of the business – office, correspondence, drapery and clothing, hardware and crockery, grocery, boots and saddlery, furniture, receiving and despatch. Jack took over receiving and despatch and his other brother Arthur (three years his junior), left his father's business, Laidlaw brothers, and took over the drapery and clothing department.

Robert walked around the premises of his new warehouse. His quick step and amiable smile were now renowned. Every morning he toured the warehouse and greeted every employee by name. Those walking with him seemed to be doing more of a trot to keep up. He reached the saddlery department on the third floor. The rich smell of leather filled the air, hundreds of saddles hung obediently on purpose-made racks.

In the hardware department immense floor-to-ceiling shelving units, crafted out of kauri, stored thousands of items from lamps to trunks to ironware – all boxed, all ready for shipping. Blackboard tally boards hung at the end of every aisle recording shipments and the movement of stock. On the top floor of one warehouse he housed the furniture department. Dozens of kapok mattresses and pillows were piled high into the roof space. On the expansive floor plush velvet chesterfield sofas, hall stands, and wardrobes all in native timbers filled the area, and from the beams in the roof hung cane chairs. Every available space was being used.

Deep in the basement under the thick floor beams lay a goldmine of stock. Heavy wooden crates, stamped and nailed, held the bulk grocery stores. Resembling those in a munitions depot, the crates stretched endlessly in the underground cavern separated only by a few narrow walkways. Echoing from the floor above could be heard the sounds of the despatch department as heavy iron trolleys wheeled back and forth loading a growing line of drays and carts for the wharf and the post office. The whole place was a bustle of activity. The first floor was his nerve centre, the general office.

In the wide open floor lined with sunlit windows two dozen typists clattered away dealing with the correspondence. To one side was his private office. Only he and his accountant had one and neither was large. In a room about 15 sq ft, with a secretary sitting close by taking letters, he directed activities. He kept a tidy desk and few papers lay around the room. By his right hand stood an ornate telephone with trumpet mouthpiece and nearby a small black filing cabinet housed all his important documents. His pride and joy was the shelf of books that rested behind him. Indexed and labelled they were his management and business texts from around the world.

By now he had gathered around him a group of 12 executives. All like him were in their early twenties. Some were Christians, some were not. He didn't believe in only promoting Christians and would not let belief hinder a talented man's progress. Around town they were affectionately known as the schoolboys of Laidlaw Leeds, but it was ironic that the 'schoolboys' were giving the other business houses of the city a run for their money.

The American management consultant A.F. Sheldon had encouraged him to see his role in the organisation not so much as manager but rather as teacher. His express purpose then was to teach the organisation, and most importantly his executives, the principles, systems, values and beliefs he wanted to see enacted. He took to this role with zest, tutoring each of his managers individually through Sheldon's Business Building Course that he had completed several years earlier, believing rigidly in the value of study.[12]

To the firm and his executive he wrote: "Twenty centuries of business have honoured this infallible Greek proverb – let it sink in – 'To earn more, learn more.' There is no truer law. The vital problem with you, is not how I scheme to get promotion, but how can I study and develop myself to fill it when it comes."[13]

Each week he held a weekly management meeting, usually on a Tuesday and at the close of business, lasting for at least an hour. After discussing merchandising conditions generally, he asked each manager to talk about any troubles they were experiencing in their departments. He also invited each to comment on every single person under his charge. By now, with a staff bordering on 200, this was no small exercise.[14]

He and his executives also spent an increasing amount of their spare time having fun together. They went to Eden Park to watch the rugby, they went hunting, fishing and boating together. These were not training sessions – just enjoyable times growing closer. It was a spirit of comradeship that spread out into the organisation.

He took the entire firm on picnics to islands in the harbour; they had musical evenings, sports days, team competitions against other Auckland firms, debating clubs, marching teams, athletic clubs and girls' social clubs. Many of the social events he paid for out of his own pocket.

To him it was all part of being a cooperative whole. "All pulling together towards the goal," he would say, and saw it as fundamental to the success of the business. "Our own ability governs the net results we each produce," he said. "Our own success consists in what we are and what we do, but our firm's success consists in the sum total of the successes of each man and girl in it. You see how inseparable our interests are. The loafer not only holds down his own success but makes it harder for his comrades."[15]

5

RAPID GROWTH

1911-1913

*"No word in the vocabulary of business is more pregnant
with significance than the one word quality. You may apply
it to goods, to service, to ability – this one truth is universally
the same; no extravagant assertion of present advantage, no
false logic of economy, can make headway against downright
merit in merchandise or men."*[1]

Robert Laidlaw, 1912.

Growth had come at a rapid pace and Robert's forethought
in all the areas of his business shone through. His concentrated
readings of *System*, the other American business books he had
purchased, and the courses with A.F. Sheldon had given him
deep insight into the planning and running of a large business
concern. He had organised every operation in fine detail, so
when expansion came, even on the scale and speed he was
experiencing, it didn't trip him up; rather he grew quickly and
easily. Four years of planning had paid off.

In October 1911 he released his third catalogue, which was
again a leap from catalogue No 2, and opened it with a warm
letter to his customers, headed up with a picture of his hand in
the position of a handshake. He wrote:

"Here is my hand, I extend it to you right heartily. I thank
you for your past support, and I want – yes, I need it in the

future if our business is to go on increasing as it did with your help last year.

"Because we never supply city trade, but deal exclusively with out-of-town people, I have come to look upon our business as belonging to you and me. A sort of mutual benefit society – to you in saving – to me in a small profit. Then let us work together through 1912. Your share to send all the orders you can. Mine, to perfect our service and to supply quality goods at our now famous prices, and next year we'll compare notes."[2]

He expanded the range of goods he carried still further and produced far more catalogues. This time he had 28,000 printed. The catalogue also jumped another 100 pages in length to 277 pages and carried over 5500 different items. He went into wallpaper, linoleum, children's toys, more lines of furniture and extended his own brand range further. He arranged for a large American manufacturer of sewing machines to produce a Laidlaw Leeds 'Rival' machine.

While sewing machines on the general market ranged in price from £6 to £12, he sold his 'Rival' machine with an unconditional guarantee at £4.19s, a third cheaper than even the cheapest machines available. He also produced baking powder, luggage trunks, writing pads and hand sewing machines all under his 'Rival' label.

Expansion didn't stop with products either. He appointed a young staff member, Frank Parkes, to the position of 'Farmer's Friend.' Not a commercial traveller, Parkes' sole responsibility was to circulate among the firm's 10,000 customers dotted all over the North Island of New Zealand and talk to them.

"I can't come myself," wrote Robert, "so I'm doing the next best thing sending Mr. Parkes as my substitute. How gladly would I spend an evening with you myself, getting to know you better.

"I feel," he continued, "that the ring of sincerity in the human voice is often lost in the written word. I feel that the warmth of a hearty hand-shake can find no expression in the 'yours truly', of an ordinary letter. I would like to know not only you, but the youngest in your family. I appreciate the fact that the boys and girls of today will be our customers of the future.

"I already have many staunch little friends among the boys and girls who have called here, and I know they will grow up into loyal customers. I would like to have such a little friend in your home.

"Mr. Parkes is not a commercial traveller; he doesn't want your orders – he won't ask for them – but he wants to meet you – to shake you by the hand – to know you; he wants to answer all questions you would like to ask; he wants to hear all your suggestions for the improvement of our service; he wants to bring you in closer touch with our organisation, because it is run exclusively in your interests, and because he feels you ought to have a say in its management." [3]

Parkes was Robert's ears in the market. No other firm had done anything like it – put a full-time market researcher in the field with no other duty than to find out how they could improve the business.

In November 1911 he barrelled ahead and launched yet another innovation publishing a company magazine entitled *The Optimist*, 16 pages long. He himself wrote and edited every edition.[4] *The Optimist* was his lifeline to the business.[5] With so many staff it was impossible to devote careful time and attention to everybody; instead he used *The Optimist* to transmit his thoughts and ideas on business, character, life and society. Each page conveyed his own brand of optimism, challenge and motivation to the staff.

He believed that continued inspiration was essential to carrying something through to the finish and saw nothing better than the inspirational lives of others to motivate himself and staff. He read the accounts of such business greats as J.C. Penny, John Wanamaker, Henry Ford, Marshall Field and the inventor Thomas Edison and passed on their stories in *The Optimist*. He also packed it with excerpts from overseas business publications. Writers like Sheldon and Casson, his favourite business magazine *System*, and others like 'The Business Magazine', 'Efficiency Magazine', and 'The Business Philosopher' he used frequently.

But *The Optimist* was not just for talking business; he also tackled topics like virtue, honour, character and his own Christian beliefs. An important part of this was the place of reward, or as he called it – the 'law of compensation.' Practically he believed that hard work brought with it reward, and that extra effort brought with it extra reward, linking these thoughts back to two verses in the Bible:

"Remember this: Whoever sows sparingly will also reap sparingly, and whoever sows generously will also reap generously."[6] "Do not be deceived; God cannot be mocked. A man reaps what he sows."[7]

To him they were like inputs and outputs: put great service in, take out profit – what you sow, you reap. He not only believed it, he saw it evidenced in the success of his business.

"The law of compensation," he wrote, "is absolute because it is a law of nature. It may work slowly, but eventually a man is sure to get his true worth in wages. If he sins he is sure of sadness. If he is virtuous he is certain of happiness. If he loves he is certain to be loved, if he hates he is certain to be hated; if he works he wins reward, if he loafs he will drift – yes, drift from one employer to another until he drifts out of the track of employment altogether till even his old companions call him a waster ...

"I am human like you men, I too feel the inclination to ease up just for a second, but the law of compensation is too exacting – the penalty of the pause is too great, neither you nor I can afford to carry such a loss. I'm right with you to help you save this loss for the coming year. Those who have brains will be keen for higher wages. If you can make any suggestions that help towards higher wages we will be glad to hear them, for our interests are mutual. Your wages and our dividends are paid out of profits, so that which can increase your wages can also raise our dividends, and vice versa."[8]

His efficiency efforts in the firm were continuous. He not only centred his activities around increased mechanisation, he also organised his reporting structure so that even with the large amount of business going through each week, he knew daily what the state of his business was and how that compared to previous months. He used ledgers and sales analysis books to show him not only daily, weekly and monthly totals to date but also kept track of expenses over a wide range of categories.

He performed ratio analysis on these figures at the end of each month to know accurately how the different parts of the business were performing, and what efforts were producing what results and how these compared with the same periods in previous years. Trade was now consistently above £10,000 every month and they were already using the larger premises to capacity. When it seemed he already had the business operating at maximum efficiency he pushed the bounds of management even further, and in February 1912 instituted a system of half-daily reports.

Jack had noticed that in the despatch floor they were getting bogged down with orders in a great rush in the afternoon rather than regularly during the day. Business was getting held up somewhere but it was difficult to pinpoint exactly where without some kind of measure on all the different departments. Half-daily reporting on everybody's progress from checking rooms to packers to typists would pick up how and why this was happening. It would also have other byproducts and by the end of three months Robert was able to ascertain the average time and output of each of the different jobs performed in the organisation. He had conducted his first organisation-wide work study. From this he increased wages accordingly for those who achieved higher than expected results, firmly believing that those who did the most work should also get the most pay.[9] Making the most of whatever opportunity you had in life was central to his thoughts.

"Lack of success, he said, "is not caused by a dearth of opportunities. Men grow their opportunities, but they fail to harvest the crop. Every day has its own particular kind of fruit of opportunity, which must be gathered on that day or never. Opportunity beckons ability. She stands with open arms. She offers prizes for effort and development. Train yourself – don't envy success. It comes with constructive work ... The world has always been full of opportunities. It exists everywhere for those who, with hands, eyes, brains, and ears, are seeking to render service that serves.

"Whatever has been done in the world's history can be done again through the operation of the same laws and forces. We can be men and women of power, or we can be men and women of impotence. The moment that one grasps the fact that he can rise, he will rise, and that he can have no limitations except those he sets for himself in the efficiency of his work.

"The world is crying out for workers who can carry things of all kinds to where they are needed. It wants workmen who can create desire for its wares where there was no desire before. It offers rewards to those willing to increase their efficiency and then sell their services at a profit to themselves and to the institution that employs them.

"We are alive to the value of a worker who strives to earn

more and is not afraid of doing more work than he is paid for, and is not so much worried about wearing out his brains as he is about using them too little. He is the sort of chap that believes that the Scripture is true in business as well as in all else, 'Whatsoever a man soweth, he shall also reap.' He sows enthusiastic, correct work and plenty of it; he's looking for a harvest of success and he won't be disappointed."[10]

Following through with the idea of forming a cooperative workforce, he had suggestion boxes made and put up all over the two warehouses, declaring to the staff that he would pay for the best suggestions. Originally deciding to rank them and pay the best suggestion £1, and second best 10 shillings, he finally settled on offering 2/6 for each suggestion put into operation. It was a good offer, over half a day's wages, and the suggestion boxes were soon well used.[11]

He reinforced the importance of these suggestions in *The Optimist* and also made available to the staff his own personal library of business books for either them or their family to use.

"For instance," he said, "you get more pay for each working hour now than you did the first day you worked. Why? Because you have put more value into each hour of your time – you have developed your efficiency. Your business efficiency grows out of your business ideas, and these come from your business knowledge. If you enrich your knowledge with the tested and proven experience of other men by reading, you save yourself valuable time, and the needless labour of studying out that which is already known – you avoid useless and expensive mistakes – you make yourself a many-brain-power-man – you add other men's business knowledge to your own efficiency – you get the best possible material out of which to manufacture new and original ideas.

"These new ideas in business are what make and break records – they bring out new ways to save time and labour –

they mark the difference between the man who gets paid much, and the one who receives little. They make business. They win and keep trade. Now if you cannot make suggestions read business books – your Department Manager will give you the right kind – let other men's ideas soak in; think about them; how can they be applied to your daily work?

"See how many useless motions you go through every day, then evolve a way of cutting them out; write it down, and there's 2/6 made in a jiffy, and best of all, your own brain further developed and ready to produce more money-saving thoughts that will help you become still more efficient, and thus more valuable. The men and girls who put brains into their work are the sort we want."[12]

Before the March 1912 edition of *The Optimist* came out he sat down at the desk of his second-floor office. Looking out through the partition at the scene before him he could see dozens of faces. Some he knew, some he barely recognised. The business was growing in all kinds of ways and still he was sure this was only the beginning. For several weeks he had been thinking about some way of capturing all the elements he had been talking about to date; about getting down in words his vision for the business – something to guide them as they grew.

Taking a pen from the drawer he began to write on the notepad in front of him. The words came quickly. It was not only a vision of where he wanted to get to, it was also the map for the journey. As the ink dried on the page he sat back and breathed a sigh. A part of him lay in those words. They were the essence of what it was to be in business, they were the essence of who he was as a businessman.

"Our Aim, to build the greatest business in New Zealand; to serve the farmers in the best possible manner, with the best possible merchandise; to simplify every detail of every transaction; to absolutely satisfy every customer with every purchase; to eliminate all delays; to sell only goods it will pay our customers to buy; to treat our comrades with kindness and our competitors with respect; to work as a co-operative whole because all at it, always at it, wins success."[13]

In March 1912 his customer base reached 11,800 and sales rose to £16,139. In April he continued with the first mass meeting of the entire firm to discuss efficiency. He had already made it clear to his customers in the third catalogue that one of the aims for the coming year was to improve both packing and service so these became as renowned as their prices.[14] Staff suggestions came in thick and fast and mass meetings to find out ways of improving service soon became commonplace and spread to individual departments. The furniture department even met in their own time to discuss efficiency methods, the elimination of waste, reduction of expenses and customer service as well as motion study.[15]

Robert also emphasised another trait in his writings which he linked to his Christian life. To him the importance of service applied equally in business as it did in life.

"He profits most who serves best, he wrote, "and if there still remains a lingering doubt in any mind as to the truth of this statement let me offer you the testimony of Him who made all the laws that govern our lives. In Mark 10:44, He says, "Whosoever of you will be the chiefest shall be servant to all." Or in other words, a man's greatness shall be gauged by the greatness of his service."[16]

The greatness of his service was having obvious effects and between March and October 1912, sales averaged £16,000 a month. It produced a record-breaking year. Staff were receiving bonuses for efficiency and being paid for their suggestions, £900 worth of prizes had been sent out to members of the Co-operative Workers League and he had realised his goal as well – business had doubled yet again and he made a net profit of over £10,000. He was now a very wealthy man.

His range of goods kept increasing, too, and when he released Catalogue No 4 in October 1912 it was 130 pages longer than No 3 totalling 402 pages. He also had an additional 10,000 copies printed taking the total to 38,000. It cost him £2287 to produce – nearly 20 times his first run three years before, yet it was more than paying for itself. He kept accurate records of how much business was done per catalogue, even per page. His first catalogue had produced £2/4/0 in sales per catalogue, his 1911 catalogue £6/1/0 per issue. To print they were only costing him a little over a shilling each.

The response to all his efforts came not only in profits, but also in letters of appreciation from customers. Often they expressed their appreciation with how well the goods were packed: one wrote in saying "I can say we have been well satisfied with all the goods received from your warehouse, and the price can't be beaten. We also found everything carefully and well packed." Other letters remarked about the keen prices and the speed at which their orders had been despatched. Another wrote in with a poem showing his appreciation for the packing of the goods he had received.

Ode to W. Hayward
Packer No. 3
Dear Number Three, it seems to me,
Though I am but a novice,
That better packing could not be,
Than you've placed at my service.
I've sung the praises of No. 4,
In full poetic measure,
And so, as well, have many more,
But three you are a treasure.
While Laidlaw Leeds' fame endures,

And packing is required,
May all their packers be with your,
Ambition fully fired.[17]

By the time the October 1912 catalogue went to print he had received over 2300 such letters, publishing three pages of them in the catalogue and offering £1000 cash if anyone could prove that any of the testimonials were false. No one did.

In *The Optimist* too he went to great pains to personalise everything that went out. Following sports days he published lists of first, second and third place-holders in individual events, the names of those who had given suggestions too he always listed, as well as those who had won competitions or solved his witty brain-teasers.

The part that A.F. Sheldon played in contributing to his thoughts cannot be underestimated. Sheldon approached commerce in a very practical way, breaking business up into parts, and this appealed to Robert's mechanical mind. In the United States his courses were well attended and by 1912, 40,000 business people had taken them. Robert communicated with Sheldon directly and offered Sheldon's Science of Business Building Course at half price to all the employees of Laidlaw Leeds.[18] In letters between the two, Sheldon challenged him directly about his role in the business.

"Mr Laidlaw I want a word with you. A great businessman said to me recently, 'I quit thinking about the success of the company dividends, etc. a long time ago, and transferred my thought to make each man and woman connected with my institution a success. As soon as I did that, I began to find that the success of the institution began to take care of itself.' If the employees in your institution are not successes, then your institution is not a success. Do you feel that way?" [19]

In his next letter Sheldon was even more direct: "I am talking with you now, Mr Laidlaw. The first thing to do is to recognise the value of Man-Power. Recognise the fact that it is the most valuable thing in your business; then recognise the fact that you are a Teacher. Approximately 98% of the world are employed by the other 2%. The 2% are therefore either consciously or unconsciously teaching the 98%. Many employers are conscious of the fact that they are teachers – Teachers of the Science of Service to their employees. Such men are the Master Business Builders. May we have many more of them. They are leaders in progress. Many do not realise their functions as teachers.

"Naturally the poor service they and their employees render to the public makes the public avoid them. Instead of graduating from the college of success the only diploma they ever receive is a discharge from the bankruptcy court. They failed, because they refused to learn."[20]

Robert wound Sheldon's thoughts into editions of *The Optimist*. He began by discussing service ... "Money doesn't make itself, it has to be made. And the necessary ingredients for making money may all be summed up in one word – service ... Oatmeal, water, and salt, plus the help of a fire, are cause – porridge is effect. It seems simple doesn't it, but it's true. Service is cause – money is effect. Correctly combine the large quantities of the right kind of ingredients together and you get much (commodity).

"Mix enough of the right kind of deeds, (the things you do) and the right kind of words (the things you say) and you then render great service and the natural result is – more profit to you. The profit you make, is the pay you get for the service you render.

"Are you aware of the fact that 95% of those who set sail on the sea of commerce fail to reach the port of financial success? Startling but true. Why? There's a reason. There is always a reason why this man wins and that man fails. Ask the next

100 persons you meet the question, 'What are you in business for?' You will get the answer, 'To make money' from at least 95% of them. That's the reason for their failure.

"When ninety-five out of every hundred can knowingly and understandingly say, I am in business, or I am working to render service, when they can say that honestly, meaning every word of it then the statistics will be gloriously reversed. 95% will win. For 95%. can win, if they will render the world the service the world needs.

"We must get back to the law of cause and effect in the world of business. Fire is cause, heat is effect. If I want heat I build a fire. Service is cause, money is effect. If I want the heat of money, the warmth of profit, the enjoyment of more pay, I must build a bigger fire of service. So must you – you who read this. So must every man who would be a business builder and a money maker. No one can escape the law of cause and effect."[21]

Robert believed that the way to success in business was not one particular thing, but rather a recipe of things that he needed to get right. He believed that if he served the customer well then he would reap profits. He saw it his duty to teach those beneath him, and that through cooperation they would achieve their greatest successes. He saw the value of education and learning, and added into the recipe providing the highest quality goods at the lowest possible price.

His quality policy at Laidlaw Leeds was simple. He saw it as his duty as a seller not to provide goods that were shoddy or possibly harmful to the customer, and at times discontinued lines that didn't meet his standards, even stopped selling cigarettes because of reports they were affecting the health of school children. Added to this were *The Optimist*, the suggestion boxes, the packaging, the picnics, the rewards for efficiency. They were all part of the recipe. They were all necessary ingredients.

Between October 1912 and January 1913 sales still averaged around £16,000 a month and it was obvious that his two four-storey warehouses could now no longer contain this amount of business. He was faced with a pressing dilemma. The lease on one of the warehouses was due to run out in February 1914 so he had just over a year to either find new premises, or build premises of his own. He decided on building and had plans drawn up for a large 80,000 sg ft six-storey warehouse.

Finding suitable financiers however proved difficult and although he made inquiries all over the North Island none would agree to backing his venture in the slightest. Nor could he finance it himself; although he had done substantial trade he had not amassed the kind of capital it would take to build a large enough building, the estimated cost of which was over £30,000.

By far the greatest proportion of his goods was sourced overseas. Much of this buying was done by agents in America and London and in January of the new year he was called on by the New Zealand representative of London buying house Laughland, Mackay & Co. They had expressed a desire to take over some of his English business from his present agents. The agent and he discussed the matter at some length and then Robert made the firm an interesting proposition.

"I'll offer you the total British and European business of my firm with one proviso," said Robert.

"What's that?" said the agent.

"That your firm, if it is financially able, allow our first £10,000 of goods as a permanent advance at 5% interest and draw drafts on us thereafter."[22]

Robert's patronage was certainly valuable but Laughland, Mackay & Co were not automatically convinced. On the other side of the world at their English premises the firm had a visit from an unexpected caller. Robert's father was on holiday in

Britain and hearing of his son's offer decided to give the firm a little encouragement of his own. Robert was soon notified of the English firm's acceptance of his terms and he got a very large and very cheap, line of credit.[23]

When news of this agreement circulated back home, other parties too began to change their tune. Part of the reluctance to finance him to date may have been the many rumours that he was in fact going broke, presumably started by his competitors. Laughland, Mackay & Co's support gave him more than just funding, it gave him a golden seal of approval, and soon an Auckland lawyer who heard of the English firm's advance contacted him and promised to raise £17,000 towards the building fund from his clients.

Money to build suddenly became less of a problem but finding a suitable location continued to be difficult. Throughout this time he had been on constant lookout for possible sites but his search to date had turned up nothing, and in the meantime the business continued to press ahead.

In April 1912 sales took another leap and jumped over £20,000 for the month and May started out just as strong. In Auckland that month, Dr Wilbur Chapman, a visiting American evangelist, was preaching in the Town Hall. It had been 11 years since Robert's conversion at the Torrey-Alexander evangelistic crusade in Dunedin, and Chapman had come to New Zealand accompanied by Alexander who had been the song leader at the original Dunedin crusade.

Robert contacted Alexander and asked him if he would hold a meeting in the offices of Laidlaw Leeds, similar to those they had held in Dunedin businesses. Alexander readily agreed and the business was closed for a special noon service with the staff in attendance.

The central office area was cleared and filled with chairs and the office manager's desk made into a temporary stage.

Robert mounted the table to address his 225 staff. On many previous occasions he had sought to speak with different ones who came into his office about spiritual things but found that often he didn't get very far with them. Changing tack he began praying on the way to work, asking God to cause them to open up the subject if he had anyone ready for him to speak to. However his heart was for all his employees to know why he believed in Christ. Standing on the makeshift platform he told them of his conversion at the Torrey-Alexander mission in Dunedin and closed with the following commitment:

"It has been my privilege to speak to quite a number of you about your relationship to Jesus Christ, but, as it would be difficult to meet you all individually, I now promise to write in detail the reason why I am a Christian."[24]

He then introduced the evangelists and after a song from Alexander, Dr. Chapman mounted the desk to speak to the staff. He gave a short address and as he neared the end drew a penknife from his pocket and held it downwards with blade drawn, pointing towards the floor. A hush fell over the staff.

"If I drop this knife it will surely fall to the floor," he said, "the law of gravitation is pulling it down and nothing can prevent it falling if I let it go. But," he continued producing a magnet from his pocket, "if I bring this magnet into contact with the knife it does not drop. The law of gravitation has not ceased its influence; it is still pulling down as hard as ever, but I have interposed a higher law which keeps it stationary.

"So does the Spirit of God with you, or your will if you let Him. Your sinful nature is pulling you downward and even if you become a Christian will continue to exercise its influence on you, but if you decide for Christ he will introduce a higher law and greater power, enabling you to conquer the old nature. He will give you a fresh impetus, a completely new outlook; His very Spirit will dwell in you, and he is able to keep you from falling."[25] The service concluded shortly afterward.

In the final week of May Robert received a phone call from the land agent. It was the call he had been waiting for.[26] The agent had found him a site on the other side of town and he hurried over to see it. There on the corner of Hobson and Wyndham Streets was a large chunk of vacant land. He stood on the street corner and looked out over the site. In his mind's eye he could see the building of his dreams. It was perfect. He turned and made the agent a proposition. "I will buy this site," he said, "if you can induce a building contractor to erect a building of 80,000 sq ft and leave payment of the last £10,000 for 12 months after the building is completed, (total cost of the building and land was to be £38,000)."

The agent was not put off and said he would approach a contractor he knew and put the idea to him. He phoned back later to say the builder was considering it.

6

TESTED BY FIRE

1913-1915

"Strive to do it better – better than your competitors, better than your associates, and above all, better than you ever did before, and your reasonable success is assured in advance. Why? Because such an overwhelming percentage of your competitors will not make the same effort, hence your success from a comparative standpoint is inevitable. The greatest purpose that could enter your heart would be to keep in constant competition with your highest previous success." [1]

Robert Laidlaw, 1913.

The working week at Laidlaw Leeds was Monday to Friday, and until noon on Saturday. At the end of the week on Saturday afternoon the 31st May 1913, Robert was sitting in his office when his office manager brought through sales figures to the end of the month. It had been another huge effort and they had again gone over the £20,000 mark recording £21,339 in sales. He felt very pleased with the progress. It was a fitting end to a particularly memorable few weeks with Dr. Wilbur Chapman preaching in his warehouse, a suitable site found for a new building, and the possibility of a building contract being signed. A new and exciting phase was beginning. Donning his tennis gear he left the building at 1 o'clock and headed towards the Victoria Park courts to play his assistant general manager David Robertson. After they had finished the game the pair called in briefly again to Fort Street at 4.45 pm then went their separate ways for dinner.

After dinner Robert was relaxing in the lounge when the telephone rang. He went to the hall and casually picked up the receiver. The voice on the other end was more distressed, his building was on fire. Grabbing his coat he dashed out of the house, over the road running for the main street. His father's car was being repaired so there was no other option but to catch the tram. As he rounded the bend one came slowly alongside and he leapt onto the front platform next to the motorman.

"Step on it," he shouted, "Laidlaw Leeds is on fire."

"Oh," said the driver enthusiastically not knowing his passenger, "that must have been the one I saw on my way out. It's a great fire."

Robert felt a strange peace in his heart. Somehow deep inside him he felt as if God had everything under control. When they finally arrived in the city he made straight for the warehouse. It was a busy night in Auckland and there seemed to be thousands of people milling up and down the main street. He pushed his way through the crowds but when he turned into Fort Street the scene was quite different. His run slowed to a walk as he joined only a few dozen spectators watching the blaze against the night sky. Looking up he could see flames flickering out the broken windows and thick clouds of smoke pouring out the top floor of the warehouse. He soon found the fire commander and began to piece together what had happened that night.

The alarm had been raised at 7 pm and the brigade had arrived at the scene three minutes later. Breaking into the ground floor they found a heap of burning soft goods and rubbish at the bottom of the lift shaft. The draught in the lift well had already fanned this blaze up as high as the top storey and so from the outside the building appeared to be burning at the top and bottom at the same time. The top floor held the bedding and furniture department, and the flames quickly devoured the large stocks of mattresses and furnishings, bursting through the roof. The fire at the bottom of the building was soon put out but the top storey proved more difficult.

The brigade brought in a telescopic ladder and running it up against the side of the building directed a hose through a window in the top floor. Hundreds of gallons of water were pumped in and eventually this quelled the blaze.[2] By the end of the night the damage was quite obvious. The top floor of one warehouse had been gutted and the stock all lost to fire, the ground and first floors had also suffered extensive fire damage.

Everything in between had been thoroughly soaked by water. More stock was lost to water damage than fire. His second warehouse had escaped the blaze but did not escape water and smoke damage to stock. Robert knew that the fire would be reported in Monday's newspaper so he immediately went round to the offices of Wilson and Horton. There he wrote a large advertisement to occupy a quarter page in Monday morning edition of the *New Zealand Herald*. Under the bold heading 'Laidlaw Leeds Fire' he stated:

"To our 28,700 country customers,

"We thank you for the loyal way you have supported us in the past and feel sure we can depend on every one of you now. The fire which occurred in our premises last Saturday night will mean a big loss to us, but it will afford an opportunity that I believe thousands of you will grasp of showing your sympathy in a practical way by sending in your orders in increasing numbers.

"Only one of our 4-storey warehouses in Fort Street has been destroyed – the other is quite intact, and, of course, our 2-storey building in Customs street is safe, so that we can fill your orders as usual.[3] By the time you are reading this notice our organisation will again be in splendid running order, and 225 employees will make redoubled efforts to fill all orders up to our self-imposed high standard of absolute satisfaction to every customer in every transaction.

"The factories will all be working overtime and additional men will be employed, so that completely new goods will be used to fill your requirements. Carefully note – As we do a cash business requiring payment in advance with order, we think it only fair to our customers to explain that in addition to being covered by an Insurance policy of £34,000, we had on Saturday last a Cash Balance to our credit at the Bank of £8,136 which can be verified on application to the Manager, Bank of New Zealand, Auckland, also a £10,000 reserve in London, so that our customers can have every confidence in entrusting us with their cash as usual. No damaged goods will be forwarded – our guarantee remains the same, satisfaction after one month's test or money willingly refunded."[4]

In a way it was strangely ironic, but he pondered what Sheldon had written to him only a few months ago in a letter:

"Think of Laidlaw Leeds," his friend had said, "the greatest business institution with which you are intimately acquainted. Having it clearly in mind now think again, and imagine that in one day, by fire, all its property could be destroyed, but that everybody from errand boys up to Mr Laidlaw stood together, shoulder to shoulder, and bound by the bands of loyalty said, 'We will hold our organisation intact. We will live on bread and water if necessary, for sixty days. We will not disband. We will start over again."[5]

That possibility had now turned into reality and the real grit at his business would now be tested. When he returned to the scene early on Sunday morning he was allowed into the building. It was a mess. Black charcoaled timbers hung broken and burned at every turn. Soggy linen lay in piles on the floor. In the basement the scene was like something from another world. Eighteen inches of water had flooded what previously had been the bulk grocery store, and broken boxes and food floated aimlessly over the cavernous room. Other floors contained so much water that holes had to be cut through the floorboards to allow it to escape. Damage was estimated at between £25,000 and £30,000.

Twenty-four hours later he had a visit from the insurance assessor. The small bespectacled man wasted no time probing all possible avenues and promptly asked for the books of the company. Robert had his manager fetch them but the assessor had no more leafed through a few pages when he looked up.

"You didn't want a fire did you," said the man almost sounding surprised.

Robert was taken aback, the possibility of deliberate arson had not even entered his head. "Have you heard I did?"

"Yes," said the assessor, "I have."

He nodded his head as it occurred to him what had happened. Obviously his competitors were busy spreading bankruptcy rumours again.

There was a slight tap at the adjoining door and his secretary came into the room.

"Excuse me sir, the builder, a Mr. Julian is here to see you."

Robert excused himself and went out to greet him. This would be an interesting discussion; it was the contractor who was considering building his new building. They exchanged formalities then Julian began.

"I have come to say," he said, "that I will build your building on the terms you specified."

Robert was more than pleased. Julian's reply had been swifter than he expected but, if nothing else, he, like many others, had obviously read about his bank balance in the *New Zealand Herald* that morning.[6]

In the burned out warehouse next door the scene was now a noisy bustle of activity. The despatch, grocery and hardware staff had all donned overalls and forming bucket chains were clearing out the basement. The drapery girls sorted through wet drapery, saving what they could and cutting remnants. Others worked away with shovels and brooms to rid the upper floors of grime and soot. Their cheery, blackened faces, united in a common cause to restore their business to its former glory. Some worked non-stop through the night, others worked the following day, a public holiday without pay.

Robert was deeply touched by their show of support and penned a letter to his staff.

"The old adage says, 'Every cloud has its silver lining.' I think I have found a golden one in mine in the loyalty of the men and girls that it is my daily privilege to work amongst. I dare not mention names lest I should overlook someone, and I would not do that, but the signal service rendered by one and all. These are expressions of sympathy that I will never forget."[7]

A week later he took out a much larger half page advertisement in the paper to advertise his up-and-coming fire sale. "Most goods not damaged by fire, only by water," said Robert in his typically optimistic manner. "But as our guarantee forbids sending damaged goods to our country customers, we offer these great bargains direct to the Auckland public." And then taking space to have a dig at his competitors added, "When a wholesale warehouse is burned, the goods are usually sold to the retailers, who add a big profit, and even then are in a position to sell the salvage goods at low prices, but we are offering them direct. They'll be as good as new when dried. You may never have another opportunity like it, so bring plenty of money. You'll be glad you did afterwards."[8]

Sales in June after the fire dropped but fortunately not significantly, returning to the previous average of £16,000. July through September were likewise and October signalled the fourth anniversary of business. Robert's sales despite the fire had been £202,142 for the year. He realised a net profit of £12,000.[9] October also brought the launch of his biggest catalogue yet – 440 pages long with 45,000 copies printed. It had been a colossal undertaking to meet the deadline in the aftermath of the fire and with the new building under way. In September when the final proofs went to the printer he breathed a sigh of relief. Yet several months of upheaval inside the business were soon marked by upheaval outside the firm as well.

In October a series of strikes around the country engulfed the ports and soon spread to other trades. Before long the country was in the throes of a general strike and trade ground to a standstill, especially the ports. Non-union labour was brought in to work the wharves and resulted in violent confrontations. In Auckland alone 8000 workers went out in support of the watersiders.

Police numbers were insufficient to control the situation, and 1600 country farmers were enrolled as special constables and brought in on horseback to break up the strike and ensure the wharves stayed open. There were running battles with stone-throwing crowds. In the midst of the unrest on November 3 1913, Robert circulated a letter among the staff outlining his position on the goings-on at the Auckland water-front. He acknowledged failings on both sides but took up the case of new workers being allowed to work in place of the strikers.

"I hear a great deal about capital versus labour," he said. "I believe both will lose heavily through this strike, but I am treating the subject now on the basis of labour versus labour, claiming that the same principle of freedom that gives the striker the right to cease, also gives the free labourer the right to work without being molested.

"Of course, it may be said that if free labour is allowed on the wharves, the strike will be broken, but true men often have to accept what seems to be temporary loss that they might hold firmly to the highest principles. Freedom of action within the scope of her just and liberal laws is the secret of Britain's greatness, and to me it is a duty to see that this lawful freedom is extended to both strikers and free labourers alike.

"May the day never come when any of you will feel the slightest reticence about discussing labour questions openly with your managers. Sincerely do I thank you all for your share in maintaining the splendid spirit of friendliness that exists in our warehouse. I will not give you all the credit, nor would I take it all for the management; it must be mutual, for just as it takes two to make a quarrel, so it takes two to make friends. You have done your part loyally; I will endeavour always to do mine."[10]

His views were soon tested when called on by his three carters who took their goods to and from the wharves. Their union had gone out on strike in support of the watersiders but these men felt a strong allegiance to Robert and found themselves in a difficult position. He was sympathetic to their case; if the men didn't join the rest of the union on strike, they risked personal injury as strike-breakers. Reluctantly, they followed his advice and joined their fellow unionists on strike. The business was now minus its carters and without the ability to get goods to the ports many customers would go without their orders.

Robert went down to see his brother Jack in the despatch department. After a short discussion they went to the cart dock, took off their jackets, mounted the waiting drays and headed for the wharf. They were soon joined by a police escort as angry strikers descended on them. Protected by a ring of horses he and Jack edged their way forward and unloaded their goods for shipment. It was a journey they perilously repeated daily for several weeks until the strike finally ceased.

In the midst of the turmoil he also took time to fulfil a promise he'd made to his staff back in May that year. At the service held in their warehouse before the fire, he had promised to write down his reasons for believing in Christ. Over several weeks he composed his thoughts in the quiet of his parents' Clifton Rd home. The result was a small 64-page booklet. He entitled it quite simply, *The Reason Why* and began with an illustration:

"Suppose that a man should send his young lady a diamond ring costing him £250, and place it in a little case which the jeweller threw in for nothing. Would he not think it strange if, on meeting her a few days later, she said, 'Oh that was a lovely little box you sent me. I am going to take every care of it. I promise to keep it wrapped up in a safe place so that no harm shall come to it.

"Such a thing is too ridiculous to be thought possible," said Robert, "yet is it not just as foolish for men and women to be spending all their time and thought on their bodies, which are but caskets containing the real self, the soul, that the Bible tells us will persist long after our bodies have crumbled to dust." (Full text of *The Reason Why* begins page 323).

Contacting publishers, he asked for two quotes, one for producing 3000 copies and another for 5000. When the prices came back there was little difference between the two and although thinking that 5000 copies would probably last a lifetime he ordered that number. The first edition was generally well received. It was freely distributed to staff and any other interested people. Some, however, in the Christian community took offence at it, believing he was using the book to further his business interests, and wrote telling him how ashamed he should be using a tract to do so. In spite of such comments the first run of 5000 copies soon disappeared so he ordered a second.

When the second edition came out, in an effort to respect the opinions of those who had complained so bitterly about putting his name on the first edition, he decided to release the booklet without his name attached. That way those who wanted to read it could do so without drawing attention to either himself or the business. Even this did not appease his critics.

Soon a second wave of letters arrived in his office in even larger numbers than the first, attacking his moral cowardice for putting out a religious tract and being too afraid to put his name on it. It seemed he was damned at every turn. Demand for the booklet grew and still more editions were published, this time always with his name on the cover.[11]

With a strike ravaging the country, business in November had been slow, but in the new year it picked up. The new year brought changes in several directions. The lease on the family's Clifton Rd home ran out, as did the lease on one of Robert's two warehouses. The entire family moved over the other side of town to the corner of St Stephens Ave and Hobson Bay Rd in Parnell, and in April 1914 he opened business in his new building in Hobson Street. The sheer size was the most impressive thing about the new structure. Sitting on top of the hill, its imposing six storeys dominated the Hobson Street landscape.

Clearly obvious from the sea, the new warehouse had over 80,000 sq ft of floor space as opposed to the 35,000 in use at Fort Street. In appearance it was dramatically functional with a combination of grey plaster and red brick infills, inside expansive floors and thick, exposed timber columns. It was still very much a warehouse and had been purpose built to act as such. He did no retail trade, nor did he sell to those within the city limits of Auckland. His business was exclusively for the farming community, although by now it was a national affair with customers in both the North and South Islands of New Zealand.

In his new building the mechanical additions to speed up work also increased. He had three lifts installed as well as 24 telephones, 38 typewriters and his original Burroughs electric adding machine was now supplemented by two more. There were also now five cart docks as opposed to three at Fort Street for the speedy delivery of goods. He was not only passionate about efficiency at every level of the business, he was also concerned about the welfare of his staff working inside, and went to some expense and design to make the warehouse conditions as pleasant as possible.

Said Robert quite proudly to his staff, "From present indications our new warehouse, with fittings, will probably cost us over £35,000. Neither money nor thought has been spared in the endeavour to make it one of the finest buildings of its kind in the Dominion. How well, or ill, we have succeeded in making it a bright, clean, airy, healthful and pleasant place to work in, we leave you to judge. It is at least a great advance on our old building, and if you and I can improve our service to our customers, our friendly, co-operative attitude towards our comrades, and our innate cheerfulness in the same degree, then indeed will the spending of the money be more than justified.

"Graven in the tiles that adorn the entrance, and occupying a space 8in. by 5 feet, the simple but sincere word 'Welcome' greets everyone right on the threshold; but, after all, the bricks and mortar are cold, inanimate things.

"It is left for you and me to supply the atmosphere that will lend them warmth and make Laidlaw Leeds so pleasant a place as to stir a friendly feeling in the heart of every customer who enters our doors. But mark well, this atmosphere is very subtle – it defies definition in concrete terms – its source is in the attitude, or, rather, the habitual mood of the mind – the disposition – it finds its expression in actions truly, but it reaches out to people in such a strange indescribable way that they intuitively feel whether we are really glad to see and serve them or not. A right personal atmosphere demands as an essential, absolute sincerity at heart, and if you exercise such toward our customers, I, too, will get to know all about it without your telling me.

"It is hardly possible to overestimate the importance of having our new building throbbing with the right atmosphere, for, personally, I would rather dwell in a humble cottage that was warm with the atmosphere of home than live in a palace that was as cold as its own marble columns could make it.

"I'm not inferring anything against the past, for we've been a happy family even in our sordid surroundings, but there is always room for improvement, and as there is always plenty of space available, let us utilise some of it in this direction."[12]

A month after they moved in on Wednesday, May 27, 1914 Robert opened the new dining room on top of their building. He supplied meals in the staff dining room at cost, and in honour of the occasion the first social was held by the newly formed Laidlaw Leeds' Staff Club, with singing, instrumental items, speeches and short dramas.

Robert's own sister Minnie, obviously keen on acting, appeared in both the dramas, 'Betsy Bold Seeks a Husband' and 'The Bashful Lover.' Robert provided everything including the supper for his 200-plus employees free of charge.

Trade during the move and the months following was brisk. He installed yet more labour-saving devices and office appliances in the general office and lifted mechanisation to new heights, purchasing a dictaphone to aid correspondence, an electric record shaver (shredder), and a comptometer – a machine for multiplying and dividing. In the grocery department he added an electric elevator and automatic weighing machine as well as a machine for cleaning currants and steaming raisins. All were used in his constant drive to greater efficiency, thereby lowering costs and prices to his customers.[13]

Peace was broken in August when Britain declared war on Germany. New Zealand and the other colonial powers followed suit and soon the world was at war. A month later his brother Arthur announced his engagement. The rumour soon went round the warehouse that Robert's brother Jack, affectionately know as Mr. Jack, had intentions of forming a bachelors' club.

In the previous six weeks Laidlaw Leeds had experienced 10 engagements and only three managers now remained unattached. War was tugging at the heart strings. The outbreak of conflict only slightly dampened sales. At the anniversary of his fifth year in business he again improved on the previous year's trade. Sales for the past 12 months were £221,379 and he reaped a net profit of £13,282. His October catalogue contained even more surprises.

"Each year, like other big firms," he said, "we have to set aside a certain sum to be spent in advertising, for no matter how good our method of direct supply at wholesale prices may be, people cannot avail themselves of its benefits unless we tell them about it. The problem that faced us," he continued, "was how best to spend this money. That was, whether to give it all to the already wealthy newspapers or give as much of it as possible back to our own customers."

He chose the customers and with every £4 order, he offered

several pieces of solid nickel-silver cutlery. As his customers ordered more so they could build up an entire set. He also guaranteed the cutlery for 25 years, offering to replace it free of charge if it proved unsatisfactory within that time.

"Because everyone is in a real good mood when gathered with the family around the table," he said, "we believe there couldn't be a better place to bring Laidlaw Leeds daily before the farmers and their families."

In addition to all the other developments during the year, his mother Jessie had purchased a small seaside house on Auckland's North Shore. Still largely undeveloped, the North Shore had become a popular holiday spot with its bushy slopes and secluded private bays. A ferry service made regular crossings between the Auckland wharves and Devonport where a steam tram ambled its way along to Milford. The Laidlaws' house was in Ocean View Rd, Milford, surrounded by only a dozen other dwellings, the beach only a short stroll away.

In November, he took his executives over to the house for their annual retreat and they spent two lazy weeks in fishing, boating, even the occasional bout of boxing. For such trips he always packed large amounts of reading material. Early on in life he used to read novels with a passion until he reached a point when he felt he was devoting so much time to them it was actually holding him back in his career. He resolved to reduce the amount he read and then after reading in one of Sheldon's letters:

"Almost without exception, no man ever did a great service, or won great success who did not have the study habit," he abandoned the reading of fiction altogether.

As to this sacrifice, which he knew some would see as harsh, he remarked: "I know it all sounds terribly strenuous, but the struggle is a joyous one. There is nothing depressing or circumscribed in competitive effort."

From then on he habitually carried two books with him at all times, a New Testament and a pocket dictionary. If he was riding in a tram to work or on the ferry to Milford, he would pull one of them out and spend his time reading rather than watching. He drove himself like this relentlessly. He saw just sitting, not exercising his brain or bettering his position, as a waste of time. Encouraging the staff to take up the same practice he offered to furnish them with a New Testament and/or a pocket dictionary – all they had to do was write to him and promise to carry it with them.

He also received an unexpected call for his own little booklet *The Reason Why*. After the Chapman-Alexander mission left Auckland the previous year they had gone on to Europe. When war broke out in 1914 they were in Great Britain. The manager of the mission team, Ralph Norton, started an evangelistic work among the many wounded Belgian soldiers who were being sent to hospitals in Britain.

Unaware of these developments Robert had in the meantime sent Norton a copy of the first print run of *The Reason Why*, thinking Norton might be interested to see what he had come up with. Norton instantly found a use for it among the troops and asked for it to be translated into French and Flemish. This was done and soon a million and a quarter copies were printed. There was no charge for the booklet and Robert personally paid for the printing.

Meanwhile the first year in the new building closed with strong sales. He spread the good cheer around by announcing a string of promotions among the staff in the new warehouse, and also reaffirmed his policy not to engage an outside man to fill a position if there was a man in the warehouse who had proved himself worthy of promotion.[14] He believed it was the best way to inspire loyalty and enthusiasm in his staff. He also had a few words to say about Christmas cheer itself:

"We all want happiness," he said, "but we are all looking in the wrong place for it. The deepest happiness of all is to be found in God, and the only other source of happiness is to be found in our fellow man, and then in nature around us. There is not one single bit of happiness to be found inside ourselves, for the self-centred person is the most miserable creature that exists, while the unselfish person, without directly looking for it, enjoys the only true happiness."[15]

7

AMERICA CALLS

1915-1918

"In this terrific, ceaseless, relentless strife, methods – ideas – are the arms and equipment as sword and breastplate were the weapons of ancient Greek and Roman. And as no nation today would think of going to war with obsolete equipment, so no businessman can succeed unless new, advanced ideas are shield and buckler. The methods that you used last year will not serve against this alert competitor of the future. Better ways of doing the things you are doing are even now being evolved. Plans, methods, systems, strategy – out of these come all business results. Are you using them? If not, be sure that some other man will soon use them against you. If you are caught napping you will go to the wall."[1]

Robert Laidlaw, 1926.

Over the previous six years Robert had poured his heart and soul into Laidlaw Leeds at a feverish pace until finally the nervous strain caught up with him and he developed a severe case of shingles. It was not surprising. Even the staff commented that no matter how early they arrived at work or how late they left he could always be found in his office ready to deal with any situation.

On doctor's advice he was told to take some time away from the business. For some time he had thought of going to America, not so much for a break but to visit some of its great businesses, so he decided to combine the two needs into one and use the trip away not only as a break but also as a business trip. His doctor's intention had been to get him away from the business, but for him that was a near impossibility. Robert's ideal in training his managers had always been that one day they could do without him.[2]

He had said to them: "The measure of a man's value to a firm is not the extent to which the business is dependent on him but the extent to which the business can do without him." The effectiveness of all his training and input into the management would now be tested for the first time as he left for this enforced absence.

Before he departed he designed all the advertising campaigns that would be launched, and worked out a secret code 'GOTSEIDANK' by which the assistant general manager David Robertson could keep in touch with him about the state of the business throughout his trip. In German, it translated 'God be thanked,' with G=1, O=2 to K=0, corresponding to the letters. Robertson was then able to cable him the sales figures quickly and cheaply. He was taking no chances as the first two months of the year always had been slow.

On Friday, March 26, 1915, he boarded the R.M.S. *Niagara* bound for America.[3] Launched only two years earlier she was the largest liner ever built for the Union Steam Ship line, and cruised at 17 knots. The comfort of her three classes of accommodation surpassed anything to date and she lay like a priceless jewel in Auckland's harbour, red and black twin funnels atop a bronze-green hull with five passenger decks.

If anything was going to rid him of shingles this luxury was going to do it. It rained steadily all morning the day of departure. His friends and family gathered at Auckland wharf to see him off.

Those lucky enough to be allowed on board explored the

finely appointed 13,415-ton steamer with its music room and library. At 1 pm the *Niagara* pulled away from the wharf and headed out into the harbour. She was soon enveloped by a low mist and disappeared from sight. For the first time he travelled First Class, and after a stopover in Suva headed to Honolulu where he changed ships for his voyage to San Francisco. His original trip was planned for only four months, but this voyage had other things in store for him and it in fact would be five months before he returned.

When he arrived in San Francisco he immediately went to see his aunt and uncle, Annie and Daniel McFee. Annie had been one of the original Laidlaws who had emigrated to New Zealand in 1886, and later had moved to America marrying Daniel McFee. Living with the McFees was a young lady, Lillian Watson, who had been staying with them since her own mother died when she was only five. Robert had never met her before but his mother Jessie had. In 1906 she had visited her sister-in-law Annie in California when Lillian was 14, and after Jessie returned home to New Zealand the two had kept up regular contact.

In 1910 Jessie had gone on a trip to London and left her son Robert in New Zealand to deal with all her correspondence. One of these was a letter from Lillian and he opened it along with all his mother's mail. The letter intrigued him. Lillian, now 18, had wanted to take up nursing, but as the McFees could not afford it, had decided instead to turn to business and became a shorthand typist.

He asked his mother if he might write back to Lillian and after she agreed, began putting Lillian through the Sheldon Business Building Course that he put his executives through. He marked all her papers and they wrote to each other regularly. As the months turned into years their friendship deepened, and he tried various means to find out if she had any boyfriends, but Lillian never let on. It seemed the master salesman had possibly met his match. His case of shingles coincided with a World Fair in San Francisco, and Lillian had been sending him pictures and pamphlets about the exhibition.

The doctor's advice to take a break away had naturally led him to think of San Francisco. He could combine many of his desires into one – a World Fair, a break away, see the world's greatest business houses, and perhaps most importantly see Lillian.

As soon as the boat docked he made his way around to his aunt and uncle's house in the picturesque suburb of Engleside. Not long after his arrival Lillian appeared. Her letters had not conveyed her beauty, and by now the young girl of 18 had grown into an attractive woman of 22, with long brown hair tied neatly back behind her neck. A finely laced dress covered her petite figure, reaching to the floor, and her white skin was offset by deep blue eyes. Robert was more than a little surprised; he was captivated. Over the next few days the two of them spent every waking moment in each other's company. They strolled around the grassy streets and went for walks in the busy shopping district.

On the 14th night after his arrival, Lillian suggested they might go for a walk in the large park over the road from their Engleside home. It was a pleasant enough evening, the end of a balmy California day. In a few minutes the two of them were strolling arm in arm down its meandering path. There was no one about and when they reached the centre they sat down next to an ornate sundial.

He moved nervously on the seat and looked across at Lillian. She was more than he had ever imagined. Although he had been excited about their meeting he had never expected what was now happening. Their friendship had quickly fallen into courtship and he found himself head over heels in love. He couldn't keep her out of his mind. He had even practised the words he now desperately wanted to speak, but his emotions had ruffled his normal self-possessed composure.

"Lillian ..." he began, his throat dry with nerves, "will you marry me?" There was silence. She looked back at him kindly and smiled. "Certainly," she said tenderly. "But you'll have to get my brother's permission first."

It didn't surprise him. Seeing her half-brother Harry Ironside was something he had already reasoned on and he had got to know him well over the last two weeks. Harry was older than he and a respected local businessman in charge of the Western Book and Tract Company, a shop specialising in Gospel publications. Both of them shared a love for the Lord.

Early the next morning he motored over the other side of the harbour to Oakland where Harry and his wife lived. In his mind he ran through the conversation again and again. How was he going to introduce the subject, how would Harry react, for here he was about to take Harry's only sister away to the other side of the world? The car finally arrived at its destination. Harry met him at the door and beckoned him in. He was a large man with a round cheery smile. Robert lingered on the steps.

"It's all right Bert," said Harry loudly with a broad American accent, "don't be hesitant. Lillian rang up her girlfriend Carol and told her this morning that you were engaged, and Carol rang my wife Helen and told her and so it's all fixed up."

Robert was flabbergasted. He walked inside, not sure whether to feel relieved or angry. A few hours later when he got back to the city he made straight for Carol's place.

"Carol," he said as soon as he saw her. "What in the world did you ring Helen about that for?"

"Oh," she said fondly, "I tell you the truth Bert, if you hadn't married Lillian she would never have married anyone else."

Robert's displeasure was defused.

"You two girls didn't have it all fixed up before I got here did you, and I just walked into the trap?" he stammered.

Carol only smiled back.

San Francisco could not hold him and despite being engaged to Lillian he still wanted to see the businesses he had come so far to visit. Leaving her in California and armed only with a letter of introduction, he set out across America. Journeying overland by rail to Chicago he was able to meet personally the man who had such a big impact on his own management style, A.F. Sheldon. The two lunched together in one of the city's better restaurants, but the event proved something of an anti-climax. Sheldon was far more impressive with the pen than he was in person, and Robert left their appointment a little disappointed with the man behind such powerful ideas.

Chicago had other important sights and he called on the offices of Sears Roebuck. Sears was the biggest mail order business in the world, and Robert estimated that they did more business than all the exports and imports of New Zealand put together. Their sales in 1914 amounted to $110 million, handling as many as 75,000 orders in one day.

From Sears he visited Montgomery Ward, the oldest mail order business in the world and whose catalogue had inspired him to begin Laidlaw Leeds. It was a moving occasion seeing the grand old firm, and he was shown around for two days by one of the top executives, and given in-depth financial and operational information on the workings of the company. He was very impressed, but the admiration went both ways and the Americans were equally taken with the scale of operations the visitor from New Zealand had built so quickly.

From Chicago he went to Detroit where he visited the Ford Motor Company. Ford's huge moving assembly lines enraptured his mechanical mind. He walked the production line and watched as the moveable track smoothly ferried along a chassis. Twenty minutes later a completed Model T emerged. He was awestruck by the marvellous combination of technological precision, and the expert work of man and machine. It was efficiency in motion, no action was wasted, and 318,000 men manufactured 1000 Fords a day.

But the works themselves were only a reflection of the maker and he found himself much more interested in Henry Ford, the man.[4] To Robert it was yet another example of a single man who, like himself in the face of established foes, took them on with grit and imagination and won. He wrote to his staff:

"Twelve years ago when Henry Ford used to go to work every morning in his blue overalls in Detroit and return home in the evening begrimed with oil and dirt like 100,000 other engineers, all men were saying 'The day of opportunity for big success is past, railways, coal, steel, mining, telephone, telegraph and shipping are all in the hands of great trusts.' The motor industry was well launched with brainy men at its head and millions of dollars behind it; even here Ford's opportunity was apparently gone.

"But Henry Ford used his brains in two directions ... first of all he analysed and then he synthesised..... To analyse is simply to take the facts and break them up into as small parts as possible, so as to comprehend exactly their significance. To synthesise is simply to use the imagination to do the opposite, that is to build up again something out of the results of analysis.

"The motor manufacturers of that day were each making a dozen different models – each of a different weight with a different horsepower engine – each model could be had in any one of eight or nine colours and possibly in several designs of body. Mr Ford saw in these facts dissipation of energy – a breaking of one of the first laws of economical manufacture – concentration. The result everyone saw – a car so costly that only the wealthy could afford to buy it. Again he analysed and found that only about 2%. of the American people had incomes sufficient to run an expensive automobile. In his imagination he pictured a model factory in which should be made one type of car only, with one type of engine and one style of body, one colour of paint, one size of tyres, one set of fittings and at a price within the reach of 10 million people."[5] Ford had done it and his success was plain to see.

From there he ventured around Lake Erie to Buffalo, the home of the Larkin soap company. Founded in 1875, it now sold over $20 million worth of soap, perfumes and essences by mail each year. Robert had first read of the Larkins in *System* and was keen to see their operation firsthand.

From there he journeyed to Toronto via the Niagara Falls travelling down the Niagara rapids to Lewiston. As soon as he arrived in Toronto he made straight for the great department store, Timothy Eatons.

It was early in the morning and as he rounded a corner heading towards the store he stumbled across a vast line of wagons of every description. There were butchers' carts, milk wagons and fancy goods carts stretching as far as he could see down the block. They formed a solid mass in the street and were making no headway. A quick inquiry discovered the reason. The traffic jam turned out to be the daily rations for Eatons staff and public restaurants. The restaurant in the store served 4000 meals daily and the staff dining rooms catered for the 17,500 staff in the store which covered several city blocks.

All the businesses he visited welcomed him openly and he was shown round in all but one, by the head of the company. He openly discussed business systems and timed operations. He checked invoices and calculated the number of orders going through mail order departments and their processing speed. It was a marvellous opportunity to benchmark his operations against what the big American firms were doing. He was particularly impressed by how quickly they put through their orders, regardless of size. Every mail order business he visited was operating on a three-hour turnaround time from the moment the order arrived to when it was sitting on the despatch floor for delivery to the customer.

In general he was pleased to find that his American counter–parts differed little from his own systems of handling goods. However, he noted that as their size increased, they tended to put responsibility onto the staff to get orders right first time as opposed to the elaborate double-checking measures he had in place. Not surprisingly, some new measures were installed at Laidlaw Leeds to improve efficiency still further when he arrived home.

Finally it was on to New York where he visited the National Suit and Cloak Company. While on his journey he also purchased two books to add to his growing library – *Scientific Management* by F.W. Taylor and *Motion Study* by Frank Gilbreth. Never far from the latest technological innovations, he also had his first flight in an aeroplane while in the States, a Wright brothers biplane. Not the brothers' original plane, but a later model with the propeller and engine behind the pilot. Robert sat on the front edge of the lower wing with the pilot, both of them holding large control wheels and spent a very enjoyable few minutes airborne.

Soon his travels came to an end and it was time to return to Lillian and San Francisco. Six weeks had passed and he was delighted to be once again reunited with his bride-to-be. A simple ceremony was arranged and they were married by Harry Ironside in the company of a few friends on Monday July 26th at 8.30 pm in a service at the Bethany Hall, 23 Avenue and 20th Street, Oakland, California.

They had decided that the trip back home on the luxurious

Niagara would be their honeymoon, and Lillian said her farewells to lifelong friends, unsure when or if she would see them again. Before leaving Robert received a cable from home. Jack and another manager had left on the *Corinthic* bound for England to enlist and would miss meeting his new bride.

When the happy couple docked in September he arrived home to a different market situation. The war was causing shipping difficulties and prices were having to be revised frequently. Yet even this hadn't dampened the jovial mood at Laidlaw Leeds, and a great reception awaited him and Lillian when they walked into the large company dining room. They were greeted with a sustained burst of applause that continued until they finally mounted the platform. All the staff had contributed to make the event possible, and the newly married couple were presented with a canteen of sterling silver cutlery.

Their 'chief', as he was affectionately known, had returned home. Every department head rose to speak and the night's reporter penned: "The writer has been associated with many functions inaugurated by our various social committees, but never has he seen such a good-natured, contented and altogether pleasing company gather together under more happy circumstances than met in our Social Hall to welcome Mr and Mrs Robt. Laidlaw back from America."[6]

Robert and Lillian moved into a two storey house at 50 Shelly Beach Road, opposite Point Erin Park in Herne Bay. Lillian settled into her new country of residence to run a big house with seven servants and Robert applied himself once again to the activities of business. In October he received news from Jack. He had just arrived in England, and although his original intentions were to enlist in the Ambulance Corps, he had witnessed first hand a Zeppelin bombing raid on London. A woman and child were killed and several others wounded. He was disgusted at such blatant attacks on civilians and immediately sought to join the small air force that was coming together to counter the raids.[7]

When he had arrived to enlist at the Navy Office he was told that they had more volunteers for pilots than planes, and asked to come back in another six to eight weeks. This was more than the young Laidlaw's patience could bear, so he called on the secretary of the Overseas Club whom Robert knew personally.

With the secretary's influence Jack was accepted into the Royal Navy Flying Corps with only one remaining obstacle. The Navy told him that although they could train him in navigation and other skills they had no way nor means of teaching him how to fly. Jack found himself a flying school, paid the £100 fee and began lessons on his own account.

The year ending September 30 1915, Robert's fifth in business, showed sales of £245,071 giving him a net profit of £14,704. So far every year sales and profits had increased. Robert also enjoyed another milestone and celebrated his 30th birthday on September 8th in the company of his new wife.

October brought the release of catalogue No 7, which again was 500 pages and he had another 45,000 printed. Wartime had increased costs and it cost £4000 to have them printed and posted but he was hoping for a big year. In the previous 12 months they had processed nearly 100,000 orders and he was expecting to exceed that this year. However the catalogue cost was not the only thing that was increasing. While the war so far had not affected his sales, the input cost of his goods was rising.

As the majority of the lines he sold were imported from overseas, he was particularly vulnerable to disruptions in supply and increases in freight charges. Both were having an effect on prices and often his profit margin. If ships were delayed through submarine action or attack and he ran out of stocks, he was forced to buy locally. This was far more expensive and began to happen too frequently. Cargoes didn't arrive, were late coming or could not be filled by the English or American manufacturer due to wartime commitments to defence forces. The prices of wire, leather and woollen products all rose sharply due to their demand for military uses.

On the open sea freight prices had also increased substantially with the risk of attack and the drop in sea trade generally. From Britain, America and Canada the cost of sea freight doubled. Back in New Zealand this meant rising prices, and retailers everywhere were soon making adjustments. As wages rose war inflation gripped the country and the prices of many goods rose 50% or more.

On March 17 1916, just three months into the new year, came terrible news. Jack had been killed at Hendon airbase. He had passed all his naval exams and had been commissioned a second lieutenant in the Royal Navy Flying Corps. All that remained was to pass his final flying test. With his naval examiner and friends watching, he flew his flimsy bi-plane over the airfield. It stalled as he executed a turn and plummeted to the ground from 250 feet. He was killed instantly.

Within hours the family knew of his death, the message flashed across the world by wire. Robert was the first to be told and it numbed him to the bone. He went round to break the news to his mother and father. Before the day was out his sister in Dunedin knew, too. She was told while sitting holding the morning's post – a fresh letter from Jack. His death brought sadness and loss to many – the business, the church, the family, yet none more so than Robert. Jack had been with him since the very first hours of trade, since they had first made up lists of customers and with all the optimism they could muster, sent out their first catalogues. Through shifts in premises, fire and strike, Jack had always been right by his side. Now he would never be there again.

Robert found it difficult to imagine. They had so many things in common, sharing many of the same interests: their love of business and mutual determination to see the work through at any cost; their love of the outdoors and their passion for speed. Some wondered later why Jack had left ambulance work for aviation, yet he knew. Nothing pleased either of them more than the roar of engines as they overtook another car with the wind in their faces and adrenaline rushing. Jack also shared his love of God and was himself a devoted Christian.

The family's reaction was mixed. His mother Jessie was devastated. Jack was her youngest boy and had been her favourite son. Robert's second brother Arthur promptly enlisted in the artillery, but there was no way Robert felt he could enlist too. He had thought before about going to fight but now too much rested on the business. Friends and family had invested thousands of pounds in its expansion and it relied too heavily on his managerial expertise.

He worked out his own grief in the next few issues of *The Optimist*. Having missed Jack's departure from Auckland made the loss even heavier; he had lost more than a brother, he had lost his closest and dearest friend. In his last letter before he died Jack wrote: "I used to laugh to myself when you told us in the managers' meetings that our success was a danger to us; that perfection meant stagnation; that to cease to progress meant to retrogress, but since I have been in London and have seen what were once splendid businesses gone to the wall, I begin to think there was truth in what you said."

Robert knew he couldn't stop. He must go on. But the journey had lost some of its sweetness now Jack would not be there at its end. For the first time ever, sales began to drop, although not significantly.

Each month recorded lower sales than the same month a

year earlier. Perhaps it was winter, or perhaps the rising prices and a nation very much in the pains of war. He once again turned to the task of putting together the catalogue for the following year, although he found it difficult to muster enthusiasm without Jack. Sales in August and September showed signs of improvement and by the end of his seventh year trading to September 1916 achieved sales of £247,937, only fractionally higher than the previous year. He reaped a net profit of £14,876.

Throughout this time Lillian had been carrying their first child. On October 7 1916, at their house in Shelly Beach Road she gave birth to a son. A perky little fellow with a large grin and grey-blue eyes, he brought new life into the home in the midst of grief. Robert, following the tradition of several generations, named the boy Robert John. The baby's second name was after his late uncle Jack, who had been born John Ritchie. The family quickly picked it up and soon the new addition was known as 'little Jack.'

October also brought the launch of catalogue No 8. It was now a steady 500 pages and had been so for the past three years. But the catalogue he released in 1916 had a marked distinction that grabbed the immediate attention not only of its recipients but the rest of the business community as well. He took the incredible step of guaranteeing his prices for an entire year writing:

"You may order from this catalogue during September, October, November or December 1916, on the understanding that the prices are guaranteed against any advance, and no rises will take place during the currency of this Catalogue in 1917 – that is until August 1917 – without being advertised in the *Auckland Weekly News*."

To ensure that he could fulfil this commitment he bought heavily, especially on all the more popular lines. No one believed it possible and no other retailer in New Zealand took the same risk. All others declared their prices were subject to market fluctuations. Certainly the low point of the war so far had been the first six months of 1916 but the price guarantee broke the drought and sales moved upwards again. November and December closed the year strongly, both over £24,000. Even January, which often had registered sales in the low teens, came in £4000 higher than the previous year.

In February he was visited at Hobson Street by an American reporter, Elmer Murphey. *System*, the business magazine that he had so avidly read over the past 12 years, now sent someone to write about him, and Murphey spent a week with Robert intensely interested in the degree of organisation he had in place. Robert showed him the card index systems he used to keep track of stock and purchases, and the bonus systems he had worked out for every job in the business and paid to staff on a weekly basis. He had previously tried profit-sharing at the end of each year but found the average worker saw the end of the year as too far off.

Murphey also attended a weekly management meeting with him and wrote: "He is informal, magnetic, and his friendly personality invites free discussion of troubles. He does not adopt a negative fault-finding attitude. On the contrary, he is positive, a booster. After a short resume of the merchandising conditions that have come to his attention, he proceeds to take up the troubles of the different department heads. This discussion before all the men of the troubles of each, serves as a continual school, and saves Laidlaw's time: the next man knows how to handle a similar difficulty when it comes up in his department."[8]

Seeing how enthusiastic and dedicated Laidlaw's young executives were Murphey wanted to know how he knew which men to promote. Robert replied that he picked only those men who were willing to study. He had put his men through Sheldon's study courses and found that those who were willing to devote their time to self-improvement outside business hours made the best executives.

Murphey was impressed. He could see the level of enthusiasm among the young managers to make Robert's business a resounding success. "Laidlaw freely delegates authority," he wrote.

"His is the only company in New Zealand where each department head does his own buying. In other places it is done by the director or a member of the firm, after consultation with the department manager.

But it is by putting authority on the shoulders of these young men that they have developed so fast; and the sum of their success is, of course, the success of Laidlaw. In this country, these methods are revolutionary."[9]

Perhaps the most astounding thing of all was yet to come. Robert took Murphey through to his office one morning and there on his desk lay a pile of 72 cheques, all signed, yet all blank. His customers trusted him so much that they merely sent their blank cheques in with their orders for Robert to add up the amounts and bank them. It was a daily occurrence.

Wrote Murphey, "It shows how confident his customers are that he will keep faith with them."

Robert's motto of 'Stern, old fashioned, unfailing honesty' was showing its fruits in all kinds of ways and, with the price guarantee, sales kept climbing. The six months to July 1917 broke all previous records and started to surge forward again.

Robert didn't drink and towards the end of 1916 and into 1917 he took more and more opportunity to decry not only the vices and effects of the consumption of alcohol, but also the negative effects it had on the nation's economy, diverting vast amounts of money into liquor when it could go to more productive means. He was not alone in these calls for prohibition but it did make him some enemies, especially among anti-prohibition sectors of the unions and media. On Monday, 25 of June, 1917 at 11 am in the Auckland Chamber of Commerce, he handed over a petition on behalf of the city to three MPs in favour of 6 o'clock closing until the war was over. The petition contained 32,000 signatures and Robert addressed the 500-strong crowd with the following remarks:

"We are gathered here this morning out of loyalty to our King, our Country and our comrades in the trenches. We are banded together to do any and every legitimate thing we can to help win the war.

"In this terrible struggle in which our Country is engaged, under God we are dependent for victory on two main forces – manpower and money power. To realise the full strength of the first we must have efficiency, and to accommodate the full force of the second, we must have economy. We contend Sir that the drink traffic strikes hard at both these main planks in the "Win the War" platform on which stand the overwhelming majority of loyal New Zealanders. Our Minister for Finance urges upon us the strictest economy, while the people waste £14,000 per working day, or over £4 million annually on drink. Efficiency is the elimination of waste in both effort and material and every thoughtful man knows that alcoholic liquor is the greatest enemy we have to contend with."[10]

He sent out the No 9 catalogue at the end of July and for the first time a catalogue had gone out early.[11] His price guarantee the previous year had worked and there had been very few price alterations during the year. He again followed through in the launch of his ninth catalogue with a further promise to keep all prices fixed unless published in the *Weekly News*. No other firm in New Zealand had been able to do likewise. His customers, the farming community, responded enthusiastically.

By now they knew full well that he kept his promises and August produced another record-breaking month. It was also time for the family to farewell another brother to the war. Arthur, now a lieutenant, had finished his training at Trentham military camp and was on final leave before venturing off to the front, saying his goodbyes to his young wife, newly born daughter and friends.

September was Robert's 32nd birthday and sales for his eighth year in business were £281,348, his own net profit over £16,000. So far he had not had a year when sales had not increased and this year was £33,000 higher than the previous one. In December 1917 he did his biggest month ever, £28,000 in sales. The past six months had broken all previous records.

Even his *Optimist* was proving so popular that an additional 600 a month were being sent to people outside the firm who had requested copies. But December also brought other concerns and on December 4 1917, he stood by the letter-box at Shelly Beach Rd holding a brown envelope in his hands. It was from the Defence Department and reading the contents for the first time he wasn't quite sure what to do. His name had been drawn along with 5000 others in the second ballot of married men and it was now time for reservist number 83794, Robert Alexander Laidlaw, to fight for King and Country.

He wasn't a pacifist and like his brothers felt a strong duty to serve his country, but he also felt an equally strong duty to his mother, father and several close friends who had invested many thousands of pounds in Laidlaw Leeds. He foresaw that if he went to war, the business could easily collapse, his family would lose all their money, and his 200 plus staff would lose their jobs. The odds of this happening were now quite high. Thirty-five men in the firm had already enlisted, including five departmental managers. Out of the nine left, eight were still eligible for service and Jack, his beloved brother and right-hand-man, was now dead. As the management structure of the firm was whittled away, his personal presence in the business became increasingly important. Each year alone he personally spent three months putting together the following year's catalogue which now stretched to 500 pages, aside from all his other duties. After much soul-searching he decided to appeal his call-up.

It was not an easy decision. The war had been on for over three years and over 80,000 New Zealanders had enlisted. There were calls from both British and New Zealand Governments that more men were desperately needed. Those men of fighting age left at home often came under scorn and ridicule in the street, and he had already endured some of this. His appeal would worsen this situation, but even he did not foresee the level of hostility and public interest he would soon face.

8

A DIFFICULT UNION

1918

"Remember that it is possible for the error of a moment, to become the sorrow of a life." [1]

Robert Laidlaw, 1912.

Appeals to be exempt from fighting were heard by the Military Service Appeal Board in both Auckland and Wellington. In Auckland the board was chaired by Major Conlon. Almost daily the details of the appeal cases were published in the country's newspapers. Any exemptions from farmer to sheetmetal worker seemed to arouse public interest but for Robert the timing of his appeal was particularly unfortunate. For some time there had been concern that the Military Service Appeal Board in Auckland seemed to show favour to the wealthy. Several recent exemptions had highlighted the popular view that political favours were being granted to the rich, and those with money could evade serving their country. While Robert was genuine, his efforts were soon cast into this basket.

At his first appearance he briefly laid out his case and the board adjourned the hearing. On February 7, he appeared before the board for the second time and his case was opened

119

up in more detail. He took the stand and outlined the number of difficulties he faced.

"One thousand pieces of mail," he said, "are sent out each day, and it is impossible to find a man in New Zealand with a knowledge of requirements so as to conduct the office service on which the structure of the business depends. Even if the specialist nature of the business is ignored, a new head would not have the vital support and experience of the departmental managers, all of whom with one exception are liable to be called up."

To Robert it was obvious that if he left, the business would then be forced to shut. As thousands of pounds of stock were already on order from abroad, closing the business could take several years. It would mean a loss to his creditors, his employees and to the community.

The head of the Appeal Board, Major Conlon, shifted uneasily in his seat. He was aware of the attention that the board's last few decisions had received, and of the stature of the man now facing him across the room. It was obvious too that whatever the outcome, this case would set a precedent for those that followed. He therefore adjourned the proceedings until a later date.[2]

On Monday, February 18, the hearing resumed. This time several witnesses appeared and Robert explained in more detail the large financial responsibilities he was facing, which in his eyes had forced him to appeal. He told the board of the large sums of money loaned to him by friends before the War. His father alone had loaned him between £14,000 and £20,000. His mother too had loaned him £1000, as had several others, and for many this was all the savings they had. Seven of these loans were unsecured, based solely on his own ability and integrity in the business.

He felt a primary duty to honourably discharge these

financial responsibilities, ensuring that those who had put money in the business were paid back in full. If his friends pulled their money out the business would close down, with the resulting unemployment of hundreds of people. The same would also happen to the factories which depended on him to take their output. Likewise enormous orders had been placed in England and America for goods to be delivered right through 1918. These goods bore the company brand so the manufacturers would not accept cancellation. One possible solution he could see would be to find someone who could act as manager in the business. However, as he had explained in the previous hearing, such a person was not easily found.

Conlon stood to give his reply. He too had been busy in the past week and gave details of his own research.

"I have given this appeal much time," he said, "and have endeavoured to get some rebutting evidence but have been unable to get any. Of the businessmen I have seen some considered Mr Laidlaw could not be replaced, others thought he could, but did not suggest a way of releasing him. If any exemption is granted," he said, "it should be clearly understood that it was not for the reservist, or for his sake, but definitely owing to possible loss to creditors and to prevent economic loss to the community by having such a business smashed in such times. Gentlemen, this case is so important the board will put its decision in writing."[3]

He bundled up his papers and left the room. Conlon was stalling for time.

Two days later on February 20 1918, he presented his verdict. "Although in general character not dissimilar to many cases which have been brought before us," he said, "it presents, in some respects, unusual features ... We have satisfied ourselves by investigation and inquiry that there is no member of Mr Laidlaw's staff, though many of them are of undoubted ability, who could carry on the present business in Mr Laidlaw's absence.

"We have also evidence to satisfy us," he said, "that, as regards the employment of a manager from outside the business, it is extremely difficult to find a man possessing the knowledge and experience necessary for the oversight and direction of such a business as Mr. Laidlaw's.

"But in cases such as that at present under consideration," he said, "where it is impossible to realise on the business, and where, for special and valid reasons, the management cannot be delegated to another, the loss inflicted on an appellant and his creditors by the enforced closing of his business would be a hardship so severe as to be justly considered undue in its character. Moreover, the adoption of such a procedure as a general practice would, by the resulting disorganisation of trade, the inconvenience caused to large numbers of people and the loss of employment to many men and women, be contrary to the public interest."

"A large amount of capital – amounting to many thousands of pounds – has been lent to the appellant by monetary institutions and private persons, and has been invested by him in the business." Now Conlon was getting to the core. "If he is removed it seems more than probable the business will be so adversely affected that it will certainly result in a great loss to those who have advanced this money. For the reasons given we have decided to adjourn this appeal sine die."[4]

Robert had not been exempted. Conlon had adjourned his appeal indefinitely and the board had made its decision by not making one. For the time being he was freed from going to war and could continue running Laidlaw Leeds, yet he was still anguished over the decision. Inside he still felt a duty to follow his brothers to the front but could see no way clear of his present responsibilities.

From an unexpected quarter, a possible solution appeared. Soon after the appeal he was approached by Auckland businessman James Boddie. Boddie was a softly spoken man and a fellow Scot. He was chairman of the Farmers Union Trading Company, one of several co-operatives that had started in the previous decade.[5] Farmers invested in the co-ops, becoming shareholders and purchasing goods. Each year the profits were returned to them in the form of rebates and dividends. The co-ops had achieved a measure of success and farmers had also launched auctioneering and fertiliser companies in like manner.

Informally Boddie suggested the possibility of selling Laidlaw Leeds to the Farmers Union Trading Company. The irony of the proposition was almost laughable. Robert's firm was a much larger and far superior business, cash and asset rich.

Over the past seven years of trading he had accumulated assets of £150,000. The Farmers Union Trading Company was a much smaller firm, and while they had great ambitions, they had little capital for expansion and were starved of cash. In any other situation such an approach might have been laughed off, but with the Military Service Board decision lingering in his mind he met Boddie and they talked further.

The offer of a buy out was not an option he had considered. It would certainly take care of the obstacles that had been discussed at the hearing. The eight personal acquaintances to whom he owed money would be paid off and David Robertson and the other young managers would not be left to run the business on their own. On the surface the offer looked like a good solution. His and Boddie's discussions soon turned to price and while Boddie himself put no pressure on Robert, the pressure outside began to increase immensely. The media leapt like wolves at the Military Service Board's decision.[6]

The Auckland *Truth* came out viciously against him labelling him 'Lucky Laidlaw' and calling him a 'Calico Jimmy.' It was an interest and slant that troubled him deeply. Robert did not object to fighting, rather he believed he was doing his first duty in what was a very difficult decision. The media very quickly made it look otherwise.

In the month that followed, *Truth* took up his case with fervour and even saw to it that it reached the ears of Parliament. The Minister of Defence, whether he wanted to or not, went to Auckland to speak with the members of the Appeal Board headed by Conlon to review their position.

Nor did the paper stop there. On March 23, it issued a challenge declaring it would set about finding a businessman or group of businessmen who could buy Laidlaw Leeds and so free Robert to enlist. Robert had been actively involved on the political platform for prohibition and the recent 6 o'clock closing campaign. Unfortunately for him, both of these campaigns had put him firmly offside with some sectors of the media including *Truth*.

It was not long before the newspaper was contacted by someone professing to have knowledge of a possible purchaser for Laidlaw Leeds. The source encouraged the newspaper enough to hastily contact the chairman of the Appeal Board, Major Conlon, who was referred to an Auckland businessman.[7] After the meeting Conlon informed the paper that he was in no doubt that a buyer could be found for Robert's business, and made it clear that he intended to reopen the case after the Easter break. Robert left Auckland and headed south for Easter participating in a series of church rallies in Dunedin.[8] It was a difficult time of year. The second anniversary of Jack's death had been on March 17th.

He returned from the South Island in early April and meeting with Boddie gave him an assurance that he would have his decision regarding the sale by the end of the week. As he did with most things he took the matter to God in prayer. By now he felt that it was the right thing to do and so his prayer was quite straight-forward:

"God, if you don't show me otherwise by Friday afternoon, I am going to sell Laidlaw Leeds."

Friday afternoon came and went. On Monday, April 8, he phoned Boddie and told him of his decision. They met and Robert signed a general agreement to sell Laidlaw Leeds to the Farmers Union Trading Company. He was now free to enlist.

Three days later, on the evening of Thursday, April 11, 1918, the day before the Military Service Appeal Board was due to reopen his hearing, there was a knock at the door of Robert's Shelly Beach Rd home. He opened it and standing in the porch was a uniformed officer, his motorcycle pulled up outside.

"Mr Robert Laidlaw?" asked the officer.

"Yes," he said a little hesitantly.

The soldier's voice lowered: "I am sorry to inform you, sir, but a cable has just been received from the front. Your brother Arthur was killed in action two weeks ago on March 27th. We have only just been notified."

The soldier's voice trailed into silence. Robert stood listless, his hand reaching for the doorframe. Pictures of Arthur raced through his mind. He saw him standing in the drapery department at Laidlaw Leeds, he saw him in his uniform, and now dead. Dead. Lillian arrived by his side and quietly closed the door.

He stood choking back the tears, his mind spinning. It was impossible. Jack was already gone. Not Arthur too. What of his wife and child? What of his own mother and father? Lillian comforted him but he had to tell his parents. Solemnly he tidied himself, picked up his jacket and drove round to their house in Herne Bay mounting the steps for the second time in two years. His mother, always pleased to see her successful son, greeted him at the door. Her eyes met his and immediately she sensed something was wrong.

"Mother," he said, the words hardly coming. "Arthur's dead."

Her face drained and she ran weeping into the depths of the house. Robert followed and his father quickly appeared. Openly the old man of commerce struggled to retain his composure. The war had robbed him of yet another son. Robert's mother grabbed the corner of his jacket and begged him not to enlist. He was bereft of words. It was all too overwhelming. It had been Arthur's first day in action. He had looked over the parapet minutes after arriving at the trench and was immediately shot in the head by a sniper. The waste was instant.

A memorial service was held a few days later at Howe Street Chapel. Robert struggled to find the words to communicate to his staff what had happened. In *The Optimist* he reprinted a short excerpt from the *Auckland Star*,

"Advice was received from the Minister of Defence last evening to the effect that Second Lieut. A.F. Laidlaw had been killed in action on March 27. This is the second son of Mr. Robert Laidlaw, Sen., of Herne Bay, to make the supreme sacrifice. On the 17th day of the same month, only two years ago, the sad news was received that Lieut. J.R. Laidlaw, R.N.F.C., had been killed in an aeroplane accident. Now his brother Arthur has fallen, fighting in the great cause.

"Lieut. A.F. Laidlaw volunteered in the early stages of the war for the Artillery, for which he studied hard for months; but when it was found there was a surplus of that branch, at the suggestion of the authorities he willingly transferred to the Infantry. Entering camp as a private, he quickly gained his stripes as a corporal, then sergeant, and then in the examination for commissions he secured second highest marks, and was duly gazetted second lieutenant. Finally he left the Dominion as adjutant of the troop-ship in which he sailed. After only four weeks in England, he was drafted across to France, where he has since been in the firing line. It is clear from the cable that he is one of the many who met death in the present big offensive. He leaves a young wife and baby girl, and a family who have now to mourn the loss of two sons."[9]

A month earlier, before hearing of Arthur's death, Robert had written a spirited piece on the soldier of ideals. Now more sombre, he closed his editorial with the following lines:

"You who do not know the deep soul sorrow of having a husband, son, or brother, go down in the flush of his youth, on a foreign battlefield, lift up your hearts to God, and thank Him that He has not called you to pass through such trial, and when you see the daily heading, 'Killed in Action', freely give of your sympathy to the new members who are being called into the growing family of sufferers."[10]

In the days following Arthur's death came some painful realisations. He was contacted by Conlon, and Robert, now the sole surviving son in the family, was granted a complete exemption from service under Section 18 of the Military Service Act. It was something he had never expected. But what of the negotiations with Boddie and the Farmers Union Trading Company? He no longer needed to sell. Yet he was a man of his word, and having signed an agreement in principle, felt he could in no way back out.

The Auckland *Truth* backed down too, and on April 20 in much more careful language wrote:

"... most people would agree with *Truth* that any family rich or poor, where two of three sons have forfeited their lives, has done its bit. It may also be mentioned, for the benefit of many who are not aware of the fact, that Robert Laidlaw is a married man with one child, a son."[11]

James Boddie, the chairman of the Farmers Union Trading Company, was a man of some capacity. He was involved on the boards of at least two Farmers Union companies. Over the previous year things at the trading company in particular had worsened. They had a plaguing cashflow crisis and had recently extended their large overdraft at the bank. The bank in turn had tightened its grip on the company and made it a condition of the new overdraft they make calls on unpaid share capital. Members had been slow paying and this was not alleviating the problem. At the same time they were having trouble controlling stock and were receiving dozens of letters of complaint. Boddie himself had had to look into these and was having doubts about the competency of the firm's manager, Donald Logan.

During the previous year the company had received and made advances to other co-operatives regarding possible amalgamations and the board at large seemed to think this was the way out of their troubles. Boddie however was a thoughtful man and realised that more of the same was not necessarily the answer to their problems. Right in the middle of the board negotiating the biggest amalgamation deal to date with three other co-operatives he had approached Robert, without the board's knowledge, regarding a possible sale.

Boddie had reasoned that the partner they really needed was one that was not only on a strong financial footing, but also displayed strong management expertise. He knew Laidlaw Leeds was a far superior business proposition than the other co-ops that had been put before the board. What they desperately lacked were systems and organisation but what Robert had in abundance was just that. It was not until April 17, five days after Arthur's death that he formally told the board at the Farmers Union Trading Company what had transpired between himself and Robert and wisely moved quickly to finalise matters. A committee consisting of himself and another board member, Somerville, was set up to negotiate with Robert over the next few days.

Two weeks later, on the April 30, a special directors' meeting was convened. Boddie and Somerville proudly produced their report on the possible amalgamation of the two businesses. It was the first time any financial information other than share sales and overdrafts had ever been discussed at the Farmers Union Trading Company. Somerville gave his breakdown of the savings that would be made by the amalgamation and it was at once apparent that Robert had written large parts of the report. In typical 'Laidlaw' language he reported,

"The total number of hands employed is roughly 300, allowing for a very conservative estimate, a reduction of 20% can be affected. The salaries paid by our company average out at £2/10/- a week, and the reduction on this basis of payment would be an annual saving of £7800. The total amount spent by the two companies annually in advertising amounts to £12,000. Now allowing for only a 33 1/3 reduction – we effect an annual saving of £4000 ..." and so it went on. Somerville concluded by moving that the board adopt the report and purchase Laidlaw Leeds.[12]

Boddie then took the chair to address the meeting and put his seal of approval on the impending purchase.

"There is a tide in the affairs of men," he said sensing the moment, "which if taken at the flood, leads on to fortune. Gentlemen, I believe that time is at hand."

After some discussion the report was adopted and Boddie and Somerville were authorised to purchase Laidlaw Leeds at a sum not exceeding £200,000. That was the last bit of good news. Things then took a turn for the worse and the next matter raised was the recently discovered embezzlement by the accountant. The matter was not pursued any further on the understanding that the accountant, Mr. Brown, make hasty endeavours to enlist and leave for the Front, thereby sealing his own fate.

On May 15, the company seal was affixed to the agreement and Laidlaw Leeds was duly purchased. The total settlement was for £175,725, but Robert had in fact funded his own buyout as most of the payment was in shares. Of the total payment £137,125 went to him, and the remaining £38,600, also in the form of shares, went to acquaintances who had invested in Laidlaw Leeds. Of his £137,125 there was a cash payment of £1000 on the 31.7.1918, a further £10,000 cash was payable on the 1.2.1919 and £5000 in warbonds. The balance of £121,125 was in fully paid 6% cumulative first preference shares.[13] Robert was now a free man.

In some ways the sale of the business had been a good thing. Since Arthur's death he had been spending much time in the company of his family, often at his parents' home. The loss of his second brother Arthur had taken a devastating toll on his mother and there seemed little that would console her. Arthur's widow and child too had needed assistance and he and Lillian had visited them often trying to ease their pain. There seemed to be new urgencies in life.

Meanwhile across town at the Farmers Union Trading Company things began to fall apart. At the annual general meeting on May 28, Donald Logan was general manager of the new combined businesses, but his position was perilous to say the least. It was clear that the management of the firm was wildly out of control. Three days after the AGM on May 31 1918, Robert was asked to attend a full board meeting of the company. They had owned his business for two weeks but already it was plainly evident how much it relied on his management expertise. The company was in deep water and the directors knew it.

The directors wanted to offer him the position of general manager and move Donald Logan sideways to manager of the produce department. Robert would have no part of it. If there was going to be any change it would be on his terms and with his people. After an adjournment and some quick talking he joined the meeting for the first time after lunch. The previous resolution to offer Logan the position of produce manager was rescinded and his engagement terminated altogether. Robert was then offered the general managership of the Farmers Union Trading Company under the above terms and he accepted.

The directors did not waste any time. Logan was notified of his termination and Robert moved in again at the helm. The next month was to prove as strenuous as anything he had faced to date as he rapidly became aware of the state of the company that had purchased his business, and the reasons for his hurried appointment as general manager.

The FUTC had been having stock control problems for some time mostly due to the company accountant who had been discovered embezzling share capital; and the warehouse manager, the second top executive in the firm, who was discovered stealing. Customers had been sent goods and never charged for them, the freight system was in disarray and customer complaints were common, especially from those who in order to cover fraud were sent accounts that they had already paid.

This however was only the beginning. One of the last acts of the previous manager Logan was to enter into a contract to purchase American made Mak-a-Tractors. These do-it-yourself kits converted a humble Model-T Ford into a farm tractor. It was a poor undertaking, and the firm in order to secure the agency of this product had agreed to purchase 500 at £58 each.

It was £29,000 the business did not have and attempts to back out of the contract had not succeeded.

If Robert had realised the state of his purchaser's affairs it is unlikely he would have sold. The buyout had been very much a one-way affair. As was the common practice investigations had been conducted into Laidlaw Leeds by the Farmers Union Trading Company, but not the other way round.

It was a difficult pill to swallow. He knew when he had entered into the first negotiations with Boddie that the past 12 months trading at Laidlaw Leeds had been his best ever. The business was still growing and nearly every month showed record sales — and profits.

He had been on target to do over £300,000 for the year and reap a net profit of at least £18,000, by far his best figures to date. He was now also cornered. There was no way he could back out even if he wanted to. The very reason he had so enthusiastically taken up the option of selling was now a noose around his neck. His father, mother and most of his friends had also not taken cash as settlement; rather, with a lot of encouragement from him, they had all taken shares in the company. His father alone was now sitting on shares valued at £20,000. If he left Boddie and the others to their own devices, it would all soon be worthless. Yet at the same time it would take him all the management ability he could muster to turn the situation around.

*Robert the young painter
in Dunedin (on right).*

The family in Dunedin. Robert at wheel, his father seated next to him. His mother Jessie, Jack, and Grandma Crookston in rear.

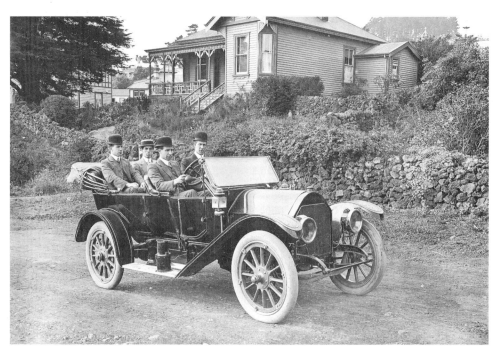

The thrill of speed. Robert (behind wheel), Jack in passenger seat. Back seat, Arthur (left), and David Robertson.

The Three Brothers in 1911.

Robert

Jack

Arthur

*The original Fort Street premises
(20ft x 30ft). Opened by Robert
and Jack, October 1909.*

*The Commerce Street premises
occupied three months later.*

*Before the first year had elapsed Robert
moved into this four-storey warehouse
across the road from his original Fort
Street premises. Staff now numbered 122.*

A year and five months after starting in business he occupied the other half of the warehouse block. Combined, he had 35,000 sq ft, nearly 40 times the size of his original premises.

The Farmers Union Trading Company pre-merger with Laidlaw Leeds in 1918.

Robert's 'Rival' brand sewing machines arrive en-masse.

The famous Hobson Street store. Opened April 1914, four and a half years after the first order was recieved from the first catalogue.

The Share Department.

The men's and boys' shoe department.

The roof-top children's playground opened in 1922.
Another view below — with electric train.

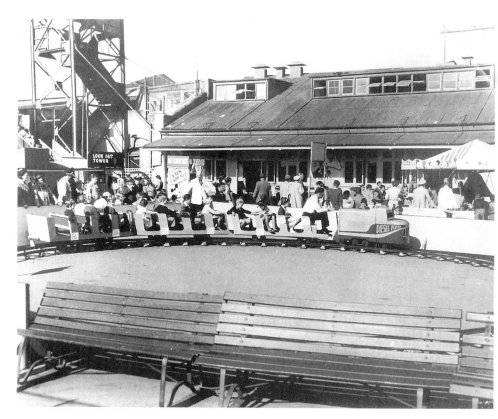

9

TURNAROUND

1918-1921

"No competitors have the youth, the enthusiasm, the vigour, and ambition that we have. The strength of our organisation is the sum of the efficiency of each individual. Are you going to be a better man or girl next week? Are you going to add your part towards the elimination of error, the perfecting of our service, the enthusiasm of our push, and the loyalty of our spirit and the triumph of our victory?"[1]

Robert Laidlaw, 1914.

Robert immediately engaged W. Wallace Bruce, public accountant, and auditor, to do a complete investigation of the company's books. He needed to get an outside opinion on exactly what had been happening to the financial accounts while under the control of Mr. Brown. A month later his worst fears were realised. The accounts had been deliberately tampered with and a trail of conspiracy woven by the company accountant was uncovered. Journal pages had been pasted together to conceal amounts, other figures blatantly rubbed out and rewritten. There was no share register and £600 was missing from the share capital account. Stock on hand had been inflated by £3000.

Overall, instead of showing a profit of £6608 as reported in the March 1918 balance sheet, the Farmers Union Trading

Company had made a loss of £11,750. Altogether they were a staggering £18,358 worse off than they thought they were.[2] If Arthur's death had given him possible reason for pulling out of the deal then this was more so.

He hastily contacted chairman Boddie and shared his concerns. Amalgamation itself had been a drawn out process and while the details were now public, no money or shares had yet changed hands. After some deliberation he again decided he must go through with the deal. His intention had never been to be involved in the running of this company. The preference shares were an investment, with a guaranteed rate of return, as opposed to ordinary shares on which the company was not obliged to issue a yearly dividend.[3] He held 70% of the paid-up capital of the company, a whopping £121,125, compared to that owned by the ordinary shareholders of a mere £14,428. To all intents and purposes he was the controlling shareholder and owner of the company.[4]

His original management contract with the firm had been for three years at a salary of £1500 a year. On June 28, with the auditor's report completed, he made his final decision. Standing at the head of the large oak table he looked around the room. The faces looking back all shared a common anguish. These men were farmers not businessmen and were now in charge of the largest mail order operation in the country. The young 32-year-old man in front of them was easily 20 years their junior, but was the only one capable of pulling them out of the desperate situation they now faced.

"Owing," he began, "to the recent events that have come to light, it is obvious that this is going to be a larger undertaking than I had first envisaged, and I will need an eight-year contract instead of the original three. At the same time gentlemen, I propose for myself a lower salary of £1000 per annum, but with a bonus of 5% on net profits."

No one disagreed. No one else knew what to do. Then with all the optimism he could muster, Robert set himself to the task of rebuilding the firm as an amalgamated, profitable unit.[5]

His immediate move was in location and staff. The firm's trade was shifted completely to his big Hobson Street premises, and all but one of the trading company's department managers relieved of their positions. Robert kept his old management structure intact. He needed to be very sure of those working under him for the job at hand. At the same time he had to reverse the hopeless cashflow situation in the firm. Before the takeover Laidlaw Leeds monthly sales were averaging £30,000, since then, even with the businesses combined, the sales figures had not moved.

All through June the business had been in a state of limbo with Robert undecided about staying, Wallace Bruce undertaking their investigations, and the two firms trying hopelessly to amalgamate. He could reorganise the business, but what they needed urgently was cash. On July 20, he dropped the old credit system of the Farmers Union Trading Company, and his strict Laidlaw Leeds 'cash with order' policy was put in place over the entire business. The effect was immediate.

Cashflow increased 30% but even that was not enough. After the National Bank declined to give the business a larger overdraft, he personally approached his own bank, the BNZ, which arranged the necessary accommodation. Messrs Stewart and Johnston (his solicitors) were also duly appointed new solicitors to the amalgamated firm and the accountant's misconduct and warehouse manager's thefts put in the hands of the police.

In August they were found guilty of stealing over £1000 from the company. Directors meetings were no longer held at the old Fort Street building but in Robert's office in Hobson Street. The seat of power was now firmly established and very soon all that remained of the old Farmers Union Trading Company – was the name painted on the outside of the Hobson Street building.[6]

The next job at hand was to bring in funds by selling additional share scrip and to get outstanding money owing from shareholders who had been sent calls on shares but were not paying up. Farmers who had taken shares in the co-operative trading company typically took up the minimum number of 10 by paying a small deposit (four shillings), but not the full price of the shares. This meant they could avail themselves of the co-op's buying opportunities without the commitment of a large investment.

When faced in October with a list of 1100 shareholders who had not paid up Robert drafted two letters. The first referred to the guaranteed rebates that would result in a great many of the unpaid calls being settled. The second, while still pointing out the great advantages to be enjoyed by retaining the shares, was accompanied by a third notice which clearly stated that all shares with unpaid calls would be cancelled. His persuasion did the trick and two months later the number of outstanding calls had shrunk by 80%.

The rebate scheme of the Farmers Union Trading Company had also lagged for some time. Paying dividends each year had proved impossible let alone paying rebates. In December he instituted a definite rebate scheme whereby they were given at the time of purchase rather than at the end of the year. In fact it was just an additional discount, but a sizeable incentive for shareholders to do more of their business with the trading company.

Rebuilding the firm was not all that grabbed Robert's attention and in the middle of this reorganisation he again threw his weight behind another campaign for prohibition. Canada had recently instituted prohibition as well as some states in the U.S., the effect of which at first looked impressive. Canada had witnessed a remarkable drop in crime figures, and as a consequence had to close several jails. There was also a resulting increase in business and retail trade. The opponents of prohibition had traditionally claimed that closing breweries would result in an economic downturn, but it was soon clear that the opposite could happen.

Robert joined a group called the Business Men's Efficiency League. This group of leading businessmen opposed the consumption of alcohol on several grounds, one of which was the waste of the country's resources in the production and distribution of alcohol that could be more profitably used elsewhere. Questions of national efficiency were of great concern to a nation channelling its resources into a war effort so, through lobbying, the National Efficiency Board again raised the question of Prohibition in New Zealand. Robert himself was a total abstainer and saw drink as a blight on the human condition that was wrecking society. To him the only possible solution was complete prohibition.

"Experience proves to every intelligent student of history," he said, "that prohibition is the only possible satisfactory solution of the drink problem."

Christmas seemed a long time coming in 1918. The war in Europe ended in November but for Robert personally it had been a long and difficult year: a very public appeal, the tragic loss of another brother, the sale of his business and the strain of turning another one around. In closing the year he wrote of peace in the midst of turmoil:

"I remember," he penned, "reading about two artists who tried with brush and pigment to paint their conceptions of perfect peace. The one chose for his subject a still, lone lake among the mountains, which mirrored perfectly on its glassy surface the bushy slopes above. The other pictured a stormy sea dashing itself relentlessly against a great rock, and in a cleft of the rock was a gull sitting on its nest in perfect peace ... It is evident that Christ brings into every life wherever he is allowed admission, a sense of peace that is immune from outward turmoil. It matters not how wildly the waves may rage on the surface, in the depth of the ocean we are told there is an eternal calm, undisturbed by the fiercest storm. Drummond says: "'Peace is the repose of a heart set deep in God; the eternal calm of an invulnerable faith.'"[7]

Lillian was now in the latter stages of pregnancy with their second child, and deciding to leave her in Auckland, Robert headed south with three of his executives for a break in the middle of the North Island. He pushed his Buick to the limits crashing through rivers at top speed and eventually ended up on the snowy slopes of Mt Ruapehu.

One of the benefits of operating a country-based business also became apparent. Overestimating the cross-country capabilities of his car one afternoon he got firmly stuck in a bog on the slopes, only to be rescued by a local farmer who incidentally happened to be a long-time customer. He returned to Auckland just in time for the birth but things did not go well.

Lillian went into labour on January 21 at his mother's holiday home in Milford. It was a long and difficult delivery and the child was eventually delivered barely breathing. There were some anxious moments before the little girl was declared fit. Robert held his precious daughter carefully. She was named Lorraine Crookston after his grandmother.

A child of unusual beauty, she had delightful rosy cheeks and thin wisps of light brown curly hair. Her eyes, however, looked far into the distance and as the days past it became clear she had suffered brain damage during the birth. Little Lorraine grew quickly but was unable to hold her balance or walk. Robert had a special swing made and attached to the veranda. In the late afternoons he would sit and push her back and forth while 'little Jack', now a toddler, ran around the yard.

Meanwhile the prohibition question had also been decided in January on the basis of personal liberty but it was a definition of liberty with which Robert took issue.

"True Liberty," he said, "can be maintained only when the liberty of the individual or the minority is made subservient to the interests of the people as a whole. The great civil war of America is an outstanding example of this. The Southern slave owners asked why their liberty to keep slaves should be interfered with. Lincoln replied:"'True liberty is upheld only when the individual's liberty is subject to the freedom of the State to govern itself as a whole.'"[8]

He was also forced over the Christmas months to do some hard thinking about customers. Robert knew that at Laidlaw Leeds to do a turnover of £300,000, he was trading with about 45,000 customers. It was obvious that he was only taking a small percentage of these customers' total business. With the amalgamation he managed to keep most of his original customers but lost many of the Farmers Union Trading Company's. When he instituted cash trading and cut their credit off, they decided to shop elsewhere.

Probably some of these customers the business could do without, but it came to his attention that shareholders in the co-operative were also now shopping elsewhere from stores where they might get credit. In an abrupt turnaround he announced to the directors in the new year that he had changed his mind on the subject of credit selling.

"It has been brought to my attention," he said, "that shareholders of the company are doing business with competitors' country stores who offer credit."

Losing customers to competitors, especially country stores, was the last thing he wanted to see happen, so the credit policy was reinstituted but was not offered to everyone who applied, only those customers who had already shown an ability to pay their bills on time.

He was also concerned that the same spirit of cooperation he had fostered at Laidlaw Leeds did not get lost in a bigger firm. To those new members he wrote: "Let me say here to some of the new members of this big new company who do not know me, that I want every one of you to enter fully into the spirit of comradeship between managers and men that it has been our constant desire to cultivate. If you have a business or a personal difficulty or financial worry, my office is always open to you, and all the help I can give, either in advice or money, if that seems the best way to assist, will be at your service."[9]

Robert was not kidding. He was already well-known for his care and generosity, funding many staff functions, dinners and entertainment nights out of his own pocket. Some of his old employees however were suspicious of the new regime. They were used to seeing him at the helm and felt uneasy about a board of directors whom they did not know. Robert as always brought such discussion from the shop floor out into the open. He took the opportunity once again to imbue them with what it was to create a company that had real worth in the eyes of the public.

"The first logical step is to give the trust an entity," he said, "a personality of its own with soul qualities – that will enable people to believe it capable of the same feelings as ordinary individuals, and the second step is by practice and precept to give this soul a character that will make it honourable and trustworthy in public estimation.

"Now there are two reasons why we do not trust men – one

because we do not know them well enough, the other because we know them too well. The big business combination built on the sound economic foundation of efficiency, and with a character that would stand the acid test and measure up to the principle that confidence is the basis of trade, had but to let its employees, and the public know it well enough to be hailed as a benefactor, instead of being treated with suspicion."[10]

By March 1919 the business was getting back on its feet and despite incurring an unexpected loss the previous year, profit to the end of the financial year was £17,831. There appeared to be a lift in commercial confidence generally with the end of the war. Looking over the previous 12 months the chairman of the company remarked that every branch of the business showed splendid development and very satisfactory results had been achieved.

With high sales farmers found too that they had excess funds, and Robert actively campaigned for these through a share selling campaign and banking department where farmers could put money on short-term deposit. In a remarkably short time he had turned the firm around and now had funds in hand.

Meanwhile, the battle lines were being drawn. The large co-operative amalgamation that was touted as a possibility before Boddie had approached Robert had gone ahead, and in June 1918 nine co-operatives joined under the banner of the Farmers Co-operative Wholesale Federation. Smith and Caugheys, the successful Auckland department store, also began offering mail order on some of its lines. Robert, however, was about to outmanoeuvre the competition on a grand scale.

In June 1919, a year after he came to the helm he put to the board his plans for expansion. In America chain stores had taken off before World War I, and there were over 2000 chain store operations embracing over 20,000 individual stores.

Woolworths, the largest, had almost 1000 stores and Robert through his extensive reading was well versed in their operation.[11]

The stores operated as distinct units, but buying, warehousing and other administrative functions were conducted by a central head office thereby leaving the stores free to concentrate on selling. No one in the mail order business, not even in America, had linked a chain store operation to a mail order house and, in a move which predated his American counterparts Sears Roebuck and Montgomery Ward by six years, he went into the chain store business.

Seven days after he announced his intentions to the directors, he purchased the 12-store chain of Green and Colebrook stretching in a line from Auckland to Taupo. Overnight the employees of the trading company went from 257 to 347. It was only the beginning. His vision was for a chain of branches throughout the whole of the North Island, and the Green and Colebrook purchase seemed to send a signal to other retailers in the country towns, because before long he was flooded with country stores offering to sell.

Incredibly, too, even country customers wrote in offering their local stores for sale offering to finance the purchase by buying shares in the company. They knew that getting one of Robert's stores in their district would not only bring in a larger range of goods, but also lower prices. Much of the remainder of 1919 and the beginning of 1920 he spent on the road with David Robertson and several directors inspecting and purchasing suitable businesses.

Nor did he stop at stores. He bought factories too, and in August he bought a furniture factory, in September, a boot factory, both of these to ensure better supply of lines to the growing business. These were then added to the saddlery he had started at Laidlaw Leeds. By November 1919 he had 19 stores. His central mail order warehouse was not excluded from his expansionist plans, and work began at the close of 1919 to increase its size to 202,500 sq ft — over two times the size of his original building.

The previous four months of trading had broken all records and as new branches were opened staff numbers grew by almost 100 a month.[12] Keen to keep motivation and solidarity high in the face of such progress he wrote to the staff: "I know some of you are asking – what does all this mean to me? First of all, it means tremendously increased opportunities for progress, because there will of course be a far greater number of responsible positions to fill. The difficulty with our business will never be money, but always men. We intend to open stores in practically every town in the Auckland Province, and will proceed just as fast as we can find men capable and reliable enough to take charge."[13]

When the balance sheet came out in March 1920, just how successful the year had really been was revealed. Total sales for the first full year in trading of the combined businesses nearly topped the million pound mark, £985,000. Sales in March alone were £114,380, the net profit was £70,510. Robert shared the success and distributed to over 700 staff a bonus amounting to 10% of the profit – £7051. The figures in other areas of the business were just as impressive and the company had nearly doubled its shareholders, an additional 4870 taking out shares in the past year. He now had 29 branches, three factories, and the Hobson Street mail order warehouse.

To date the mail order business had sourced nearly all its goods overseas. At times it had proved difficult to ensure continuous supply and quality over such long distances, and now with so many branches to cater for as well as the mail order operation, he suggested the company should open its own offices in London and New York. This was agreed and he prepared to travel overseas intending also to investigate chain-store methods in England and America. Just before he was due to leave, his daughter Lorraine died.

At home the past year had been particularly difficult. Robert found illness difficult to cope with, and had spent most of the time away heading the expansion programme. While Lillian still had the help of the servants, his absence had been noticeable. Lorraine over these months had deteriorated. At first she had seemed quite healthy but during March and April she had become increasingly unwell with severe stomach problems.

On Saturday, April 10, Robert called in his Howe Street Assembly colleague Dr. Pettit to their home at Shelly Beach Rd. Lorraine had deteriorated further and had begun having convulsions. She died the next day. There was a private family ceremony on Monday at Waikumete cemetery and the directors expressed their deep sympathy at their meeting two days later.

Robert did not cancel his trip but rather took Lillian and 'little Jack' (now four), with him, setting sail a month later on the *Maheno*. They were also joined by William Mackay, one of his managers whom he had decided to put in charge of the New York office. Arriving in Sydney the following Tuesday they spent a pleasant few days taking in the sights.

Robert had been terribly sea-sick on the trip over making several hurried departures from the saloon, and when he arrived in Sydney he announced to everyone he was taking the train to Perth where he would once again rejoin the group. A few days rest however improved his constitution and he decided to take his chances at sea.

While travelling up the Red Sea on the steamer *Orsova*, he and William Mackay hit upon the idea that while the ship was making its passage through the Suez Canal they might engage an aeroplane and take a short jaunt to see the pyramids. Robert sent a wireless message from the ship to the African Coast, which was forwarded as a telegram to Thomas Cook and Son.

However, as the boat reached Suez, they were notified that this particular adventure was impossible because there were no commercial aircraft available. Lillian chipped in and suggested that they might fly from Paris to London. Robert took to this idea immediately since it would not only save time, more importantly he could possibly avoid another bout of seasickness. Landing at Naples, the party split up. William Mackay took John and his nurse on to London and Robert and Lillian set off together to explore the continent by rail. Their first stop was Pompeii. Walking over the remains of the preserved city he wrote:

"I used to think the destruction of Sodom and Gomorrah was an example of God's severity, but after visiting Pompeii and seeing in the Museum at the entrance pictures which depict the utter depravity and lasciviousness of the people, I could not but feel that to let the city exist for over 600 years was an example of God's long suffering."[14]

Leaving Italy, they travelled up through Switzerland and France on a 28-day sojourn full of scenic, historic and business interest. In France they visited Arthur's grave at Albert. Surrounded by row upon row of plain timber crosses Robert stood by the graveside. His brother was but one of thousands. In his mind's eye he could see Arthur's smiling face and thought of how things had changed.

If he had only lived but a few more months there would have been no more war to fight. Robert bent down and unwrapped a package he'd brought with him all the way from New Zealand. It was a white wooden cross about four feet long with a circular epitaph to his brother. He pushed it in the ground at the grave site and paused for a photograph. His face showed no emotion.

From Albert he and Lillian made their way to Paris and after a few days' sightseeing left for their trip across the channel. On a dull overcast July morning they huddled together at an aerodrome outside Paris, and after strapping on lifebelts clambered aboard a flimsy, single-engined biplane. The conditions were anything but ideal. There was just enough room for them and the pilot with their knees doubled up facing each other. Commercial air travel was in its infancy and this was one of only two flights daily between England and Paris. As optimistic as ever Robert loudly declared to Lillian and the ground crew: "Who wouldn't have this, as against a dirty trip across the Channel?"

The attendants on either side of the plane moved it into position and on the pilot's signal let go of the wings. The engine roared and the small plane shot down the runway. Robert looked over at Lillian. The noise was deafening. The plane lifted off, climbed to 2000 feet and careered towards the Channel at 110 miles an hour. Air pockets and heavy winds played with it like a toy and it dropped 20 or 30 feet at a time without warning.

He had heard the term "bumpy passage" before but didn't know what it meant. Now he did. The colour drained from his face as he felt the characteristic surgings of nausea. Pulling back the window he pushed his head out and was violently sick, staying there for the next two hours in the backdraught of the propeller. Lillian watched but could do little to help. As the English countryside came into view Robert managed to prop up his Kodak and take a shot over Dover, but it was only light relief. His body was overjoyed to be reunited with the ground when they finally landed at Croydon.[15]

London on the whole did little to bolster his spirits. Although ostensibly the English summer, it rained constantly and he found himself dressing in heavy winter clothes which he disliked. But it wasn't only the weather that was bad, economic conditions were also changing for the worse. For the past year and a half the world had been enjoying a post-war boom. Factories in Britain and America geared back into civilian output and were producing goods as fast as they could, yet even this could not satisfy consumer demand and prices had risen sharply as a result.

Europe was a different story. Torn apart by four years of war it could not hope to re-establish itself overnight and in the summer of 1919, continental businesses on a wide scale began cancelling orders for goods from Britain. It was more than the fledgling market could take and as fast as it had surged up it began to head back down again. As he and Lillian toured the counties they saw an increasing number of factories closing down. The management he talked to described very different conditions from the boom economy which still had hold in New Zealand.

Robert knew that it would not be long before the effects of what he was witnessing in Britain travelled to New Zealand. Three weeks after he arrived, on August 21, he sent an urgent cable back home. The message was short and direct.

"Indications prices breaking, buy short and often."[16]

He knew that the company's stocks in New Zealand were high and when he left this had not been a problem. They had been placing large orders for some time as had everyone else, and the market was buying up all they could sell. In the business they had seen a string of record months and even the company's large overdraft had not been a concern. Now it looked as though the situation was going to reverse.

His cable would at least stop their own buyers entering into long-term contracts for goods, which would give them some protection from the falling prices. If he did not do it, the firm would be left with several hundred thousand pounds worth of goods bought at top dollars on a falling market. It could bankrupt them.

Leaving London he and Lillian went north to visit the Lever Brothers works at Port Sunlight, and Cadbury's Garden Village at Bournville. Robert wanted to learn more of their staff welfare work and was very impressed.[17] At Port Sunlight, Lord Leverhulme had transformed the community into a self-contained industrial unit. The factories were well lit and ventilated, and they had dining and tea rooms where food was supplied to the staff at cost. There were restrooms with hot baths and a modern surgery for the workers. In the town itself was a free library, museum, art gallery, technical institute and staff training college.

He and Lillian also called on the Boot family at Nottingham. Sir Jesse Boot, the famous retailer, had been confined to bed with arthritis for the past 17 years but despite his infirmity had developed and managed a chain of 600 chemist stores, the largest in Britain. Robert and Lillian had first acquainted themselves with the Boots five years earlier on the ship back to New Zealand after their wedding. There they had travelled in the company of Sir Jesse's sister, and now accepted an invitation to stay at their gracious home in Nottingham.

Sir Jesse was wheeled about constantly on a mobile stretcher, but it did not restrain his alert and talented mind and he and Robert spent many hours discussing business matters in depth. Sir Jesse had recently sold his chain of chemist stores to the American-based United Drug Company for £2,170,000 in cash and said to Robert:

"I didn't want shares in a business that I no longer owned and managed, so I demanded the full amount in cash and got it."

Reflecting on his past two years at the Farmers Union Trading Company, Robert could now see full well the wisdom of Sir Jesse's actions. If only he had done likewise. Soon it was time to leave for New York to establish the company's buying office in America. They set sail on October 9th and after finding premises, he, Lillian and John said their goodbyes to William Mackay and left to travel around the United States. They made their way across by train and in California Lillian was able to catch up with her beloved half-brother Harry Ironside whom she hadn't seen for five years. They were soon swamped with invitations from many friends eager to meet them and little Jack. For one particular function Robert required an evening shirt and headed into the city.

An American friend had specifically told him not to go to the upper-class men's outfitter, Roos Bros. because of the high prices, and following their advice he sought out a large mainstream store on Market Street. A few minutes later he located the shirt counter and found three salesmen engrossed in conversation. No one turned to serve him and momentarily he spoke up.

"Would one of you gentlemen please show me a pleated front white dress shirt."

"What size?" said the assistant bluntly.

"Fifteen please."

"Haven't got any," and with that he turned his head and carried on his conversation.

Robert was horrified and immediately left the store, crossed the street and entered the prestigious Roos Bros. Cordially greeted by a salesman he was quickly served with a shirt and induced to buy a set of matching front studs and tie. He inquired about the Government war taxes which he had seen added onto the price of goods and the courteous salesman led him through to the store's main office where he received a complete schedule. This was the kind of service he was used to.

Later, he returned to buy a young friend an overcoat for Christmas and had the same pleasant experience. He was shown a selection of coats and after picking one the salesman suggested that if it was left it with them for the day he would have the sleeves taken up and the belt lifted. He then told the boy that if he brought the coat back a year later, they would let it out to its original size free of charge.

The American multi-millionaire Rockefeller had said that success came by doing the common everyday things of life uncommonly well – it was a motto that Robert fully understood and wrote to his own staff back home.

"It is not always easy to be pleasant – physical disability within, pressure of business without, and cross, hard-to-please customers make it mighty difficult to always maintain an unruffled pleasant expression; but, thanks to natural gift of self-control, we have quite a number of sunshine salesmen and girls that any business might well be proud of. If you are not already there, join the ranks of those whom customers seek out the second time because of the courteous service you render them." [18]

Meanwhile, news from home suggested that so far the fall in prices that he had witnessed in England had still not reached New Zealand. Monthly sales were averaging £120,000.[19] News had spread that the firm's managers had stopped buying, and rumours again circulated that the business was on the verge of bankruptcy. Fortunately, the extensions to his original building at Hobson Street were well under way and in October, the doors of the new-look building were opened to the public for the first time. Inside the transformation was astounding.

The utilitarian warehouse had been converted almost throughout to a modern department store. Now three separate functions were run under the one roof – mail order, wholesaling to branches, and retailing.[20]

To follow up the inaugural move to retail, a 'Buy in November' sales campaign was launched to clear out stocks and it produced a record month. The firm did a colossal £175,150 worth of sales and Robert was thrilled with the result. In America he was in constant contact with David Robertson his assistant general manager back in New Zealand, and after adding up the month's sales scribbled at the bottom of his cashbook: "Some month."

While they were away Lillian became pregnant again, and by January, when they were scheduled to make their trip home, she was almost due. It was an uncomfortable crossing. They arrived home in February to what was again another warm-hearted welcome. The company hired the concert chamber of the Auckland Town Hall and on February 7,400 members of the staff put on a reception and musical evening for their beloved 'Chief.'

Once again Robert's cheery 'Good Morning' was heard echoing in the halls of the Farmers Union Trading Company as he went about his rounds. His return could not have been more timely, though perhaps a little late. The acute fall in prices he had seen in Britain had moved right across the globe. Sales at Sears Roebuck in America had collapsed from $233 million in 1920 to $159 million in 1921. Stock levels had become wildly out of control and instead of making a net profit of $11 million, they made a net loss of $16 million. At the world's oldest mail order house, Montgomery Ward, a similar pattern occurred. Sales dropped 32% and they, too, recorded a $10 million loss.

It appeared as if the Farmers Union Trading Company might be headed for a similar situation. When he got home in February the bank overdraft was a staggering £116,000. Something had to be done and done quickly. But it wasn't the sales level that was the only problem; in the past few months stock levels had gone through the roof.

10

NO PORT IN THE STORM

1921-1925

"For the last 12 years the two businesses I have been connected with have 'been going bankrupt' according to the man on the street, who has inside information on every business in the City except his own. I have often thought that Mr. Clarke, the Income Tax Commissioner in Wellington, as he raked in the shekels we have had to pay, must have smiled to himself and devoutly wished that every other business in the Dominion was in a like rickety condition."[1]

Robert Laidlaw, April 1921.

During the post-war boom many retailers had great difficulty getting stocks from overseas and factories in Britain and America often had far more orders than they could possibly fill. British manufacturers in particular, many of whom were a year to 18 months behind their production schedules, stated that they would fill orders only in the sequence they received them. If a firm wanted to receive goods regularly, it had to keep placing orders continuously, regardless of the delays.

At any one time a business might have multiple orders placed with a single factory. In the throes of an economic boom this was not a problem because the rapid escalation in demand meant that all over the world, goods could readily be sold.

However, as recession hit Britain this situation changed dramatically and with their European markets closing, British manufacturers pulled out their backlog of orders to the colonies and started filling them as fast as they could.

At the Farmers Union Trading Company, the stock level at which Robert routinely kept the business (for both Hobson Street and the branches) was around £350,000. At this figure he could turn the stock over three or more times a year and generate a modest profit on sales of around £1,300,000.

With British firms sending him old orders in quick succession by March 1921 he had an enormous stockpile of £673,050 worth of goods, and all at prearranged boom prices. If that was not bad enough another three months worth (£80,000), was already in boats and on its way to New Zealand. He had enough stocks of most items to last him for over two years, and they were still coming. The firm would have been bankrupt already had he not ordered the department managers to stop buying last August.

"Travellers were still being deluged with orders everywhere," he said, "and when our department managers turned them down and explained that they had instructions to hold off, out went the first whisper that the company must be in financial difficulties. Had it not been for this prompt action taken last year, we would to-day have one or two hundred thousand pounds worth more stock than we have."[2]

Why he did not simply cancel dozens of out-of-date orders must have seemed strange to some, yet it was an extension of his beliefs about commerce in general. His motto since 1909 had been, 'stern, old fashioned, unfailing honesty,' and he extended this to not only customers and staff, but also to his suppliers. To cancel hundreds of thousands of pounds worth of orders was contrary to everything he believed in. In his mind, it was up to him to make the very best of a bad situation.

When the final accounts for the year came in they had narrowly averted a disaster. Sales for the year to March 1921 were £1,484,513.[3] Many goods had been sold at cost if not below, and this was how they achieved the high turnover. The firm had managed to turn a small profit of £20,719 (1% of sales), but it was a dismal result. It should have been six times that at least.

At Laidlaw Leeds he consistently turned a net profit of 6% on sales which on the latest figures would have been over £120,000. It was a blowout in nothing but stock. His working expenses had not increased. He consistently kept these around 14% of total sales and for the 1921 year they had dropped to 13%; all possible profits were being spent on stocks.

He never conveyed the results to his customers, staff or the directors in these terms. He knew very well the actual state of affairs and the kind of returns the business should be generating. In his optimistic way he ignored the poor profits completely and, focusing on the sales figures (which had increased 50%) and the numbers of shareholders (which had increased 49%), he said: "Our financial year ended on 31st March and we take this prompt opportunity to acquaint our 15,944 shareholders of the phenomenal progress made by their company during the past twelve months.

"Every one of our thirty-one branches as well as the business in general, show very substantial increases in sales. This wonderful success demonstrates the splendid loyalty of our farmers to this Co-operation. It also shows the uniform strength of this business in that not a single department or branch has failed to register steady increases. Our factories have also been highly successful.

"The furniture factory was greatly increased in size during the year, our saddlery factory more than doubled its capacity, while our boot factory, which is one of the best equipped in

Auckland substantially increased its output. Not a shareholder has more reason to be proud of this great institution than the men and girls who daily contribute to their share of service to the success of this great undertaking. As rumours seem to be particularly rife at the present time, keep this *Optimist* in your pocket, and when you hear your company attacked by competitors, produce the above figures and ask them if their businesses can show a quarter of the progress yours has registered in the past twelve months.

"Boost for your Company every opportunity you get, and accept my assurance, not only of its present absolute substantiality, but of the fact that it is destined to be the greatest and most successful commercial undertaking in Australasia."[4]

He needed more cash however if this 'successful undertaking' was to stay afloat, and this was not going to be easy. Financial conditions in New Zealand had become so tight that on March 21 1921, the Government passed the Moratorium Extension Act.

This effectively froze all large deposits made before that date, which could not be withdrawn until December that year. Things had not gone well for the farming community either, and in addition to falling retail prices the international prices of wool, mutton and grain also dropped.

Many companies and local bodies around New Zealand (as did the Farmers Union Trading Company), ran banking departments offering customers competitive interest rates for both fixed and call deposits. However, the tightening economic conditions caused a run on withdrawals and many of these institutions did not have the funds to repay depositors. When the councils and businesses turned to the banks for help they too did not have sufficient funds. To prevent a financial catastrophe the Act was passed giving all these institutions protection for another nine months.

Without deposits coming into the banking department Robert had to look elsewhere for money to fund the company's day-to-day needs. He made further calls on unpaid shares and issued more B preference shares. Then in May he issued £250,000 worth of 7½% bonds. It was an instant success.

Three days after they were announced £21,000 worth had been sold.[5] But in reality he was just juggling numbers and he knew it. Unable to borrow from the banks, he had effectively borrowed from his customers to finance the company's shortfalls. It was only a short-term remedy. He still had to meet the high interest rate and repay the bonds themselves in 1925. Undaunted he remained optimistic.

"How is it," he said, "that, in spite of the persistent opposition from without, our sales should be steadily rising, our Bonds selling, and our business progressing? May it not be that the FUTC is destined to succeed? Personally, I believe it is."[6]

On April 24 1921, Lillian gave birth to a third child in his parents' home at Argyle Street. They had now moved out of their Shelly Beach Road home and were living permanently at his mother's beach house in Ocean View Road, Milford. Lillian however wanted to be in town for the birth and after a smooth delivery their second son was born on the sewing room table in the big house. He was named Arthur Lincoln, Arthur after Robert's second brother. It had been a year since Lorraine had died and Lincoln, as he came to be known, was a very happy addition to the small family.

Flying kites was a popular pastime and together Robert and the boys made several large fabric kites with 6 foot wingspans which they took to Milford beach. Controlling these monsters in the wind proved problematic so it wasn't long before they too were the target of his innovative flair. Robert had one of the servicemen at the Farmers convert a 'Unity' sewing machine into an electric winch and on their next sojourn to Milford they were airborne with style.

Meanwhile in the business monthly sales remained around £100,000. His share and bond selling campaign had brought new customers but there remained one nagging problem: it was obvious that he not only had too much stock but also that much of it was unsellable, especially in drapery and womens wear. He had not experienced anything like this before.

Until 1917 Arthur had run an efficient soft-goods section at Laidlaw Leeds, but he now lacked anybody with similar experience. As a result the business had accumulated £180,000 worth of largely out of date and worthless drapery. In March, he held a stocktaking sale in the drapery department at Hobson Street. This he followed with a competition to pay £20 to the person who bought the most drapery on every day in May.

It was a popular drawcard and May sales were again over £100,000. He kept pushing and marked many surplus stock items at half price for the month of July. Normally 500 customers a day came to the store and for the half price deals he was expecting to see double that number, encouraging the staff to grasp the opportunity.

"You hold the full power in your hands," he said. "The quality and the prices are right, but these are only the first half of a satisfactory purchase. What of the service? You will be labouring under all the disadvantages of a rush, but if you can keep smiling and give polite, prompt, efficient service, you will make so many new customers that we will be looking for more employees to take care of our growing sales. No one can be left out," he commanded, "We must all help. The sales staff, the office, the dispatch, and even the motor-men who deliver the packages to the door must each contribute their share of that subtle yet essential thing called service."[7]

The campaign took off with a vengeance and the stores were

besieged with customers. They were six months into the new financial year but he was still worried. He had managed to make a dent in the piles of stocks coming from Britain but these were not high-margin sales. Prices kept dropping and he was selling some goods below their landed price, purely because by the time they arrived in New Zealand the ruling market price was lower than what they had been bought for. Grocery lines had been knocked down up to 33%, drapery up to 38%, hardware up to 40% – some items up to 50%. By September he had moved £50,000 worth of drapery alone, but at a £14,000 loss.

In September he also celebrated his 36th birthday, yet how different from that which he experienced 10 years earlier. Then he was installed in his double four-storey warehouses and was enjoying the first-fruits of the incredible cash-rich growth at Laidlaw Leeds. He had come full circle and was now desperately trying to pull a large concern, starved of cash, back into line. September was also marked by the absence of *The Optimist*. He decided that in light of the severe financial strain the business was under they could no longer afford it. It was a sad moment. *The Optimist* had been a precious little book and a vital link in the business. In the closing pages of the August issue he published some thoughts from his mentor A.F. Sheldon. In essence it summed up many of the things he had been striving for over the last 12 years.

"I believe that the science of business is the science of service. That he profits most who serves best. That the success of any institution is the sum of the successes of the people engaged in its service. That no house is greater than its representative, and that everyone connected with the house is its representative. That a house is known by the customers it keeps. That both the getting and keeping of customers depends upon the efficiency of its representatives."[8]

These beliefs were now being tested at every turn. By the time the 1922 accounts came out in March the following year the business had suffered a £58,000 loss. It was the first he had ever experienced in business. Ironically sales had still been over £1 million but the margins too small. The loss had been further aggravated by the numbers of debtors on the company books. Credit selling meant the firm was carrying over £260,000 worth of debtors and it was a cost it could not afford. He made no allocation for bad debts in the accounts but this was not realistic and he would soon find out that the firm's financial position also reflected that of its customers.

Nor was he alone in these difficulties; trading firms all over the city were experiencing the same kinds of problems. Looking back on the past few years the financial writer of the *Truth* newspaper wrote:

"The complete collapse which for a while staggered the whole commercial community, brought about mostly by the slackness followed by most of the mercantile quidnuncs, who unwisely trusted too greatly the honour of British merchants and manufacturers ... This country was made the dumping ground of Britain.

"Our importers should have repudiated millions of pounds sterling in overdue orders, just the same as British importers who were in the habit of sheltering themselves from the effects of falling markets by declaring 'the goods were late in arriving,' or 'that the goods were not up to sample.'

"Business contracts which are based upon order, should be rigidly framed and carried out to the letter. The future business of this country will have to be conducted on better lines and our trading community must see to it that never again will the dear old British manufacturer get an opportunity to use this country as one of the dumping grounds. The truth is, that we are tricked, if not swindled, by the people at the other end of the world in the matter of supplies."

The writer then singled out Robert in particular, "The general manager, young, enthusiastic and brimful of ability, has measured up to his job with points far exceeding champion honours ... The 16,000 shareholders in this concern are very fortunate in having the services of this talented young businessman at their beck and call. He carries a huge responsibility, and time will prove how much the membership of the company is indebted to him for the manner in which he fought the 'slump' in values. No man could do better."[9]

The reporter's words were to prove prophetic but Robert was not out of deep water yet. He knew that he must make some serious changes in the business if he was to pull it out of its current difficulties. He could not go on propping it up with more and more short-term cash. Over the year stock levels had dropped to £485,000, but it was still £135,000 too much. He would need another big year to move this amount of stock and wipe out the loss. The previous August he had sent the branch managers a letter informing them to stop credit for customers with accounts three months overdue, and began to tighten up credit.

In March 1922, he opened two cash-and-carry stores to boost sales but the figures did not respond. Unbelievably the opposite happened and March sales fell 45% followed by the same in April.

Robert recalled William Mackay from America and closed the New York office. The next two months picked up slightly but the damage had been done. Things were getting worse not better and for the next five months the business stagnated.[10]

The Hobson Street store had never been designed as a retail outlet and although the extension and renovations in 1920 had helped, the main shopping area of Auckland city was Queen Street. Hobson Street was a steep climb up from Queen Street and the long and arduous walk was obviously deterring shoppers. If the people were not going to come to the business on their own accord then he would bring them up. He commandeered a truck from one of the firm's branches, had it converted to hold passengers and the first free bus service in New Zealand, or 'traffic truck' as it was known, was launched.[11]

At first it lured few passengers. In 1922 Aucklanders were not used to a bus service let alone a free one, so Robert induced his staff to ride on the bus in their lunch hours and gradually its popularity grew. Holding up to 15 people at a time, in its first few weeks it carried around 90 people each day. On Christmas Eve that year it carried nearly 4000 shoppers chugging up and down to the store for 13 hours.[12] Robert also opened another first during the year, a large children's playground on the roof of the building complete with battery-operated pedal cars, scooters and tricycles. It proved immensely popular. Customers could now dine at the rooftop tearooms while their children played in the playground, or if they wished, stroll on the promenade taking advantage of the unprecedented panoramic views of Auckland that the hilltop building offered.

Sales slowly picked up but before the March 1923 balance sheet came out he had to face the inevitable. There was at least £70,000 of stocks that were never going to sell. Some of it was even left over from when he had purchased branches four years ago. It was obvious too that there was a hard core of accounts that were never going to be paid (debtors had increased to nearly £300,000). In the balance sheet he wrote off £69,169 worth of stock and £10,000 worth of bad debts. He had made a total loss for the year of £86,394. When this was added to the £58,000 already sitting on the books from last year, it rose to £144,400. It would take some doing to ever return this to a profit situation.[13] For the second year in a row ordinary shareholders received no dividend and losers too were his friends and family who had also taken preference shares. His father alone was now owed in excess of £2400.

As the new financial year began in April 1923 sales improved but the stock problem and debt servicing costs were sucking money out of the business at an alarming rate, and the overdraft began increasing £20,000 every month. Robert attacked efficiency in the firm with vigour. He appointed William Mackay as full-time efficiency manager and looked at new ways of eliminating error, improving service, and minimising costs. Together they cut back on pencils, string, wrap and even replaced light bulbs with less powerful ones.

"My mental attitude has changed," he said, "and frankly, from today, we are on the warpath after that small percentage of mistakes, and if you will change your mental attitude like I have, it will solve half the problem before our new efficiency methods get properly started.

"Every worthwhile man and girl wants to work for a firm that is famed for its high standard of efficient service, and that covers invoicing, department staffs, assembly checking, packing, despatching, accounting, and correspondence. Whatever the price in discipline, hard work, care and thoughtfulness, I want you to join me in aiming at a reputation 100% high for efficiency in service ...

"Take these actual instances from the past few days – lbs. typed on a seed order instead of bushels; two articles ordered and sent but extended on invoice at price of one, 6 lbs. of currants sent for raisins; instructions on order to forward with other goods overlooked; goods consigned to Whakapara instead of Waipawa; lawn mower sent off without the handle; drapery substituted without any explanation; and so we could go on with a frightful list of small irritating mistakes that lose us hundreds of customers, and annoy many who still keep ordering.

"Will you join me in this crusade against these simple, yet silly, errors resulting from lack of concentration on the particular work at hand – easy to make, yet hard to remedy and costly beyond computation in lost business and lost prestige."[14]

In June he, Lillian and the two boys moved out of their Shelly Beach Rd home over to Argyle Street in Herne Bay. His father had purchased a substantial house there in 1917 and Robert bought it from him. The house stood like a landmark in the Herne Bay area. Only a few houses backed down on to the beach, and none were as large or as imposing as number 45. Called 'Norwood', the big two-storey home was made entirely of timber and painted a light cream colour, its windows and facings picked out in chocolate brown.

A square cut hedge on a grey stone wall marked the property's road boundary and large wooden gates opened to a spacious driveway. Walking through the front door, the grandeur of the house was instantly apparent. A panelled hallway disappeared into the heart of the house and an expertly crafted staircase wound up through a series of landings. On one side of the hall stood ornately carved occasional tables from India, on the other a grandfather clock and fearsome tiger skin. Affixed to the wall panels and just within reach rested a pair of crossed bayonets, and above the door to the rear rooms a sword and scabbard. All over the polished wooden floors Robert put thick Persian silk rugs connecting the various rooms.

A door to the left led through to the formal dining room where a black 12-seater oak table barely pushed the room for space. On one wall stood Robert's glass-fronted book cabinet that held his leather-bound classics, and on top a marble statue of Dante's head watched over the collection. On the wall facing north a large bay window gave an uninterrupted view of the harbour and parklike gardens.

Across the hall was the drawing room and large fulsome seats in the latest styling as well as a baby grand piano graced the wide room. Robert collected statues and paintings on his overseas trips and had brought back several from Italy. His statue of David sat on the fireplace and in a hexagonal bay window a bust of Venus de Milo surveyed the room. To the front and rear of the drawing room were two more rooms. One was a sunroom and at the rear of the drawing room was what was affectionately known as the 'snuggery.' A smaller room, quite oriental in flavour, with cane sided chairs and heavily patterned tables again filled with books, pictures and statues, this was the room used to entertain a lesser number of guests in a more informal setting.

The house had four live-in helpers: a downstairs maid, upstairs maid, a cook and a governess for the children. A full-time gardener was employed to look after the gardens. Around the walls of the house at strategic points were buttons for summoning the help, and inside the kitchen a small box on the wall with stencilled numbers showed which room to attend.

The second floor was full of bedrooms and Lillian's sewing room. It was used as the family room and there they spent most of their time together. It was in the south-west corner of the house and again the room had a large bay window looking down on Argyle Street. This was the children's room, complete with cosy fireplace, comfy chairs and a large rug, and the boys could scatter their toys without always having to clean up.

Robert and Lillian slept on the second floor too, but not in a bedroom, rather on the veranda directly above the ground-floor sunroom. He believed that sleeping outdoors was healthy and with the cedar shutters providing a measure of privacy and protection from the elements, they made the journey out to the open part of the balcony and through to the sleeping porch regardless of the weather.

By now there were more and more calls on his speaking abilities and in June he journeyed to Wellington. The year before he had been approached by a Canadian representative of Rotary and had helped to establish the first club in Auckland. He was serving as a director and had been invited to speak at the Wellington convention, taking as his topic 'friendship.' Standing in front of a room full of well-dressed businessmen he opened his address:

"It has been said," he declared, "there is no sentiment in business. But, we all know there is. The world may live on results but it runs on feelings, and I am pleading now for more real sentiment, though not for sentimentality – for more frank friendliness and less suspicion – for more thinking aloud and less secret scheming – for a little less fear in expressing those feelings which, if we only realised it, are common to all men.

"Rotary," he continued, "is doing a mighty service to humanity in the cultivation of friendship, both national and international, and we can best help it forward in our club and community by cultivating it in ourselves, and for this purpose let me recommend our own homes as the finest practice ground in the world. That is where all the hog that is in a man comes out, and remember, a man does not need a high-powered motor car and a dusty road to show how much of a hog he can be. On the other hand show me a gentleman within the four walls of his own home, and I will show you a gentleman in all walks of life.

"I know a man whose little boy, when asked who he is, affirms that he's daddy's pal, and I know of no finer tribute that could be paid to any man than he should be such a friend to his own boy that he would grow up to emulate his dad as the finest type of man he knew. That is not to be attained by making great self-sacrifice; that privilege falls to few. Life, for most of us, is made up of minor details, but as dripping water wears away stone, so many acts of simple kindness leave indelible marks for good in the lives of those we meet."[15]

Returning to Auckland however was not so pleasant. All his efforts in the business could still not control the overdraft, and by September it reached £138,330. He had had enough of credit selling and on September 1, the mail order business and all trade out of the Hobson Street premises was once again put on a cash-only basis.[16] Much relieved he wrote in the new catalogue:

"We have tried both cash and credit and have given credit a fair trial over two years of prosperity and two years of depression and, without being vulgar, the credit system has proved to be rotten through and through. Here is what the credit system is costing our shareholders each year as per figures taken from our last year's balance sheet, but applicable to any other years:

7% interest on £270,000 Book Debts	£18,000
Bad Debts, conservatively estimated at 5% of the amount outstanding, but should be more. Ask any man in the credit business.	£13,500
Bookkeeping Staff, Clerks, Collectors, Ledgerkeepers, etc. Actual wages paid annually	£10,968
	£43,368

In September he refunded to the company part of the interest he had been paid on his preference shares and in a letter to the board of directors wrote:

"In view of the difficulties through which our company has been passing, I feel I should not take the extra 1%. now being

167

paid by the company on my preference shares as per agreement dated June 13 1921, and have therefore paid back to Mr Crouch the sum of £2620, thus refunding the 1%. from the commencement to even date and have instructed him to calculate interest on my shares at 6%. in future.[17]

His refund was generous but it was only minor compared to the firm's financing commitments. It was clear that with the existing level of sales and profitability, it would not be able to pay back the bondholders when they fell due in 1925. In December, he put forward a plan for converting the depositors and bond holders into secured debentures, at a lower rate of interest and with repayment not until 1930. They accepted his proposal and he bought himself some more time.

By March in the new year 1924 he had reduced the overdraft to £108,977, opened more cash stores and instituted a bonus scheme for management in addition to the efficiency drive. Sales for the year totalled £1,168,000 and the business was able to turn in a small net profit of £10,209.[18] What he did with it however caused major upset among the shareholders.

Many wanted it written off against the loss still on the books but family and friends who were A preference shareholders had prior claim and wanted their money. If they were not paid, they had the power to liquidate the company and this was openly discussed.[19] He was caught between them and the company he was trying desperately to restore. The company lost and the A preference shareholders were duly paid the profits towards their outstanding dividends, and for another year the firm carried a colossal loss on its books.[20]

By August 1924, four months later, he could count some successes. Three years after the stock blowout occurred he had at last returned it to its previous level and it stood at £350,000 for the entire business. Sales were averaging around £90,000 a month which was not high enough, but without dead stock the margins were improving. In August he relaunched *The Optimist* after a gap of three years.

"First let me confess," he said, "that I was wrong in ever ceasing to issue *The Optimist*. If I ever needed it, it was in those dark days of three years ago when the clouds of trade depression hung lowest and the fight was most uneven. The compilation of its matter would have been an inspiration to me that must have found its reflection among the rest of you, for, as the hero or the 'Go Getter' says, after describing the influence of his captain at the Front, '*Esprit de corps* filters down from the top,' and I see now that one of my major duties during the difficult days of the past was to help maintain the right spirit, for after all it is better to die glad than live sadly.

"Then I was striving to avoid defeat. Today I am striving for victory – but the fact is I got so absorbed in the conflict that I forgot the main issue – that true satisfaction is not to be found in the avoidance of defeat nor in the attainment of success, but in the strife itself. I mean that the man who smiles when the sun shines and frowns when the storm gathers is but a creature of circumstance, whereas the joy of life ought to come from the process of living, not from the surrounding conditions. I feel a particular regret that I have been fighting so grimly instead of joyously, because I profess to draw my inspiration from a source far above the influence of either trade booms or depressions, and reflection on the experiences of the past has served to show me how weakly I have permitted great truths to grip me."[21]

His enthusiasm was short lived for by November it was clear that customers who were unable to pay their accounts owed tens of thousands of pounds. Sales too had been slow all year and indications were that the firm was going to take another loss for the fourth year in a row, possibly over £200,000. There would be no dividend yet again and on top of this there were still overdue dividends owing to friends and family who owned A preference shares – now a whopping £38,600 and he was still under mounting pressure to sort this out.

That Friday afternoon he sat alone in his office. He had been thinking over the situation for weeks, but could see no way out. Turning around in his chair he looked out the window. From his second-storey vantage point he could see right across the Hobson Street wharves and into the harbour. The inviting waters glistened in the sun but his mind was elsewhere. It had been a long struggle and he had given more and more of himself. He had spent hours upon hours inside these walls and Lillian and the family had seen less and less of him.

Directors' meetings and the many meetings with managers and clients had consumed his time and energy. He had beaten the stock situation, but the company was still going further and further into the red. It would take him 10 years or more to get rid of the losses, let alone repay all the outstanding dividends. Even if he was able to do this, he would never be able to pay out the quarter of a million pounds worth of debentures when they matured in six years' time.

Reluctantly, he faced the inevitable and picking up the phone asked to be put through to Joe Johnston his solicitor. The conversation with Joe was brief but painful. Holding back any emotion he instructed him to draw up the necessary papers to liquidate the business.

Packing his bag he took the stairs and left the building. It was a strange sensation. Hard to believe that it had finally come to this. Motoring home to Lillian, he put the children in the car and left town for the weekend. He could not face being in Auckland at the moment. They journeyed south to a remote holiday spot but the situation played heavily on his mind. He thought of the shareholders and the money they had invested in the firm. He carried their trust, and defeat did not sit easily on his shoulders.

Suddenly, an idea flashed across his mind. It was unheard of, but it was a way out. Instead of trying to find new money to get the firm out of its financial strife, he would use the money that was already there. Each shareholder could personally take a portion of the loss off the existing value of their own shares. Everyone would lose some of the money they had already paid in on shares, but it would wipe out the loss.

It was an exciting option. From the firm's point of view it was just moving figures around on the books, it was the shareholders who would feel the pain, but with no losses the company could begin paying dividends. If they could return a dividend, then they could also start selling shares again and further strengthen the capital base of the company for future growth. Hurrying back to Auckland he filled in some of the details and on Wednesday, November 12, put his sketchy plans to the board. No one opposed him; the alternatives were too dire to consider.

Robert was firing again. His mind was alive with ideas for pulling the business back on to its feet and as the solicitors drafted plans for the share write-down he launched an offensive that would go down as his masterstroke: he began selling consumer goods on time payment. The company had previously sold a few items like this, but it was only a very limited range and amounted to a few thousand pounds in sales each year. No one had ever thought of extending it to everyday items and on November 8th he took out a large three-quarter page advertisement in the *New Zealand Herald*.

"Furnish Today – Twelve Months to Pay," he decreed. "Our convenient plan of supplying Phonographs, Pianos, and Sewing Machines has proved so successful that we have decided to extend it to General Furniture."

While the critics mocked and waited for his inevitable

financial collapse the customers flocked through the doors. It was a resounding success. The cash came in either weekly or monthly and he soon found an unexpected bonus: sales on a Friday evening out of Hobson Street soared as customers came in to make their payments.

Christmas seemed a long time coming this year. It had been a particularly arduous few months. On Tuesday, December 23, 1924, at 5 pm, a large gathering of staff and their families assembled on top of the Hobson Street store. He had planned a special party; it would be a Christmas to remember. A sumptuous meal was put on for everyone in the staff dining rooms then after dinner they were led out onto the rooftop playground. It was a warm summer's evening and as the children played on the pedal cars their parents chatted and took in the sunset views of Auckland city.

Suddenly there was a commotion at the door leading to the playground. It was Santa, and 250 children left their playthings and ran simultaneously across the building to greet him. Surrounded by the delirious youngsters Santa led his followers out along the rooftop promenade. The lights came on and there against the night sky was a towering Christmas tree, its pine branches draped with every decoration imaginable. But it was what was at the foot of the tree that left the children speechless. Robert had been busy and there lay a vast mountain of presents. He stood by and watched as Santa mounted his seat and gave out gifts to all the children. It was a magical evening.

11

GROWING AGAIN

1925-1930

"Never prostitute your faculties or energies to the accomplishment of that which is low, grovelling and unworthy of your noblest self or unending destiny. Live above deceit, set your face like a flint against lying, white or black, keep your hands clean and your heart stainless. Moral honesty is comparable with business success. A Christ-like character is the sole secret of business integrity and business success. Every life has its limitation, every task its temptation; but with ceaseless vigilance and scrupulous fidelity the very difficulties may be compelled to pay tribute to personal character, increased opportunity and exalted victory."[1]

Robert Laidlaw, 1914.

1925 looked to be a good year. With stocks under control, time payment surging forward and his capital reconstruction plan under way, Robert began the year with fresh enthusiasm.

"Where are we going this year?" he asked. "Upstream or down, forward or backward, to nobler things or baser, to greater accomplishment in business or less? Frankly have we made any particular plans – have we any special goal before us, or are we content to start 1925 with no worthwhile purpose in view? The same law seems to operate whether it be spiritual, moral, intellectual or business advancement we are seeking, that unless the fire of aspiration is constantly fed, it quickly

173

dies down, and failure to appreciate this is causing many who make great resolves to become completely disheartened.

"To take an example," he said, "a young man reads the account of a poor boy who started out in life with little education and no natural advantages, but who, by persistent application to work and study eventually made a great success of life. The story seemed so real, so reasonable, that it was easy to picture oneself rising to the same success. A little voice whispered, 'What man hath done, man can do,' and in the enthusiasm of a moment there was born a thoughtful determination to match that man's performance. For a month everything went well – textbooks on English and bookkeeping were purchased and a definite, keen interest was taken in business.

"Gradually the ardour died down, the nights in became irksome, and soon indifference had taken the place of enthusiasm, and a young man, with all the possibilities of a successful future had drifted back into mediocrity. Why? Because his enthusiasm had not been fed. Had he kept on reading inspiring biographies, and studying the records of successful business men, he would have fired his own enthusiasm and would have kept himself eager for the work which had become irksome.

"Who among us cannot look back on some meritorious line of action we once decided on, but which has long since been forgotten? Let us find out what was the motive that impelled us to make that decision, and reaffirming the resolve begin to feed that same motive until it burns brightly again, and the fire of enthusiasm rekindled will enable us to accomplish now what we might have accomplished long ago had we not overlooked this vital point."[2]

He also threw his enthusiasm behind an inner-city mission in Auckland. For five weeks over Christmas and into the New

Year a tent in Auckland civic centre was filled with large crowds of people. The work was carried out under the oversight of the United Churches Tent Campaign Committee and Robert along-side other clergy in the city opened the campaign. In turn many of the city's popular ministers also spoke in the weeks that followed including Evan Harries, Lionel Fletcher and Joseph Kemp.

Sales in the business to the end of March 1925 were £1,180,000. The firm turned a net profit of £30,201, but this had to be written off against losses. £71,000 was written off as bad debts and a further £17,500 off stocks. Indeed the total loss now on the books had gone well over £200,000 to £241,110. At the annual general meeting the capital reconstruction proposal was put to shareholders. It was a difficult pill to swallow but even more unattractive was liquidation. The A preference shareholders had their shares reduced from £1 to 17 shillings, the B preference shares to 14 shillings and the ordinary shares to eight shillings. Spread over all the shareholders the writedown provided another £240,800 in capital which was then used to pay off all the losses.

"Many times a surgeon refuses to operate," said Robert, "until the health of his patient has been sufficiently restored to stand it. To operate with the patient in too weak a condition would make the operation which was intended to save his life the means of destroying it. We believe the right time has been chosen to write down our capital and completely wipe out our losses, which under present circumstances could only have hindered the payment of dividends had they been left on our balance sheet, and our shareholders, by an overwhelming majority, have endorsed this opinion.

"We would like to make it quite clear," he continued, "that the writing down of capital does not mean the loss of a single penny. Writing down the capital simply clears the loss already incurred off the balance sheet and enables the company to pay dividends on its ordinary shares instead of holding them back for many years to offset the loss. This puts the annual profit in the hands of the ordinary shareholder, who can set it aside and build up his own capital again, or spend it just as he pleases."[3]

The plan had written off the losses but it had not endeared the company to many of its customers. Those who had the value of their shares written down lost a real part of their investment despite Robert's rhetoric, and throughout the year there were still no new applications for shares. Of all his innovations the time payment business was proving the most popular and in August he presented a report to the directors outlining the success of the scheme to date.

So far over £27,000 worth of goods including furniture, pianos, cycles, sewing machines and gramophones had been sold. The firm was carrying 1360 accounts of which 1096 were paid up to date. They were making 10% interest on all the goods sold and bad debts looked to be only about 1%. It was a tremendous start.

Robert pushed ahead in his next catalogue spreading the range of goods offered on time payment still further to include crockery, cutlery, blankets, curtains, kitchen utensils and soft furnishings. Considering the extension into these items too risky no other firm followed suit, and he quickly established himself as the leading time payment business in the country. In September he took a full page advertisement in the *New Zealand Herald* to launch a summer cycle sale on time payment.

The terms were £1 down and 3/6 each week for a year. Customers flocked in their thousands to buy the £10 bike and over the next six months the company sold over £20,000 worth of cycles on terms. September also marked another milestone and he celebrated his 40th birthday. March 1926 was the first full year of trading since the capital reduction and the launch into time payment. The figures proved the success of both schemes.

The firm produced a profit of £58,072 on turnover of £1,219,000 – a return of 5% on sales. All arrears on A preference shares were at last paid off and a dividend declared. At the annual general meeting the firm dropped the word 'Union' from its name. Now officially the 'Farmers Trading Company, it soon became known quite simply as 'the Farmers.'

A fresh wind also blew through the Laidlaw home. In the five years since Lincoln was born, while the business was in some of its most trying times, Lillian had given birth to another son, Andrew, but the infant had survived only for a day.[4] It had added sorrow on sorrow, but now on the morning of March 2nd 1926, Robert arrived at the warehouse with a particularly happy smile on his face. On the front page of the *Herald* that morning he had placed the following notice: "Laidlaw – On March 1, at their residence, 45 Argyle Street, Herne Bay, to Mr and Mrs Robt. A. Laidlaw, a daughter." A perfect little girl in every way she was named Lillian, after her mother.

It signalled the start of a new period in his life. These past few years had been his darkest days. At times he had wondered if the firm would pull through at all. The losses borne by many friends and family had soured some relationships, especially between him and his father.

There had been times when he thought he might lose all he had built up and worked so hard to achieve. He had often thought about that fateful Monday in 1918 when he had signed the agreement with Boddie. How different things might have been if he had waited just another three days. The events of the past few years had taken a toll on his health. The country had been in the grip of an influenza outbreak and Robert had been struck down with a weak heart. It confined him to bed for several weeks and he found he lacked the same physical energy as before. Yet reluctant to follow doctors' advice he strove to continue his many interests. For the second year in a row he joined with clergy and other speakers in the city for the annual united churches' tent campaign in the civic centre. Almost every denomination in the city was represented and alongside Joseph Kemp, Robert was joined by Lionel Fletcher, his Brethren colleague Dr Pettit and others.

The mission began in December and lasted for five weeks. Plain wooden planks stretched across benzine boxes formed the pews and sawdust and woodchips were scattered on the ground to form a carpet. The pulpit itself was little better and another box did for a piano stool. Yet the crowds inside were matched only by those outside who strained to hear what was going on inside. The audiences were limited only by the capacity of the tent itself, its sides having to be lifted up to accommodate the overflow.

His work in the tent campaigns was mirrored in other areas of his life as he began to put more of his time into Christian work. Over the past five years he had been involved as a director of the first New Zealand Bible Training Institute. In July 1921 he and a group of like-minded businessmen in the city joined with well-known Baptist minister (Rev. Joseph Kemp) to plan a Bible training school for missionaries and Christian workers. In 1922, the Institute had opened its first building in Ponsonby and had taken in 10 students.

Rolls had grown considerably and they had quickly outgrown their premises. Recently Robert and the other directors had been looking in earnest for a new location for their fledgling college.

On the April 27, 1926 the students of the Institute set aside a day of prayer, hopeful for a new building. On the other side of town, unbeknown to them, Robert and another director were looking over a piece of land at the top of Queen Street and negotiating with its owners. The price being asked was £5500. Robert thought carefully. He told the vendors that they wanted the land for religious not commercial purposes and asked them to consider reducing the price.

The negotiating parties retired for lunch and when they returned the owners offered to donate one portion of the land to the institute worth £3000 and sell them the other at £2500. It was a generous offer and Robert and the other director accepted on the spot. Building soon began on a block that would house 60 students as well as the necessary classrooms. It was an important part of his life; he was vitally interested in spreading the gospel through missions and became increasingly involved in the institute's activities.

The foundation stone of the new institute was laid in a simple ceremony on Saturday November the 20th 1926 at the site in Queen Street. A group of friends and supporters of the institute were there as well as the students.

The men who gathered were common faces at such forward efforts around town: Robert, Rev. Joseph Kemp, Rev. Evan Harries and paper merchant R.L. Stewart. Lillian also got involved in the work and was elected first president of the ladies' committee organising all the finer details of their events. The new building itself was completed and officially opened in September 1927.

Back in the business he made continued headway in time payment. In July 1926 he brought carpets into the range of goods and made a bold offer on the entire carpet range – 5/ down and 5/ a week on any size, any quality. It was an immediate success and cleared out the firm's entire stocks. Carpet was sourced from all over New Zealand to fill the demand until new stocks arrived from Britain. Time payment was having a big impact on the company and sales in hardware, furniture and phonographs had risen 100% over the past two years. His success did not go unnoticed and soon a controversy erupted as to whether this new way of selling was in fact a blessing to the country. Robert found himself right in the middle of the fray and was attacked by both the Christian and business communities.

Wrote one opponent: "At a meeting of the Council of the Auckland Chamber of Commerce opinions were expressed by certain businessmen that the extension of the hire purchase system to articles of luxury was a menace to the prosperity of the Dominion. These opinions have wide acceptance as the menace is causing anxiety, consternation and distress both in New Zealand and Australia. No doubt it has caused the present depression in trade and consequent unemployment."[5]

Robert was of course closing the gap between rich and poor. People no longer needed large amounts of cash to purchase items which could improve their standard of living, and a more affluent middle class was emerging. This was uncomfortable for some but he replied directly to those mounting attacks against him. He took the responsibility of people's indebtedness very seriously.

"After considerable experience of the hire purchase system," he said, "it would seem to me that the articles opposed to it, which are frequently appearing in the press, are inspired by those whose goods do not lend themselves to this method of selling, or are written by those who know little about the subject from a practical standpoint, for the statements made and the deductions drawn are quite erroneous.

"Pianos, furniture, sewing machines, separators, milking machines, farm implements, etc., have been sold for many years on time payment," he continued, "but purchases have been so conservative that no honest investigator could charge the buyers with wild extravagance. Those experienced in both lines of business know that ordinary credit on open accounts leads to more extravagance than the time payment system, which requires the hirer to sign a legal document – in fact, the time payment system, instead of leading to extravagance has led to systematic and regular saving, and the final owning of many useful and artistic articles that never would have been possessed had it been necessary to save the amount in cash beforehand.

"It is a very common thing," he said, "for people, having completed one purchase on the time payment plan, to state that they have found it possible to set aside 5/- or 7/6 per week as the case might be, and immediately make another purchase, involving the same weekly payments. This definite setting aside of part of the weekly income for a specific purpose no doubt leads to minimising a lot of wasteful extravagance that previously went on in a small way, which resulted in the same person frittering away on non-essentials what is now being saved and put into permanent improvements in the home."[6]

With the growing success of time payment in 1927 the firm again produced another good year recording a profit of £50,246. Robert was keen to establish some permanent way of contributing to staff welfare, and set up the Laidlaw Brothers' Memorial Trust in memory of his brothers Jack and Arthur. He donated 5000 A preference shares to fund the trust's activities which in the main amounted to making loans to staff who might need assistance to purchase homes or small sums to meet urgent needs. Trust funds provided extra living rooms, bathrooms, improved drainage and electric lighting, helped staff with medical expenses and other urgent needs.

It also gave every girl leaving the firm to be married £5, and each married man received the same in the event of a birth in his family. These were not small amounts and could easily be two and a half weeks' wages.

The worries of the business over the past few years had devoured much of his time and energy. He had spent many long evenings in the board room and managers' meetings. With finances now on a firmer footing, he began to allow himself more time away from the firm. Christmas 1923 had been the family's last holiday at Milford and for the past few years he and the family holidayed at a farm at Gordonton near Hamilton which took fee-paying guests.

When he had come back as general manager of the Farmers Union Trading Company he had written into his contract that he could have a month off each year at the time of his choosing. He worked this in with school holidays and the children began to see more and more of their busy father. By now both John and Lincoln were at primary school and his daughter Lillian was aged two.

Robert was not a relaxed holidaygoer and took to such breaks with the same level of activity that he threw into business. Their Gordonton holidays were the first of his great rabbit safaris. It was the Laidlaw spirit of adventure at its best with minimal physical effort. Bustling the kids into the back seat of the car he clambered onto the Buick lying between the right front mudguard and the bonnet with his legs stretched back along the running board.

Lillian got in behind the wheel and with him directing activities she drove off down the bumpy country road. The area around Gordonton had seen little human habitation and was prime hunting ground. Rabbits were plentiful and, cradling his .22 rifle carefully in his arms it wasn't long before he had bagged dinner and the party returned to base.

Such chases proved so exciting that it wasn't long before Robert and the boys launched an innovation on the hunt and found at dusk they could have just as much fun getting their prey without the use of a firearm. Driving down the country roads it was never long before a long-eared bunny was lit up in the head lights and with a little acceleration from Robert and a small bump, dinner was again caught. Soon however the rabbits grew weary of this line of pursuit and instead of freezing in the headlights bolted for the grass verge only to find a one-ton Buick careering through the grass after them.

It became affectionately known as the 'huntin, shootin fishin' car and once, while on an excursion up Muriwai beach with some of his managers, Robert glimpsed a large fish splashing about in the undertow of the waves. Without hesitating he swerved the car towards the sea and drove straight in. The surprised manager bent down from the running boards, caught the large fish by the gills and Robert swung the car back up on to the beach again.

On several occasions he and Lillian had visited Lake Taupo in the middle of the North Island. Both were keen fly fishers and had often gone trout fishing together. It was on one such trip in 1926 that he decided Taupo would be the location of their next holiday home. Exploring the shoreline he stumbled upon a picturesque spot at Two Mile Bay, just south of the Taupo township. With some sticks he marked out a small isolated plot of bare land right on the water's edge, and contacted a local solicitor to find out who owned it.

The lawyer soon found the owners. The plot he had chosen was part of a larger parcel jointly held by 184 Maori. After some discussion they agreed to sell him a quarter acre for £1 each. It was no bargain but the spot had captured his interest. He paid the £184 and in doing so established a new high for land sales in the area.[7]

While sitting on a rock overlooking the land he had sketched on the back of a used envelope the layout of his future house. It was a simple design with a large central living area and picture window to the lake, and three bunk rooms and a kitchen off the main room.

When he arrived back in Auckland he gave the envelope to Auckland builder Roy Page, whom he used for much of the building work at the Farmers. Plan in hand Page knew exactly what to do. Assembling a team of builders and a load of materials he set off for the Taupo site. Several weeks later the new holiday home was up.

In the August school holidays that year the family set out for their first stay at their new retreat. Going to Taupo was a major expedition and it would take a full day to drive there. The roads were mostly dirt and gravel and the only local store did not stock fruit and vegetables. Robert packed a large trailer with everything they needed for a two-week stay and hitched it onto the back of the Buick. He, Lillian and Lincoln sat in the front seat while John, young Lillian and her governess squeezed in the back.

By the time he reached the Bombay Hill 25 miles outside Auckland city, rain had set in and turned the rough metal road into a quagmire. He had brought chains for such conditions but was impatient to get under way. Deciding not to stop but rather take the hill at speed, he accelerated through the approaches to the hill. Halfway up the weight of the trailer and the slippery conditions proved too much and the wheels began to skid uncontrollably in the wet and the car came to an uninspiring stop.

Climbing out, he and the boys collected bracken from nearby bushes and placed it under the wheels to try to give some traction but it was no use. With each attempt the heavy trailer only pulled them further backwards. Backing down the hill to take another run looked the final option but Robert wasn't used to driving with a trailer and soon became hopelessly jack-knifed in the ditch on the roadside. He got out of the car and surveyed their situation. The rain beat upon his oilskin hat and dripped down his face. This was not the kind of start he had envisaged.

Lillian, who by now knew exactly the kind of man her ambitious husband was, smiled humorously from the cover of the car. There was a noise in the nearby paddock and he looked up. Over the crest of the hill came a farmer with a team of horses. He had seen their predicament and had come to help. The large draught horses made quick work of the car and soon they were under way again.

Robert took to the roads with renewed gusto and it wasn't long before he caught up with the daily Auckland-Wellington express. Drawing level with the engine he tooted the horn and the children waved madly. The train crew took their greeting as a challenge and with a fresh belch of smoke fired up the boiler. Robert was not about to be outmatched by a train and putting his foot to the floor squeezed every last inch of speed out of his trusty car.

In the train the passengers crowded to the carriage windows to watch the race unfold. The steam engine barrelled along the tracks, neck and neck with the car. With road metal flying and the trailer tossing madly about behind Robert edged the Buick up to 60 mph. It could have been anyone's race but the train engine had to slow for its next stop and Robert and family roared victoriously on ahead.

As they neared Taupo they came across the white volcanic pumice roads. These had been badly weathered and deep corrugations laced them. The Buick shook and rattled over the pitted surface. He slowed to a crawl but found it less severe the faster he went. The children loved it, and lifting the speed to 50 mph he found he hardly noticed the bumps although he had the benefit of the steering wheel. At around 6 pm they pulled into Two Mile Bay and there by the water's edge was their new, freshly painted holiday home, just as he had drawn. It was a trip they would make many times.

The house was only about 50ft from the water and with a large picture window in the front room had an unimpeded view right across the 26-mile lake with the snow-capped Tongariro National Park in the distance. Settling into their new accommodation they decided the house should have a name. A few suggestions were made and Lillian, who had learnt Spanish at school in America, offered 'Monte Vista' (mountain view). It was approved, and the family began their first holiday at 'Monte Vista.'

While the holiday house was being built Robert also had under construction at an Auckland boatbuilders a 17ft kauri speedboat powered by a 32-horsepower, 4-cylinder Johnson Seahorse outboard motor, then the biggest available on the market. He named the boat after the motor, 'Seahorse,' and began taking to the water in his new possession.

The only way to start 'Seahorse' was with a pull cord. It had no reverse gear or clutch so had to be fully laden with passengers and pointing out towards the middle of the lake before any attempt was made to start it. As soon as the engine fired, 'Seahorse' leapt into life. Doing roughly 25 mph, the boat was the fastest on the lake, and Robert intended it to stay that way.

At Taupo he relaxed. As a family they went fishing, exploring and shooting in the surrounding hills. He spent many long hours tinkering with the boat engine or waxing the hull to give it even greater speed. On the walls of the living room he began hanging pictures of all the fish he and his companions caught on the lake. He found that even fishing was something he could mechanise, and while motoring around in 'Seahorse' dangled a line off the stern. Often they packed their things in the boat and took excursions down the lake, fishing for lunch and cooking it over an open fire. At night they gathered round the large fireplace where Robert entertained young Lillian and anyone else who was listening with the wild adventures of Poppy Porpoise, his imaginary talking dolphin who ventured to all kinds of marvellous places around the globe with a little girl on his back.

The past two years had been quite difficult for him physically. The heart condition he had suffered from in 1925 had lingered and he struggled to find the same levels of physical energy. The Laidlaw Brothers' Memorial Trust which he had established in memory of Arthur and Jack had been generous to staff in all kinds of ways. It had made final payments on mortgages sometimes amounting to several months' salary, it had met interest payments and expenses for staff in difficult times, painted houses, paid for drainage to be installed sometimes even hot water.

But feeling his own frailty more than before he put in place another scheme for a further contribution to staff welfare. In a letter to the directors he laid out his plan.

"Having had a number of applications from our men from time to time for assistance to acquire houses, I have decided to make a gift to H.O. staff, for this purpose, of 5000 'A' preference shares, to be administered by a committee, on terms similar to those following: That each girl leaving the firm's employ to be married be presented with £5. That each married man, in the event of a birth in his family, be given £5 maternity allowance. That the balance of the interest and the principal be utilised to advance money to the members of the staff for the purpose of paying the deposit on a house, an endeavour be made to keep these deposits in the region of £100.

"The committee," continued Robert, "would also be open to consider any appeals for temporary loans on behalf of members of the staff who, through sickness or other cause, urgently require money. The committee would have the right to lend the money with or without security at their discretion, at a rate of interest not exceeding 6%.

"My reason for addressing you is to ask if our board will allow this committee to have an overdraft against these shares to the amount of say £4000, so that they can immediately be in a position to help a number of our men to purchase or build homes for themselves. I believe it would be good business on the part of the company to agree to this, as it will give the committee the opportunity of assisting a far greater number of staff than before."[8] His attendance at work, too, in the wake of his illness had for some time been sporadic. He felt the physical strain of the long days and other commitments outside work hours.

"As you are aware," he said, "I am keenly interested in Church work in the city, which occupies every night in the week, either at meetings or in my study in preparation for same, excepting only Saturday evenings, which I keep free for my wife and children. Since I strained my heart two years ago, I have been feeling these long hours a considerable tax, and for some time have been looking forward to our business being in such a condition as to allow of my having more free time.

"I therefore propose for your consideration, that unless there is anything special demanding my attention, I be free to leave at 2 pm each afternoon. Mr Robertson would be available for callers, and the general run of matters that need attention, while anything vital to the business he would hold over for discussion with me as in the past. As a matter of fact, I have never known of anything of great importance cropping up during the afternoon that could not wait till the following morning for a decision, but if such did happen, I would always be available on the phone and could run down if required.

"As my reputation and financial interests are at stake, I

would not propose this if I felt it would in any way interfere with the efficient working or profits of our Company, but to make quite sure, after discussing the position with Mr Boddie, we have tested it out for a month, and it has worked very satisfactorily. I suggest that my salary be reduced by £500 per annum."[9]

While the directors approved of his suggestion and gladly accommodated whatever working relationship suited him best they outrightly refused his salary reduction. Robert tried leaving at 2 pm for the next few weeks but found in the end that it was preferable to start later in the day and work later at night.

In August 1926 with the company back on a profitable basis he looked to further strengthen the capital base of the firm by issuing £200,000 more shares, seeking to raise its capital from £300,000 to £500,000. In a letter to the board he laid out his idea:

"While I have been away I have given considerable thought to the affairs of our Company, and now submit the following for your consideration and that of our Board of Directors. Believing from figures already available that we will have a profit September 30th of over £30,000 I feel the right time has come for facing the only remaining problem of a major kind that confronts the Company; that is, bringing our capital into a more satisfactory relationship to our liabilities.

"Our capital at March 31 1926, was a little less than £300,000 and our liabilities over £1,000,000, or in other words we are trading on about £700,000 worth of borrowed money and credits. Not only do we know that over £300,000 of this money (Debentures) must be repaid in the next few years, but a time of depression, and such times are sure to come in the future as they have come in the past, would again jeopardise our whole undertaking"

"While we have no choice as to the raising of new capital if we desire to put our undertaking on a sound footing, even if we had there is much in favour of share capital at 10% as against Debenture capital at 6½%, for the ordinary dividend need only be paid in good years when we can afford it, whereas the debenture interest <u>must</u> be paid in bad years, when we may actually be trading at a loss. And again, the ordinary capital is an asset, and a help to financial strength, whereas the debenture money is a liability , and at any time may be a source of real danger to the very existence of the Company."

Having said that he also made it quite clear to the board where he felt the company's obligations lay though the ordinary shares were due no dividend by right.

"The company would in no way be committed," he said, "to pay 10% on Ordinary Shares, but would be guided by the profits available from year to year, but I take it that to sell shares to Debenture holders on the above basis, would imply a moral obligation to the Board to recommend a 10% dividend for at least the next few years, if the profits were available."[10]

By now many of his earlier initiatives had become standard practice in the firm; each year the catalogue was over 500 pages long and there were more and more giveaways and special offers. There were free home trials of sewing machines, even raincoats. On a variety of goods he even offered to pay the freight to the customer's door anywhere in New Zealand, always guaranteeing that the prices that the firm offered were the lowest in the country.

If a customer could purchase cheaper elsewhere then he guaranteed to meet the lowest price. If the customer later found out that they could have bought the goods cheaper elsewhere on the same day, he would give them a credit to that amount. He had even opened a carpark in an unused portion of land over the road from the Hobson Street store, and in 1928 it was the first free customer carparking area in Australasia.[11]

Further modernisations had been carried out in the store itself which now boasted electric lifts, interdepartmental telephones, automatic weighing machine, bookkeeping machines, listing and adding machines, calculating machines, cash registers, dictaphones and even duplicating machines. His policy of absolute satisfaction still remained in force, that if after using the goods the customer was not satisfied they could return them and the firm would refund the cost of the goods and repay the freight both ways. The free bus service to the Hobson Street store operated every five minutes in the working day, and he still received up to 70 blank cheques each day from customers for him to fill in and bank. There was no business in the country like it.

In March 1928 the firm recorded yet another profit of £42,561 and in 1929 this increased to £49,334. For the fourth year in a row Robert reaped the dividends on his own shares, plus his salary, plus 5% of net profits. The average wage was still about £1 a week, and rumours went around that he was earning the unimaginable amount of £100 a week. They were wrong, it was over £150. He was a very wealthy man, yet he still stayed true to his pledge to God and was giving away many thousands of pounds.

Nor was his giving confined to the church. He had been concerned for some who had borne the brunt of his capital reduction scheme and in 1926 had freely distributed some of his own shares among them. At the Bible Training Institute in Auckland he was particularly generous. Some students had their fees paid anonymously. Other missionaries who often were not particularly well endowed found at Christmas large parcels turning up for their children – dolls, steam engines and colourful boys' manuals. One had an all expenses paid trip to Rotorua to recover from exhaustion, someone else received new carpet for their home, a church worker while driving down country was met at a bridge by a local garage owner. Escorted to the garage there he found a new car waiting for him. In Auckland a young family lost their house and all their possessions in a fire. Robert didn't turn up for work the next morning, but the staff knew where he was.

During the year he also had their Herne Bay house altered. On the second floor he had one bedroom converted into a bathroom. It was tiled throughout in white with a striking black border round the edges. The towel rails were ceramic and the shower was the latest innovation. Tiled on the inside, it had three curved pipes each with a separate water control enabling a complete spray from all directions as well as above.

Robert then had the roof space converted into a top storey for the house with more bedrooms and a study. A small tubular looking room facing north; it was about 10 ft wide and 20 ft long. The ceiling on both sides sloped and along each wall was a row of bookshelves. From the window he had a commanding view of the harbour and Auckland's North Shore. There were two desks in the room, one directly under the window with a small table lamp, the other, a more elaborate writing desk, just to one side. Pictures of family and friends were pinned on the wall and at the far end of the room a well-worn armchair sat warmly inviting any takers.

In this room he wrote and rehearsed all his addresses and John and Lincoln, who slept in the next room, could hear him practising late into the night. He wrote out many of his speeches in full (Lillian and his secretary would type them for him), and the stories or anecdotes he used he fully indexed in small, leather-bound folders. The files grew and grew and soon he had over 600 illustrations to draw from. This was the room where he spent most of his time.

Every night after dinner if there was not some meeting to

attend he would go upstairs to the study, sit down in the brown leather chair next to the writing desk and write, think and pray. Here he got close to God.

He also began taking more opportunities to speak at different church gatherings and missions. In 1929 he travelled to Sydney to speak and spent three weeks at a mission in Christchurch where he gave 13 addresses and saw 167 become Christians. Christmas that year he again participated in another united churches' tent campaign and afterwards headed for Taupo and 'Monte Vista.' Not long after they arrived Robert heard that an American film-maker was making a film about the Maori Wars at the southern end of the lake. He was keen to see this and estimated that the journey down in 'Seahorse' would take him about an hour. He and a few friends could spend the day watching the film crew and still be back in time for tea at night.

Leaving the women and children behind they left early the next morning for the 25-mile jaunt down the lake. The trip took much longer than expected, but eventually he found the film crew and spent the day watching the filming. In the middle of the afternoon they again boarded 'Seahorse' for the return trip home. The weather began to change for the worse and the further they ventured up the lake the rougher it became. In Robert's little open-top boat the situation soon became dangerous so they decided to turn back and wait out the storm. Lillian and the children further up the lake in the warmth of 'Monte Vista' waited anxiously by the window for the party to return.

At dawn the following day he again put the boat out trying to make as much distance as possible before the wind set in. It was no use. Soon he and his friends found themselves again caught in the middle of a storm tossed around at will by the waves. To make things worse the fuel began to run low. He had additional supplies on board but there was no way he could stop the engine to fill the tank. With the boat under power he could at least keep facing into the waves but if he turned the motor off, they would certainly be flipped. Having survived that experience once in his life it was not something he wanted to repeat.

Foraging under the coats and baggage he pulled out a jerry can and began to fill the tank. The fuel spilled perilously over the hot motor as the boat rolled in the storm. Mercifully the engine did not catch fire and once again they continued their journey up the lake. On the shore the family had woken from their restless night and were again crowded round the large window looking for any sign of their father in the storm. Finally, around lunchtime one of them saw a black spot on a waves. As it got closer they made out the shape of 'Seahorse' and ran to the beach to greet the weary travellers. As he and his exhausted passengers clambered ashore one thing went again and again through his mind as he walked up the beach: he needed a bigger boat.

12

CELEBRATION

1930-1932

"So much for the past – what of the future? Those of us who know the inside facts and figures of the business can assure you that the prospects have never been brighter. Our financial position is very sound: our popularity with the public and the rapid growth of our sales are a source of constant wonder to the business community, and with faith in the future of this wonderful Dominion, faith in each other, and with an unwavering faith in God, we can look out upon the years to come with absolute confidence." [1]

Robert Laidlaw, 1930.

1930 was a year of celebration, it was 21 years since Robert had started out in Fort Street and accordingly the business celebrated its 21st birthday. It had strengthened considerably over the past five years. The free bus service had grown from one old converted truck to seven dedicated buses operating from different parts of Auckland city bringing customers continually to Hobson Street. The free parking area was up and running and now held 160 cars.

More branches had been added to the business and now stood at 45. With this expansion the number of staff had grown too and the firm had a total of 1021 employees throughout its Hobson Street store, factories and branches. Total sales for the business in the financial year ending March 1930 were

£1,407,950 and the profit for the year was £60,422. Over half the firm's entire business was conducted from its Hobson Street premises which had become a city landmark. With the influence of time payment on the business it began to move more and more towards a stronger hardware and furniture section.

In 1924 the furniture department business amounted to only 7% of Hobson Street sales yet by 1930, five years after he instituted time payment, made up 24% of all sales. In June he was invited to speak to the Auckland Creditmen's Club on the subject of modern business organisation. He was 44 years old, and having traversed both the height of success and the verge of bankruptcy, he could look back on the last few years and examine what he had learned about commercial life. The creditmen welcomed his well-seasoned advice and Robert outlined the important points as he saw them.

"The first essential in a successful business is a satisfactory gross profit," he said, "to build a super-structure on any other foundation is so much waste time. The second essential is low enough working expenses to leave a satisfactory margin of net profit. Some businessmen are satisfied if they attain these two, but both of these may be perfectly right, and still the business be a most unsatisfactory one.

"Our third essential is therefore a satisfactory number of stock turnovers per annum, the fourth – low book debts in proportion to sales; and the fifth – a reasonable amount of fixed capital in proportion to productive capital. If any business can measure up on all of these five essentials the net result will be a high rate of profit on the actual capital invested."

He went on to deal with each of these in turn in more detail and then drew the salient example of a fruit vendor to illustrate his point. "I often say," he said, "that the fruit vendor with his banana stand on the corner of the street is the finest merchant in New Zealand. He buys 30/- worth of fruit each morning and has sold it for 50/- by night, leaving a gross profit of 20/-. Deduct his wages of 15/- per day, bad stock and depreciation 2/- per day, and we have left a net profit of 3/- per day on an investment of 30/-. Or, 10% per day for 300 working days in the year, equal to 3000% per annum on his capital.

"In organising a business, let us remember that balance is the great consideration. There is in mechanics a law known as the law of diminishing returns, and this law operates relentlessly in every avenue of commerce."

He used his knowledge of mechanics to drive the point home. "We get a good illustration," he said, "in the steam boiler. The steam escapes through the chimney and makes a greater draught through the firebox, and so the fire burns more brightly. The hotter fire makes more steam and the extra pressure creates greater draught still, and so action and reaction go on until the draught is so great that it carries the heat units up the flue before they can become effective in heating the water further, and here we reach the point of diminishing returns where more draught is a disadvantage instead of an advantage.

"This law of diminishing returns applied to business gives us the following – too big a gross profit, prices too high – people cease to come and soon no gross profit at all. Too small a gross profit through price cutting – net loss and business goes bankrupt.

"Too low working expenses – in endeavouring to get these down we reduce staff too much and give poor service, result customers don't come and up goes wage expense as sales fall. Or too high working expenses because too much service and no net profit. Too many stock turnovers and poor assortment, down go sales and kill the number of stock turnovers, and so it goes on right through. Too much laxity in credit and many bad debts, in addition to a large amount of capital tied up. Or too much strictness and customers are driven away and good sales lost.

"My endeavour has been to indicate only the broad lines along which every business should be organised, leaving you to fill in the details, which must be adapted to suit the particular requirements of each particular business. But the great aim should be to arrive at the point of perfect balance in every activity where the maximum return is obtained, and that point is just before the law of diminishing returns begins to operate.

"In conclusion, let me again remind you that no business is rightly organised unless it includes provision for its accountancy department producing figures each month which reveal not only where the business is, but how it has reached its present position, and what direction it is headed in. Don't be misled by that old and trite saying 'Knowledge is power,' – applied knowledge is real power – knowledge is static; applied knowledge is dynamic, so that the furnishing of complete information about a business is so much waste effort unless it is definitely acted upon and a strenuous effort made to rectify every weakness."[2]

To coincide with the birthday celebrations the store had been greatly modernised. All the departments had been enlarged and rearranged. A large extension had been built at the rear of the building to house three of the firm's factories and the front facade of the building plastered and painted a light yellow tone. With six acres of floor space, Hobson Street was now the largest department store in the country.

While the extensions were still in the planning stages, he pushed for a new dining hall to be built with views of Auckland city and harbour and employed an architect at the then unheard of figure of £20,000, to do the design and interior decoration of the room. A lavish hall was planned with a vaulted ceiling, panoramic windows and stone interior. It would be grandeur on an unprecedented scale.

Although he approved the working drawings, he wasn't allowed in to inspect his new hall until it was nearly complete. Finally, towards September with the paint still fresh, he was shown in while its constructors stood proudly by their creation. He looked at the scene before him. The sunlight poured in through the generous windows reflecting around the ornately plastered room. Robert's keen eye caught something and he turned to the architect.

"That column's out of line."

An embarrassed scuffle broke out, and the column was checked for level. It was a quarter of an inch out.

Dutifully replastered, the perfected dining hall opened in September that year.

He released 70,000 catalogues to mark the celebrations and made a number of generous offers to his customers. A set of Royal Doulton jugs were offered at 3/11 with every £2 order which was a quarter of their normal retail price. In addition customers whose total cash purchases before July the following year amounted to £100, could present themselves at the Hobson Street store and ask for any of the following – a 59-piece cabinet of cutlery, a gents or lady's cycle, a Westminster chiming clock, a gents solid gold hunting watch, lady's gold wrist watch, silver plated tea service a 4-drawer sewing machine, or an easy chair. The scheme was a resounding success and repeated in later years.

However, it was also clear that economic conditions were once again changing for the worse and the country as a whole was entering yet another depression. In a hand-written letter to all the shareholders, he wrote:

"From market reports the year we are now entering is likely to have many trading difficulties, so it is more important than ever that you do your best to ensure a good profit this year by purchasing your total requirements at the Farmers' and by inducing as many of your friends as possible to buy from us. This is the surest way to increase the value of your shares and maintain good dividends.[3]

In the Christmas holidays that year he took delivery of his new boat at Taupo which he named Piri Pono (faithful friend). The building of Piri Pono and her impressive sea trials in Auckland created quite a stir. Manufactured by Auckland boatbuilders Messrs. Collins and Bell she was made entirely of mahogany and powered by a very fast 150 h.p. straight-eight Niagara engine. She was 28ft long and weighed just over one ton. However it was one thing to build such a boat, it was another to get her to Taupo 200 miles away. He had a special trailer constructed from the chassis of one of the original Farmers buses, and together boat and trailer weighed in at over two tons.

This in turn was pulled by a two-ton truck carrying spare tyres, fuel and supplies for the journey. The total entourage weighed in at over six tons and set out early one morning towards Taupo at a top speed of 10 miles an hour.

The long rough road to Taupo was going to take some negotiating. Twice the boat haulers were held up by traffic inspectors concerned about the size of the load and wanting to see special permits. Four times they blew tyres and ended up using a solid tyre on one of the wheels. The radiator consumed over 200 gallons of water. Three days later the boat finally neared its destination and a very tired crew of three, who had driven 13 hours each day, greeted Robert who was waiting expectantly at Wairakei for his Christmas present.

It was a short drive to the river mouth where Piri Pono under his command was slipped gently into the water. He fired the gutsy Niagara engine into life and motored carefully out into the lake. Opening the throttle he sped off across the water towards Monte Vista. He was overjoyed. At last he had his bigger boat and was once again king of the lake. He rewarded the weary crew with a night's rest followed by an afternoon's fishing the following day on the lake in Piri Pono. They then returned to Auckland taking with them 'Seahorse,' which fitted comfortably on the back of the truck without the use of the trailer.

He did not have the pleasure of his new toy for long. The Laidlaws journeyed back to Auckland in January, the children got ready for the school year, and he and Lillian prepared for a long-awaited break away – a year-long world tour together. He felt completely at ease about taking the trip. It was clear already that despite the downturn in trade, the company was on track to put in another healthy profit of around £50,000. This time they would face the downturn a lot wiser and on a much stronger footing than the difficult times of 1921-22. On the second floor of the Hobson Street building at a farewell evening in the directors' boardroom he took opportunity to address his managers and the directors:

"I know that it is trite to tell such a body of men that boom and depression follow each other as night follows day," he said. "The far-sighted businessman should conserve in times of boom, because he knows an economic depression is coming, and contrawise, in times of economic depression he should have his head up and his heart full of confidence because he knows an economic boom is ahead.

"We all know this in a sort of abstract way, and our intellects assent to it as true, but it is somewhat difficult to get one's emotions in line with these facts, so that we will be sure to take up a conservative attitude in times of boom, and a confident aggressive attitude in times of depression. Because so few of our competitors act on this basis it becomes more effective than ever for those who conserve their resources in times of prosperity, and liberate them in times of depression. Some of the greatest fortunes in the U.S.A. have been made by men of foresight and courage buying up businesses in times of depression, when everyone else was frightened to death, and willing to sell at a fraction of the real value.

"Because I have faith in the future is one reason why I am going away with confidence; the other is because I have faith in you men around this table. Faith born of long years of experience through good times and bad, and my confidence is not only in your capacity to carry on for twelve months, but to carry on indefinitely.

"Fear plays a greater part in the lives of most men than they are willing to admit," he continued. "Men are afraid to decide and act for fear it may not turn out right; a sort of nameless dread of the future paralyses their initiative and keeps them far below par. On the other hand, faith enables us to look forward with confidence – it tones up the whole system so that we think clearly and act boldly. Today fear is gripping our business competitors, so there is an added premium on courage and faith and foresight, and because I believe you have these qualities I am sure we will come out of this depression stronger in personnel and in finance than we entered it.

"When Alexander the Great was entering on his campaign against the Persians, his spies reported that there were myriads of them. Said Alexander, 'What are one thousand sheep to the butcher?' 'But,' said the spies, 'the arrows of their archers darken the sun.' 'I prefer to fight in the shade,' was his laconic reply. It was not by superior numbers nor better armaments, but by the spirit of indomitable, infectious courage that Alexander's armies became invincible. We must accept the challenge of these difficult times in a spirit of courageous confidence that will permeate our staff and thus ensure success for the Farmers in spite of depressions. Over these outside conditions we have no direct control but we have control over our reactions to them."[4]

While his wishes were encouraging he still took no risks and gave Boddie, the chairman of directors, a letter to be read out at the next board meeting. It would further placate any fears they might have being left alone in the middle of a depression without their 'chief.'

"I wish, gentlemen, to convey to you my heartfelt thanks for the opportunity you have given me of taking this trip abroad. I would not have thought of going under present circumstances had it not been for my unbounded confidence in Mr. Robertson and the executive of the business to carry on successfully under your guidance.

"Arrangements have been made so that I will be in cable touch with head office at least once a month until reaching London, so that if the necessity arises I can return at any time. Meantime I am only booking through as far as London, and will expect full written reports there at the London office. If you think it advisable I can come back from there post haste, through the Panama Canal, arriving here about August, so that I would then have been absent only six months. If however in your opinion there is no necessity for this I will then go on to Europe as planned.

"Meanwhile I shall welcome the opportunity of discussing with leading businessmen of America how they are facing the problems of the depression there, and will also have the pleasure of meeting our London staff after an absence of eleven years, and of seeing first hand how our compatriots are meeting the present situation. Besides this the rest and change will be of great value to me in solving business problems which may still be confronting us when I get back.

"As farmers I know you are all feeling the stress of these

days, and I extend to you my sincere sympathy in the personal difficulties you are facing. Sincerely trusting that the depressed conditions will not be so protracted as one might at present expect, and again assuring you of my deep appreciation of your action."[5]

A few days later in early February, he and Lillian said their goodbyes to their young family and friends and left on the first leg of their tour. It was a pleasant trip across the Tasman, and in Sydney they ventured out to the city's main department stores to see if the stories they had heard about the depressed state of trade were in fact true. Many of the city's firms had put their staff on holiday one week in every five. Robert as always was keen to test the quality of salesmanship. He had already used mystery shoppers in the Farmers back home and in Sydney in such tight times expected to find staff thirsty for sales.

Entering a large chemist shop in the city centre he made his way to a counter where a middle-aged man was engrossed in his docket book. The salesman didn't look up, rather waited for him to speak. Robert was not going to play this game and waited too. An awkward silence ensued until the man finally raised his eyes.

"A bottle of Cascara Evacuant please," said Robert looking straight ahead with his usual grin.

The assistant produced the smallest bottle he had.

"Can you give me a large bottle," inquired Robert?

"The next size will cost you 3/9," said the salesman surprised.

"Thank you," he said, "I will have that one. Can you also transfer it into a screw top bottle so that it won't leak while travelling."

"Haven't got any," said the assistant vaguely interested, "but I can give you an extra cork if you like."

His patience tested, he took the extra cork and left, hoping for better results elsewhere.

Over the street was a smaller but seemingly well appointed shop and he approached the counter.

"Have you a pair of smoked glasses suitable for the tropics," he asked politely, yet received no reply.

The sales assistant bent down and pulled out a selection of cheap glasses from a drawer. Robert awkwardly tried a couple of pairs on and in desperation pleaded, "haven't you got any better quality?"

"Oh," said the assistant, "you can bend those if you put them in hot water."

He was disgusted, but now running out of time took them and left in search of yet another shop. Writing home to his staff he expressed his displeasure.

"After such experience I could not help but feel proud of the men and girls of the Farmers' sales staff. The whole of Sydney sales people seemed to be seized with a cheap complex. Without being asked for it they all show the cheapest they have, and scarcely ever think of mentioning that they have anything in stock of a better quality."[6]

Later that day he joined the Sydney Rotary Club for lunch at David Jones, and then met Lillian to visit the Berlei Corset Company. In the afternoon he spent two hours walking over the construction site and workshops building the Sydney Harbour Bridge. His mechanical mind worked overtime as he eagerly copied down all the various details of the bridge's construction, noting sizes of bearings and strengths of concrete and construction methods.

The next day (Wednesday February 18), they set sail at noon on the plush Dutch steamer *Nieux Holland* en route for Singapore. Stopping at Java, he and Lillian left the ship with a party of other passengers to see the tropical island from the road and meeting up with a native guide travelled some 650 miles further down the coast. The roads were mostly sealed and it was a pleasant trip through the lush green tropical island with its terraced hills and rice fields. Their guide for the trip was a Buddhist and when he found out that Robert and Lillian were Christians remarked, "Buddhism is much better that Christianity."

"Oh, no," said Robert, "Buddha taught that life was a curse, and said that you were to seek self-extinction, and be lost in Nirvana as the great objective, whereas Christ came that we might have life, and have it more abundantly, and put before us life everlasting with intensification and perpetuation of personality as against your doctrine of self-repression and life-extinction."

The guide was not put off. He had experienced first hand the varying standards and harsh treatment of the Europeans who to him were all Christian.

"But," he said, "Christianity is no good. First you send your missionaries with fine words and a cross; then your merchants follow with trading practices that impoverish the natives and enrich you; and then you send your soldiers with a sword to protect the profits of your merchants."

Robert could see his point. "In some instances," he admitted, "that is perfectly true. But because we are nominally a Christian people that does not mean all in our race are true Christians."

"Well is your King a Christian?" asked the guide.

"Yes," he said, "I believe His Majesty is a true Christian."

"Then," replied the guide, "your soldiers always use the sword in his name."

Robert reached down and pulled out his Bible. He opened it at Christ's sermon on the mount.

"But I say unto you, love your enemies; bless them that curse you; do good to them that hate you; and pray for them that despitefully use you and persecute you. Therefore all things whatsoever you would that men should do unto you, do you even so unto them."

The guide looked thoughtfully over the fields.

"Ah," he paused, "that is very beautiful, but why don't Christians carry those instructions out?"

He had not seen such things acted out among the Europeans he had met so far, but then he remembered something.

"What do you think of the Salvation Army?"

"Why I think a great deal of the Salvation Army," Robert replied," My wife and I have left a Salvation Army officer in charge of our children, and a beautiful Christlike character she is."

"Well,' said the guide thoughtfully, "I only know one thing about the Army. Two of our Buddhist Priests were caught out in a country village in a rainstorm, and as night was coming on they sought lodgings, but none of the Mohammedan villagers would take them in. At last one man said, 'There is a Salvation Army Officer who has come to live in our village, try him.' When they knocked, a man came to the door and without asking what kind of priests they were he said, 'Come in friends, welcome to my home.' He prepared food for them and lodged them for the night." The guide added, "I think the Salvation Army must be good people, but I am a Buddhist, and nothing on earth could ever make me change my religion."[7]

From Java he and Lillian travelled on to Singapore where they visited missionary friends then boarded a Japanese ship bound for Hong Kong, Shanghai and Japan. They arrived at the port of Kobe on Monday March 23, in the late afternoon. Robert again booked a guide to motor them around Japan by car, and the next day after arriving was taken to an art studio where Satsumaware was produced. The proud owner showed him in great detail the process by which the earthenware was baked and then coloured through its different firings. As he did so his wife busily prepared a cup of Japanese tea and biscuits for their guests. After their tour of the studio, he and Lillian graciously accepted their hosts' hospitality for some refreshment. While sipping on their tea the owner politely produced several fine pieces of work from his studio and told him the prices.

He was stuck. He had spent a marvellous afternoon in the company of their kind host, admired his studio, now even partaken of his hospitality, but he didn't want to buy anything. He could only think of one excuse.

"We have come all the way from New Zealand," he gestured, "and are travelling around the world and so cannot burden ourselves with breakables."

His Japanese host, like his guest, was a master salesman.

"But, I will pack it well, and post it, and will guarantee safe delivery to New Zealand. I will also," added the host, "make out the customs papers for your country, so that all you need do is pay me and forget it."

He had been outmanoeuvred and graciously purchased some pottery.

Travelling on to Osaka he saw at first hand the increasing industrialisation of the Japanese economy and thoughtfully pondered where it might lead.

"As Japan becomes more and more industrialised," he said, "she will be increasingly compelled to look to the outside world for her food supplies, and this means a rapidly growing trade for whatever countries like New Zealand care to intelligently and promptly break into this great market."[8]

Overall he was much taken with the colour and charm of Japan – especially the politeness of the people. Everywhere he went he was bowed to and treated with the utmost courtesy from elevator boy to hotel manager. At 10 o'clock one night he saw a shopkeeper saying goodnight to his three assistants. They all smiled and bowed to each other.

"The Farmers' could add 20%. to their sales within a year without spending an extra cent on advertising," he said, "if, from the general manager to the latest office girl, we were all as sincerely polite to each other and to our customers as these Japanese are."[9]

From Japan he and Lillian crossed the Pacific to Vancouver. They toured Canada then made their way down into the United States where once again they renewed their friendships from earlier trips. In Los Angeles and San Francisco Lillian caught up with her old friends while Robert spoke at different church meetings. Crossing the States they ventured as far down as Austin, Texas, then back up to Chicago where they met up with Lillian's half-brother Harry Ironside. Harry was now pastor of the Moody Memorial Church and Robert was invited to speak at the 3500-strong church as well as the Moody Bible Institute. After a short stay they said their goodbyes and left for New York and on to Britain.

In Britain they made their way up to Keswick in the Lake District where each year since 1875 an annual Christian convention had been held under canvas. Robert had heard about the convention and was keen to see it at first hand. Thousands gathered from all over the world to hear different speakers. There were large meetings of young people and many important times of prayer and challenge for the church at large. Robert did not speak but caught the fire of the Keswick message, a life of liberty and power through unreserved surrender to God in Christ. It was something he believed with all his heart; risking everything for God was what he had built his life on.

From Britain they crossed to Scandinavia and visited Norway, Sweden and Finland then down through Russia into

Europe. Criss-crossing their way through Europe they stopped in Poland, Czechoslovakia, Germany, Holland, Belgium, France, Spain, Morocco, Algeria, Tunisia, Italy, Austria, Hungary, Jugoslavia, Rumania, and Turkey. From Turkey they headed towards the Mediterranean visiting Greece, Syria, Palestine and Egypt. Leaving Egypt they took a ship to India then to Australia and back home to New Zealand.[10]

They returned home by the *Maunganui* from Sydney on January 26, 1932. Overall they had covered 33 countries in 11 and a half months. It had been an important break away for them both, but for Robert it was chiefly a business trip. He had made many new contacts and noted business conditions wherever he went. He had also indulged his new passion and moving up from his trusty Kodak he had purchased a hand-held movie camera, taking over 7000ft of film.

13

ENDLESS INNOVATION

1932-1938

*"People make the excuse, 'I did it on the spur of the moment.'
That is no excuse. 'As a man thinketh so is he.' The true man
appears on the spur of the moment. If we think noble thoughts
we won't be sneaks on the spur of the moment. If we think
kind thoughts, we won't say hard things on the spur of the
moment. If we think honest thoughts, we won't steal on the
spur of the moment. The spur of the moment actions don't
make the man, they only reveal him in his true character. A
young man rushes into danger to save someone, and we say
he is now a hero. But he was always a hero. The brave act
doesn't make a hero, it only reveals him."*[1]

Robert Laidlaw, 1912.

Trading conditions at home had worsened in his absence
and it was clear that the company had to pull back its expenses
still further. His first move was to suspend production of *The
Optimist* again for 12 months. The business was pulling out
all the stops in measures to attract customers to the store and
secure what sales could be made. While he had been away
there had been many different and varied promotions in order
to entice customers, including a free gift hunt and free tram
concession cards. In January when he returned home there
were 10 days of automatic reductions where a large range of

goods all across the store were reduced 10% each day until someone bought them.

If the goods still remained unsold at the end of ten days after being reduced 90%, they were given away. In February he went even further and gave away beach sections on Waiheke Island. For seven days one section was given away each day to the customer who made the largest cash purchase at the Hobson Street store or in the mail order business.[2]

While things in the firm were certainly not easy, his earlier predictions that they were in a much stronger position to face the storm had proved correct. At the close of the March 1932 financial year they again showed a profit of £25,148 on sales of £1,186,587.

Wrote Robert, "It is not pessimism to look the facts squarely in the face, and then attack them with courage and perseverance. Such a view of the future reveals considerable difficulties ahead for New Zealand and the world in general, that will challenge the best that is in us, but we are so much better equipped in personnel and finances that we were in 1921, that while there is no doubt about the outcome we must not be satisfied to let profits slip on the side of loss.

"The cumulative effect of one thousand staff, all keenly interested and loyally helping to keep down expenses and to push up sales, could work wonders even in such times as these, so that while difficulties must be faced, I believe we have the courage and the will to meet and defeat them and come through this depression with flying colours."[3]

In May Robert travelled to Wellington with five other directors and lecturers from the Bible Training Institute for BTI Week as it was called in the capital. The objective in part was to arouse wider interest in the Bible Training Institute, either through supporters or possible students. On the opening night, Saturday, May 18, Robert gave a motion picture lecture on

Palestine which attracted so many that the 800-seat hall was filled to capacity and 200 had to be turned away. On Sunday he again spoke, this time giving an account of his visit to the Keswick Convention in England. At the Sunday gospel service he gave his own personal testimony, and several came forward on his invitation at the close of the meeting to make commitments to Christ. At the end of the week he returned home.

In the country as a whole the depression tightened its grip and with the National Expenditure Adjustment Act, salaries were reduced between 5 and 12%, mortgages and rents by 20%. In the firm, rather than make anyone redundant, he cut salaries by 10%.The preference dividend was reduced to 5%, down from seven, and the directors took a 10% cut in fees. The large reductions in general expenses however only bolstered the downturn in trade. The firm was still getting as many customers through its doors, but they were spending far less and for the 1933 year the firm's profit dropped lower to £14,200 on sales of £1,168,175. With continuing fluctuations in prices and the need for further cutbacks, after much thought he suspended his original mail order catalogue.

Such actions and the drop in profits started rumours once again that the company was going bankrupt. To some it may have looked as if the firm was headed down the same road it had travelled in 1921. It was not the case. He no longer had the stock problem and in fact had reduced the imported content of his stocks considerably with 68% of his goods now produced locally. This time he publicly took the rumours head on and turned them around to his advantage. In a bold move he took out a half-page advertisements in the Auckland papers.

"£5 for the biggest lie about the Farmers' Trading Company sent to us before the end of May. Must be absolutely bona fide – in general circulation – and must not be manufactured by the person who sent it in."

He then listed several of the lies currently in circulation together with the accurate details,

"Lie no. 1 – That the Farmers' Trading Company is going bankrupt.

"The Truth – Our balance sheet for the twelve months ending March 31, 1933, shows a profit of £14,000, which compared with heavy losses made by most farmers' companies throughout the dominion, must be considered very satisfactory in these days.

"Lie no. 2 – That Robert A Laidlaw, our General Manager is selling his shares.

"The Truth – Mr Laidlaw has not sold a single share for five years; but has actually purchased during the past few months 1,300 of the Company's ordinary shares in the open market.

"Lie no. 3 – That our General Manager is leaving the Farmers.'

"The Truth – Mr Laidlaw has a three years' contract with the company."

He concluded his challenge with a little note on Disraeli, "When Disraeli, the famous Jewish Prime Minister of England was climbing to power, a friend said to Disraeli's mother, 'I am sorry that the papers are criticising your son.' 'Oh are they,' she replied, 'Then he must be doing something.' It was the same with Robert.

Towards the end of the year David Robertson, the assistant general manager resigned. Robertson had separated from his wife Min, who was Robert's sister. It caused an irreconcilable difference between him and Robert. By now Robert had a large group of veteran managers to choose from, yet he approached none of them and instead went to see Bill Mackay, his old New York buyer and manager, now living in the South Island.

Although he had no intention of stepping down, he was 48 years old and knew that his next assistant general manager would likely be the one that would succeed him.

He trusted Bill Mackay who, like him, was a devout Christian and had by now become a good friend. Mackay had joined him as a despatch boy in 1911 when he was 15 and had worked for him ever since. In 1928 Mackay had left the firm to launch out on his own, and went to the South Island to start his own chain of furniture stores. Robert had financed his friend into the stores from his own personal overdraft, and became the largest shareholder in the new business.

The chain now boasted several stores and he had kept in constant contact with his younger friend. Now he approached him about the vacancy as assistant general manager. Mackay was at first reluctant, knowing that some of the other department managers were more senior, but he eventually agreed and, installing a manager to run his own stores, followed Robert back to Auckland.

The Farmers chain now had 60 branches and five factories and the largest retail store in the Dominion. Back in town Robert put his plans into operation for a Christmas spectacular for 1933. Several of the other department stores across the city put on special shows at Christmas and included in their store a Santa for children to visit. Robert had in mind to do exactly that but even more so. He had his display department construct a huge ice castle on the ground floor of the Hobson Street store and 'A flight to the Great Polar Cave' was born.

Children and parents boarded a mock aircraft and were flown through the clouds to the polar cave. Past the explorer and fighting the bear, past the penguins, and the polar bears, past the friendly walrus and eventually landing at the grotto of the Silver Princess to receive a present from Santa's helpers.

His innovation was met with some direct competition from

merchants Milne and Choyce in the city. They too launched their Christmas Aeroplane trip to the North Pole in the 'Flying Bluebird.' Robert was not outdone. He posted a children's Christmas essay competition with a first prize of return flights to Hamilton then took the inevitable next step. He brought Santa to the Farmers by aircraft. A week or so later Santa circled the city and landed at Victoria Park at the bottom of town. A little shaken from the experience he emerged from the small plane and was immediately swamped by hundreds of gleeful children. From there he was driven to the Hobson Street store where he took his place in the Great Polar Cave.

The following year was even more spectacular. Another department store, George Courts on Karangahape Rd, brought Santa to their store on a decorated float with much advertising. Hundreds blocked the street to see the red man himself take up residence in their decorated 'Wonderland.' But Robert was not about to be outdone and the very next day on the Saturday morning November 24, 1934 staged his first 'Grand Parade.'

At 10.30 several highly decorated carts pulled by gaily decked horses left the warehouse accompanied by a bevy of colourful characters, Waggles and Goggles, The Fat Boy, Man and the Giant and the Big Fiddle. They went up Pitt Street past their rival George Courts, along Karangahape Rd, down Queen Street and back up to Hobson Street, where Robert's Santa took up his residence in the magical Waitomo Caves. The stage was set for some yearly competition and innovation but Robert had led the way twice.

By March 1935 the firm reaped a profit of £41,277 on sales of £1,339,286. The business had regained the position it was in before the depression hit, and on Wednesday, May 22, 1935, the *Auckland Star* discussed the financial results.

"Best Results since 1931 at the FTC," it claimed. "It was a touch of genius," said the paper, "which inspired the management to arrange some years back to convey its customers free in buses from the crowded Queen Street area up the hill to its comparatively isolated warehouse in Hobson Street. Two years ago there was a bank overdraft of £121,000 and £14,000 cash in hand at balancing time. In the last year's balance sheet the overdraft had disappeared and cash in hand had increased to £41,424. This latter item now appears as £72,733 so that in two years the cash position has improved by over £179,000."[4]

International speaker and evangelist J Edwin Orr also visited New Zealand. Robert organised his itinerary and while in Auckland he stayed with them. Orr travelled up and down the Dominion, speaking at churches and gatherings far and wide. It was at a frantic pace. Robert had booked 100 meetings into Orr's five-week tour. On the April 12, at the close of the New Zealand tour, he and Orr sailed for Australia, and Robert took the main stage with him at a series of church missions in Sydney and Melbourne. Robert was there for six weeks and spoke to capacity crowds and gave over 35 addresses. While he was there he was awarded the King's Jubilee Medal and William Mackay in New Zealand reported his award to the firm:

"We are all delighted that His Majesty the King has been pleased to present our General Manager with a Jubilee Medal. No man in Auckland has made greater contribution of his ability and energy to the Christian and business life of this city, and we all feel proud that this has been recognised in such a signal manner."[5]

On Wednesday 22nd of May he arrived home. Ten days later on Queen's Birthday weekend he travelled with a group of young people to Rangitoto Island in Auckland harbour. The group were bible class members from Brethren churches all over Auckland and Robert was the current president of the

Assembly Bible Classes (ABC). They had decided to make a day of it and climb the dormant volcano to have a picnic. Together they eagerly boarded the ferry and headed off into the harbour.

He and the ABC secretary Frank Bardsley leaned on the railing of the boat on the way over talking. They had been discussing for some time the possibility of a campsite for the young people in Auckland. Holiday times were important yet with the effects of the depression still being felt few could afford to travel let alone afford a holiday. Robert was keen to find a place that was both accessible and enjoyable and as the boat went past the Tamaki Estuary he spotted a beach surrounded by open land along the coast.

"What's that beach over there?"

Frank was immediately enthusiastic. He knew the beach that caught Robert's attention, having investigated it only a few days previously. "That's Eastern Beach," he said, "There's some Education Board land there which isn't going to be used. It would make a great site."

By the time Robert had reached the top of Rangitoto he was absolutely enthused about it. His young companion was commissioned to look into buying the land, and after several months the negotiations were completed and two acres of beachfront land at Eastern Beach, on the outskirts of Auckland, were duly purchased with final settlement in January 1936.

On September 8, 1935, Robert celebrated his 50th birthday. Nine days later on Tuesday night the September 17, 800 members of the Farmers' staff from all over the North Island gathered at the Hobson Street Store to celebrate with him. They put on a concert programme like none before – the staff orchestra performed, there were sketches, songs and even a slide show of the development of the firm since 1909. One after another the firm's managers stood up and paid tribute to their 'Chief.' They praised his ability, his courage, his energy and the high ideals he possessed and his friendly warm personality which had won him the affection and unswerving loyalty of every member of the staff.

The directors presented him with a gold watch, his executives gave him a new desk and chair, his Hobson Street staff a pair of binoculars, and the branches, knowing their 'Chief's' love of travel, a Morocco travelling case. He stood up to reply to his beloved staff.[6]

"We have learnt hard lessons from the past," he said. "The intervening years have been spent deepening the foundations of the company, rather than increasing in height its superstructure. The result is that we have come through the depression unscathed, and now possess the best chain of stores in the Dominion. To the staff," he concluded facing the rows of adoring faces, "the company owes much of its success."[7]

Christmas time and once again he resolved to outdo his competitors when it came to Christmas attractions. This year in a effort to parallel his activities, George Courts department store paraded its Santa up Queen Street accompanied by the Boop family of Giants. Robert the next day once again paraded his Santa right around the city, accompanied by even more storybook characters, fairies and clowns and a band. But it was his destination that was even more remarkable.

He had had his designers and builders create an enormous 'mice city' on the ground floor of the Hobson Street store, inhabited by 300 performing mice. No detail was left out and the city was complete with furnished bungalows, shops, a working railway, a home for blind mice and even a service station for cheese. At the end of the display every eager little visitor received a present from the 'Gipsies of the enchanted forest.'

In December the family once again headed south for Taupo

to 'Monte Vista.' By now their holiday home was well established. Robert had had a large boatshed built on the edge of the lake to house his launch Piri Pono, and a petrol generator installed at the back of the house to provide lighting. At night he cranked it up and round the fire they would swap stories to the distant chug chug of the motor. Over the past few years the popularity of Taupo as a holiday spot had increased, and although still quite remote it became an annual retreat for several other business friends and their families.

During the year a prominent local Taupo businessman named Gillies had a 22ft speedboat built and fitted with a powerful Dodge motor. It was about half the weight of Robert's Piri Pono which was longer but heavier. Occasionally during the next few weeks the two boats met on the lake and neither he nor Gillies could resist seeing who had the faster boat – sometimes it was Gillies, sometimes Robert and Piri Pono.

It was decided to hold a regatta on the lake at the end of January, and among other events the question of who had the fastest boat on the lake would be decided. Three days before the race Robert hauled Piri Pono out of the water to let the timber dry and lighten the boat. His younger son Lincoln, now 14, was selected as crew and despatched under the boat to wax the hull, while Robert changed the spark plugs and worked on the motor. To further reduce the weight he pumped out half the 80-gallon tank leaving just enough fuel to complete the race. Everything was unloaded apart from the essentials – a fire extinguisher, a few tools, the anchor and a couple of life jackets.

Finally race day arrived. He had hoped for rough weather which would favour his heavier boat but it was a bright, calm January day. A large course had been marked out on the lake and contestants were to do 20 laps. He and Gillies pulled up at the start line, the engines impatiently ticking over. As the starter's flag dropped they roared off into the lake and Gillies leapt ahead. By the first bend Robert had caught up but couldn't pull ahead. This happened at every turn. Gillies took the lead, he caught up but was unable to nudge ahead far enough to turn first. Robert trailed an unacceptable second.

In earlier trials he found he could squeeze out a bit more speed with more weight in the back and barrelling at top speed he sent his young son to the rear cockpit. Lincoln's weight was not enough and Gillies still retained the lead. A few laps later Lincoln clambered back over to the front, dug around under the fore deck, and returned to his rear seat clasping the anchor. Robert pulled wide at the next turn and came up on the inside. By the end of the straight he had edged forward enough to pass. Among cheers and flying spray he took the lead and retained his title as fastest man on the lake.

The Brethren churches in Auckland held four rallies annually for young people known as the ABC Quarterlies. Every three months on the first Wednesday of each of the quarterly months, young people from the 35 different churches in the Auckland area gathered at Howe Street Hall. Several hundred would meet and after sharing a meal different groups presented items with competitions and invited speakers. At the June meeting in 1936 Robert stood before the packed gathering and told them of the proposed campsite at Eastern Beach. With his usual enthusiasm he outlined the scheme.

"We've bought a property at Eastern Beach," he said, "and want to develop it. We need to raise £2500 to build an accommodation block for 350 campers with the necessary dining and meeting facilities."

He had already agreed to underwrite the project but wanted to inspire the young people to get behind it. "For every pound that you put in, I'll give a pound," he declared.

There was a buzz across the room and soon, though many

earned less than a pound a week, hundreds of pounds started coming in. Robert matched them and in September work began on the two-storey accommodation block. Within a few months it was completed, debt free.

In December he spoke at the Bible Training Institute graduation then went on to the inaugural Christmas camp at Eastern Beach. Several hundred gathered, and Robert delivered 10 addresses. After camp he and Lillian and the family motored to Taupo to spend the rest of the holiday relaxing at 'Monte Vista.' In the May school holidays the following year with assistance from some energetic teachers' college students, he launched the first boys' camp at the Eastern Beach facility and in October attended a camp for missionaries. His speaking engagements began to take up more and more of his time as he travelled around the country speaking at church meetings.

By now Robert's annual Christmas parade had become a city event. But he was still out to differentiate himself completely from his competitors. For the 1937 Christmas attraction a complete Babes in the Wood in Fairyland set was constructed, but as to how Santa would arrive Robert was keen to do something completely different. He had his advertising manager come in for the briefing.

"How are we going to bring Santa in this year?" asked Robert, but his manager could tell that an idea was already brewing in the mind of his general manager.

"Um ... well ... we brought him in by plane in '33 and that was a pretty good show."

"Yes I know but we ought to do something even more sensational this year,"

"How would it do to bring Santa down by parachute into the harbour?" Thinking of his very fast boat Piri Pono he added: "It would be no trouble to pick him up by speedboat."

The advertising manager tried to look enthusiastic but pointed out the risk of Santa getting smothered in his parachute before the boat might reach him.

"No, you're right," said Robert, "That would be too risky. Well then what about the Domain? That should be safe enough, yes, we'll bring him down there."

So the plan was put into action. At first the city council forbade such an event claiming that the stunt would possibly endanger the lives of the spectators. But after many assurances and no little amount of convincing by the infectious Robert, who was now convinced of the soundness of the plan, it gave way.

On Saturday, November 22, 1937, a large crowd assembled at the Domain in Newmarket. It was a popular recreation area and passers-by couldn't help but stop and look skywards. There a lone, single-engined bi-plane came into view. It circled over the park and below Robert and several hundred spectators, parents and children eagerly craned their necks to see what would happen next. Suddenly against the sky a figure parted from the plane and a gasp went up from the onlookers. Santa really was coming down.

A few seconds later a large white parachute ballooned out against the sky and the waiting crowd put up a cheer. As the figure got closer Santa in his red costume could be clearly seen descending towards the earth. A minute or so passed and as he got lower and lower it became clear that he was being blown off course. Robert held his breath. Santa was heading on a collision course with the Wintergarden glasshouses.

Santa jerked frantically on the parachute lines trying desperately to manoeuvre his descent away from the peril but it was no use. As Robert watched the spectacle play out before him a single thought raced through his mind: "I'm going to be the first man to kill Santa Claus."

Santa flew over the roof missing the glass by inches and

seconds later there was a tremendous splash from behind the buildings. He had landed in the middle of the lily pond. After being welcomed by the children and greeted with some relief by Robert, Santa took his place on a decorated float and was driven in triumph to the Farmers Hobson Street store.

In April Robert headed down to the South Island to conduct a church mission. He was accompanied by singer Murray Fountain and it was a trip of some nostalgia because he planned to end up in his old home city, Dunedin. Beginning on Saturday, the third of April, in the Victoria Hall in Invercargill, each meeting followed the same format with community singing, then Robert gave his address. To the opening on Saturday evening he brought his moving pictures and gave an illustrated address on Palestine explaining the customs, habits and garb of the Middle East. There wasn't even standing room in the hall.

On Tuesday the mission resumed and every night during the week. The meetings followed the same format. The following Saturday, Robert again put on a moving picture display showing the places St. Paul visited in the Holy Land, then on Sunday evening he spoke on a favourite topic, a talk he was to give many times, entitled 'Forbidden Subject.' Every seat in the dress circle and stalls were taken anxious to hear what this might be.

"Such subjects," said Robert, "as sex, crime, politics, economics and almost every subject under the sun are welcomed and allowed as a matter of discussion. But immediately the subject of personal salvation is mentioned there is constraint and silence." The hall was hushed. Every soul in the place knew he was right and some were terrified as to what he might say next. "But don't take my word for it prove it yourself – introduce it at the next bridge party." This interjection broke the tension and the audience broke into laughter. Robert continued.

"But why, should that subject which vitally affected every man and woman eternally be avoided?" He then went on to deal one by one with the excuses normally intelligent people made, then reasons men gave for not facing the issue of personal salvation in Christ.

Overall he was on the road for nearly five weeks. On the second to last night of the mission he delivered his own testimony. Late-night shopping made no difference to the attendance, and a full hall listened to him give his personal testimony entitled 'From Fear to Faith.' Always keen to bring his illustrations to life he immediately related it back to business.

"The wagging tongue of the satisfied customer," he said, "is the greatest advertisement for any business house. Similarly, if Christians would only tell what Christ has done in their lives and can do in the lives of others, such testimony would be the most successful sermon that could be sounded forth.

"Once I felt the restraint of my puritanical home life where there was no gambling, no cards and no dancing, but later I lived to bless God for every restriction I had known. My first lessons were not nursery rhymes, but the first story I knew was that God so loved the world that He gave his only begotten son, so that whosoever believes in Him should not perish but have everlasting life.

"Now here is the question: Did a boy like me brought up under such conditions need to be converted to God?

"Opportunity makes patent what hitherto was latent. Given a certain set of circumstances every person is capable of committing anything in the calendar of crime. The disciples in Christ's day lived for three years with Judas Iscariot, but when Christ said, 'One of you shall betray me,' not one of them said 'that's Judas.' But each of them said, 'Lord is it I?'"

"Judas," said Robert, "had been a magnificent hypocrite, but the final opportunity had shown what was in his heart all along. At my grandmother's knee I learned the 300-odd promises in the New Testament concerning Christ's return to earth. Consequently my greatest fear as a boy was that Christ would come for the Christians and that I would be left.

"Several times I have faced death by accident or drowning but not once in these crises had the thought of God entered my head although I fully intended to die a Christian."

He then spoke at length of the Torrey Alexander mission in Dunedin in 1902 and his eventual salvation. Concluding the mission that Sunday he headed back to Auckland. His speaking engagements increased in the next year and in February 1938 he spoke seven times at meetings in St Heliers, then in April he travelled to Palmerston North and gave five addresses at a conference after attending the Ngaruawahia Easter Convention, where again he was a main speaker.

The Easter Convention had close links with the BTI and often the speakers were drawn from institute ranks. This occasion was no different and on the Sunday evening Robert gave the address. Over 600 packed into the marquee to hear him. In July was the first Winter House Party at the Eastern Beach camp.

Many young people in the farming community were unable to attend the popular Christmas camp because of farm commitments, so a 10-day winter house party was launched during the slower winter months. It was an immediate success; hundreds came from all over the North Island and again Robert was a keynote speaker.

On Tuesday, July 12 in the Milne and Choyce reception room he presided over the first meeting of the Christian Business Men's Association (CBMA) in Auckland. About 150 gathered in the plush surroundings and then met thereafter every second Tuesday. The New Zealand organisation was modelled roughly on its American counterpart, the Christian Business Men's Committees.

It was a time of new beginnings and in August he called a young man into his office to talk about the Postal Sunday School Movement.[8] Five years earlier such a movement had started in Sydney and Robert had seen it in operation while on tour with Orr in 1935. Now over 10,000 were enrolled.

Wanting to start such a scheme in New Zealand he formed a committee consisting of himself and fellow BTI directors Sir Albert Ellis and Dr William Pettit and entrusted the day-to-day workings to Gilbert Hicks, a graduate from BTI. With some office space in High Street, Auckland, and a small staff it was launched. The requirements for entry were almost the same as doing business with Laidlaw Leeds. Children if they wanted to be on the roll had to live outside a 10-mile radius of the Auckland Central Post Office.

The lessons and material were provided free, all monies coming from those who, like its originator, felt it a worthy cause. Like his many other activities it took off with a rush and he placed advertisements in the main Christian magazines as well as on radio. In addition Farmers was now issuing a monthly catalogue in place of the yearly mail order catalogue and he placed a special insert in successive issues about the Postal Sunday School Movement. Within a few months there were nearly 4000 children on the roll. In October he travelled north to speak and in December again addressed the graduation ceremony of the Bible Training Institute and the Christian Business Men's Association. By now preparations were well underway for another overseas trip and he and the family attended the Eastern Beach Christmas camp before travelling to Taupo. It would be their final break together at 'Monte Vista' before leaving New Zealand.[9]

14

TRAVELLERS ALL

1939

*"Travel is a great education and inspiration and I suppose
we all look forward with anitcipation to a trip to a foreign
country, but one of the finest things about a trip abroad is the
joy of coming home again."* [1]

Robert Laidlaw, 1932.

In late January the family returned to Auckland and began
packing for their first overseas trip together. Eight years earlier,
Robert and Lillian had ventured around the world alone, this
time they intended to take the whole family with them
travelling by boat to America, overland through the States, and
then on to Britain and Europe. Hitler had already overrun
Czechoslovakia, and Robert knew before they left New Zealand
they were taking a risk. However, the prospect of war in
Europe had been looming for several years. Even as early as
1936 he had delayed extensions to the Hobson Street building
on account of an early war. [2]

The year ahead seemed an opportune time for the children
to see something of the world before they settled down into
the next stage of their schooling. John was now 22, Lincoln 17
and had just completed secondary school, Lillian 12, and had
just finished intermediate.

Their transportation was the Matson Shipping Line boat

Mariposa. The speed queen of the Pacific, her six steam turbines powered her along at a massive 22 knots.

Easily recognisable her distinctive yellow and blue funnels were each emblazoned with a large M, and a row of lifeboats lined the sundeck on both sides. A crew of 350 serviced the 475 first class and 229 cabin class passengers in style; the most talked about innovation was the fully air conditioned first class dining room. On February 6, family and friends bid them farewell as the boat sailed out of Auckland Harbour towards the open sea on a beautiful summer's day.

The first stop on the journey was Fiji and the ship berthed for a day. Robert hired an island taxi and the family left for a tour of the island. None of the roads outside Suva was sealed and the taxi lurched over the rough island roads. Halfway around the suspension gave up and they found themselves stranded only two hours before sailing time. Shortly before 5 pm an old wooden-decked truck with no sides and a motley canvas top came to an abrupt halt on the docks next to the liner. Perched on the bare wooden seats sat the Laidlaws. They were quickly hustled up the gangplank, the last on board before the ship set sail.

From there the ship pressed on to Honolulu. Again they stopped only for a day. Robert was eager for the family to see Waikiki Beach and have a chance to relax so he hired a large beachfront suite at the Moana hotel. Once again they drove round the Island although this time without incident. A spectacular Honolulu farewell complete with streamers, hula dancers and brass band saw the ship farewelled on its final leg to Los Angeles.

After a few days in Los Angeles they journeyed up the coast to San Francisco where they visited the World Fair. Robert was quite relaxed; news from home was good. As the 1939 financial year closed in March the business had broken two records. For the first time sales went over £2 million for the year reaping a profit of £125,316. The company had repaid all its mortgages and was now debt free.

While in San Francisco he unexpectedly developed a sore back and, unsure what to do, paid a visit to a local chiropractor. He had no sooner entered the chiropractor's rooms and mentioned his back was sore than he was cut off midstream.

"Your problem is that your right leg's longer than your left one," said the chiropractor. "What we will do is put a lift of leather on the heel of your left shoe which will straighten up your hips, and you won't have a sore back any more."

"But how do you know what my condition is without even examining me?" probed Robert.

"I noticed when you came into the room," said the chiropractor, "that you used your right hand to open the door and close it again. So I deduced that you are right-handed. As with everyone who is right-handed your right side develops more than your left side. Whereas in a left-handed person your left side develops more than your right side. In an ordinary right handed person their right leg is slightly longer than their left one. You are walking with your pelvis slightly twisted," making the gestures with his hands as he went, "and your spine is slightly bent. If you straighten it up you'll overcome your back pain nine times out of ten."

The doctor's argument seemed well-reasoned so Robert got a piece of leather placed in his left shoe and soon his back felt better. A firm believer that what was good for him was good for the rest of the family, he felt that they too should have the benefit of this relief. One by one they were sent down to have little pieces of leather put on their shoes as well. Now complete with raised left heels and 'straightened spines,' the family continued on their holiday after their knowledgeable father.

At San Francisco he also bought a large, black straight-eight

Chrysler Imperial and together they headed off in the direction of Yosemite National Park. Robert was behind the wheel driving with his usual gusto when there was the unmistakable sound of a police siren behind him. Looking in the rear-view mirror he saw a motorcycle cop riding a large Harley Davidson beckoning him to the side of the road.

He slowly glided to a halt. He had been doing well in excess of the speed limit. The cop got off his bike, walked up to the car and in a rich North American accent began to lay down the law.

He hardly got a chance. Just as the officer was beginning his dressing down, Robert broke in.

"Excuse me officer," he said, "but I'm from New Zealand, and I've got my whole family here and we're making a movie of our trip across America. I'd very much like to have a shot of you coming up behind the car, with those lights flashing and your siren blazing. That would look just terrific."

The officer's eyes widened but Robert was only warming up.

"Let my son drive the car instead of me," he said getting out of the vehicle, "and I'll lean out the back with the movie camera and take you coming up behind."

The officer was stunned. Robert's outburst had completely disarmed him and he didn't know what to say. Scratching his head he turned around and walked obediently back to his motorcycle as the family took their positions. The camera started to roll and the officer kicked the Harley into life. With sirens screaming and lights flashing the movie train made its way up the incline, only this time with a little less speed. When they reached the top, actor and director shook hands, smiled, and parted company the best of friends.

Over the next two months the family ambled their way across America in no particular hurry. From Yosemite National

Park they moved on to Salt Lake City where they toured through the Mormon Temple, (at that time) the largest single-span wooden building in the world. They headed down through Colorado stopping to see the Bryce National Park and Grand Canyon and, staying in cabins, they lived simply. Breakfast was always the same, bran crackers and canned grapefruit juice. Their appearance came as quite a shock to most of their American hosts since the cabins had been snowbound that winter and the Laidlaws were the first travellers they had seen.

Of course, there were mandatory stops along the way. Following behind their father they went into nearly every department store in every city. Both Robert and his sons made exhaustive notes on business details.

From Colorado they travelled into Mexico long enough to see a bull fight and the new Kress store at El Paso. Leaving Mexico and heading up through Texas they finally arrived at one of the highlights of their American leg, Chicago. For Lillian, Chicago was once again a chance to catch up with her half-brother Harry Ironside.

The Ironsides now lived in a small hotel across the boulevard from the large Moody Memorial Church in Chicago and while they were there Robert booked rooms in the same hotel. This gave the family more time to catch up with Uncle Harry, but was also a marvellous base for the men to investigate the famous department stores. He and the boys went to Marshal Fields store and within a few blocks, Sears Roebuck. There were also Mandels, Montgomery Ward and Wiebolts, a regular department store heaven.

As their Chicago stay drew to a close they said goodbye to Uncle Harry and headed up towards Canada, stopping off in Detroit to visit the Ford works taking in Henry Ford's birthplace and the first Model T. Much of this trip brought back fond memories for Robert as they retraced the journey he had first trekked in 1915 when he and Lillian met. Their journey into Canada was the same. The first port of call was Toronto and staying at the Royal York Hotel the family soon headed towards Canada's most famous landmark, Timothy Eatons Department Store, whose sheer size had impressed him so much the first time he visited. While in essence the trip away was a family holiday he also used the time to speak and whenever he could delivered addresses to church groups.[3]

From Toronto it was up the coast to Montreal where the all-Canada ice hockey finals were being held. It was the top event on the Canadian sporting calendar and stopping at the hotel lobby Robert asked the concierge if they might get tickets.

"No, I'm sorry sir," replied the smartly dressed assistant. "They sold out weeks ago. There is no way you will be able to see that event, might I suggest."

But his urgings met with thin air for Robert was off. He quickly bundled the family into the car and drove straight to the stadium. The car park at the stadium was relatively quiet, the games had obviously already started. Robert walked up to the manager's box at the ticket booth with the family a few paces behind. A short knock at the door produced a competent-looking fellow who surveyed the small group in front of him.

"Good evening sir," Robert declared sticking out his hand.

"Er, yes, hello."

"I've come all the way from New Zealand and I would like my family to have a chance to see your spectacular show."

"Well ..."

"Could we possibly have a look? Even if we were just standing at the back."

The manager's eyes flickered to the corner of the room where a young assistant was watching to see what he would do next.

"Take this gentleman and his family into the stadium," he

said puffing his chest. "They've come all the way from New Zealand to see the show."

Their young escort obediently led them through a series of corridors and mounting some steps they emerged at the back of one of the seating areas. A huge crowd completely filled the icy arena and a deafening cheer went up as a the two teams clashed below.

Robert, who had been talking quietly to their assigned guide, reached into his pocket and slipped the young man a few dollars. The usher disappeared and was soon spotted again at the front of the tiered seating waving them down. Within minutes the family found themselves munching popcorn in prime ringside seats.

After Montreal they drove further up the coast towards Quebec, but soon found their journey cut short because no cars were allowed on the roads. Quebec had been snowbound that winter and with the spring thaw large blocks of ice were slipping across the roads. Some trucks were being allowed through, but it was still regarded as too treacherous for cars. Again such protocol was not sufficient deterrent for Robert and some time later a lone car approached Quebec down the highway, packed full of wide-eyed Laidlaws. After a short stay they drove back down through Maine and Boston, travelling the Merritt Parkway and curving their way through the low foothills between Boston and New York.

After a jaunt to Washington the family settled into the St Morritz Hotel near Central Park, New York, where they were joined once again by Uncle Harry. He had relatives in England and, as a way of spending more time together had decided to accompany them on their trip to England. While they were staying in New York Robert developed a sore throat and again had to visit a local doctor. Upon closer examination it was obvious that he had tonsillitis and they needed to come out.

More than a little curious at how they intended to do this he inquired about the operation.

"Oh," replied the doctor. "It's nothing. We just give you a local anaesthetic and whip them out."

Quite impressed with these newfound capabilities of medical science he promptly had his tonsils removed. It made such a remarkable difference that he booked the entire family in for the same procedure. Dutifully the Laidlaw family lined up one by one, as they had done in San Francisco, and had their tonsils removed.

The operations occurred just before boarding the *Queen Mary* for England. The first-class dining room on board the *Queen Mary* had the reputation of being able to serve any dish from anywhere in the world. While Robert and the family ate ice cream, Uncle Harry and Lincoln, who had had his tonsils removed earlier, partook of the ship's cuisine, much to the envy of everyone else.

The *Queen Mary* took its usual four days from New York to Cherbourg and the following morning docked in Southampton. Travelling to London they booked into the recently completed Cumberland Hotel by Marble Arch. Robert bought another black Chrysler Imperial, this time a seven-seater, and the family spent a couple of weeks taking in the sights. They went to the tower of London, Greenwich, Buckingham Palace, to Kew Gardens and took a trip on the Thames. Their hotel was over the road from Speakers Corner in Hyde Park and in the evening they walked across to listen to the speakers.

One weekend there was an unusual amount of activity in the park and a large three-storey structure was hastily erected. The auxiliary fire service intended to put on a public display and had built the mock building meaning to burn it down later that evening. Such was the size of the display that the Princess Royal was the guest of honour so Robert eagerly grabbed his movie camera and set off for the event.

As dusk fell the structure was set alight and when it was burning fiercely a wide assortment of fire crew and tenders arrived to put it out. Robert filmed the proceedings for several minutes then quite undaunted pushed past the police cordon and went up in front of the royal box. Squatting down in front of the Princess he resumed filming. Everyone including the police thought he was a press photographer and no one attempted to stop him. He had an unparalleled view of the night's events. When the show was over, he raised his hat to the Princess, smiled, and returned to his place in the crowd.

From London they journeyed west to Bath, then north to Stratford on Avon and worked their way up to Scotland. In Edinburgh they watched the Tattoo and caught up with friends. On the way back from Scotland Robert stopped at the Lake District for the Keswick Christian Conference. He and Harry Ironside were both guest speakers. Robert gave the opening address. The meetings lasted a week.

Returning to London, Harry Ironside and the family parted company. Harry returned home to Chicago and Robert and the family took their car over to France in mid-August 1939 to begin their European tour, making their way through France, Belgium and Holland towards Germany. The border crossing was nearly empty; only a couple of cars were pulled up waiting to go through. Robert edged forward alongside a German sentry who beckoned him to stop. He looked dubiously at the car, surprised that a family might be wanting to enter Germany at this time, especially all the way from New Zealand. He motioned for Robert to get out of the car and he was escorted to the gatehouse.

He informed them that they were on holiday but that he might be speaking to different church groups. Suspicious of what he was up to the guards questioned him at length and took careful notes of the route he intended to take and all the hotels they'd be staying at. Finally he was released and they were free to carry on their holiday. Their first stop was Osnabruck, 50 miles inside the German border. An aircraft factory had been built nearby and he and the children spent the morning watching the planes being put through their paces overhead. They had never seen aircraft fly as fast as these and climb at such remarkable rates. Little did they know they were watching Messerschmitt 109 fighters being flight-tested for combat.

Later that night in the hotel after dinner Robert was approached by a tall blond German in his early twenties. He, too, had eaten in the dining room and had been watching the family with interest.

"Hello," he said in perfect English. "I was wondering if I might join you?"

"By all means," said Robert and pulled a chair out at the table.

"Thank you. I couldn't help notice you speaking English," said the German. "I have been studying at Oxford but in Germany my English gets so little practice it is nice to use it from time to time. What are you doing in Germany?"

Robert told him about their holiday plans but as the two of them chatted the conversation turned more and more to him and less and less the German. He asked Robert what he thought about the German economic miracle, and about Robert's philosophy on life. They talked for over an hour. Then, without warning, the young man broke off the conversation, excused himself and left the hotel. Outside a large black Mercedes was waiting. The German slipped into the back seat and was driven off at speed into the night. Robert had passed the Gestapo test.

From Osnabruck they made their way across to Berlin where

they saw the very first Volkswagen, one of three handbuilt by Porsche to show what the 'people's car' would look like. Overhead the Swastika banners were clear evidence of the grip of Nazism, yet there was little animosity shown to the tourists except from the Hitler Youth who took objection to the GB number plates on their car.

Their tour had been progressing quite well until they headed south from Berlin. Driving along the autobahn Robert noticed that all the petrol pumps said the same thing, 'Leer,' empty. When he inquired why, he was told that petrol was being used for Army manoeuvres. It seemed a logical explanation. They had already seen large numbers of troops moving around. What they didn't know was the so-called Army manoeuvres were the imminent invasion of Poland, and all available fuel had been sent to the Polish border.

The problem grew increasingly difficult. Some stations were giving 10 litres at a time others none. The British Consul in Hamburg permitted them to fill the tank at the only station supplying foreign consuls, which gave them enough petrol to get as far as Munich, where one of the boys found a garage delivering fuel in unlimited quantities. They rushed the car in and the hungry Chrysler was filled up and then driven to the underground carpark of the hotel where they were staying.

The next morning after packing all their belongings Robert turned the key but the Chrysler refused to start. A local garage was called in and soon found the fuel they'd been sold was not petrol but diesel. He and the boys quickly dismantled the carburettor and filled it with petrol. Once started the robust Chrysler engine then continued firing on diesel. However, the fuel problem was becoming more than just a nuisance. Munich had been their last refuelling stop. The quickest way out of Germany was to take the Simplon tunnel through the Alps into Switzerland, but the Germans had closed this to traffic.

Robert was left with no alternative but to take the mountain route over the Brenner Pass in the Bavarian Alps and into Northern Italy. A worried look came over his face but he tried not to pass his concerns on to the family. If the fuel didn't hold out they'd be stranded. Thoughts of having to abandon the car and find their way out by train crossed his mind.

He pressed on towards the mountains and up the Alps they motored. The winding roads seemed to stretched for miles as the Chrysler chewed heavily on the tank of diesel. On and on they drove, the petrol gauge descending relentlessly towards empty. As darkness fell they crossed the top of the pass and began to head down the Southern slopes towards Italy, yet they were still miles from the border. Flicking his eyes down he saw the gauge was now showing empty.

Ahead his headlights picked up a little shack by the side of the road and next to it stood a petrol pump. For a moment it appeared they had been saved. Robert stopped the car and the family disembarked behind him. There was no one around. The boys spotted a wooden house perched up on the hillside but it was shrouded in darkness. Robert poked his head inside the car and leant on the horn. Several attempts later there was a little bustling and a light. A small, rather annoyed, Italian woman in her dressing gown wound her way down towards them holding a lamp.

Sensing she was obviously in the presence of foreigners, she held up the fingers of one hand and pointed to the car as if to ask how many litres did they want.

Robert wanted as much as it could take and held up both his hands, twice. As Lincoln pumped the gas, John filled the tank until the petrol spilled onto the ground. They reached the border a few hours later and before long were enjoying the comforts and pleasures of Venice. From there they made their way through Florence and on to Rome. A relaxed pace set in once again and with the assistance of a Swiss guide they took in the sights of the Italian capital. At four in the morning on their third night in Rome there was a violent banging on their hotel door. Robert stumbled out of bed and turned on the light. Opening the door it was their travel guide, fully clothed and out of breath.

"I have just heard on Swiss radio," he spluttered, "the Germans have marched into Danzig."

Robert shuddered. Danzig meant Poland and everyone knew the British had signed a treaty with Poland to come to their aid in the event of war. Chamberlain had openly said if Germany invaded Poland he would declare war on Germany. His mind raced. If Britain declared war on Germany then Italy would surely join their axis ally and declare war on Britain as well. He was caught in the wrong country at the wrong time. Immediately he phoned the British Consul in Rome. The official at the consulate agreed they should leave, but suggested they wait till morning before attempting the 600-mile journey along the Vittoria Highway from Rome to Genoa.

The next day they crossed the border into France, and once again relaxed having reached the safety of the French Riviera. It did not last long. The British Consul in Paris broadcast a message to all expatriates advising them to return to England at once. Robert placed a call through to Thomas Cook to book the car on the ferry, and the channel dash was on. He opened up the throttle, and the family sped towards Calais.

They were not alone; hundreds were making the same trip in the same haste and arriving at the seaside port the scene looked hopeless. There was a vast traffic jam of cars and trucks. Some were even sitting empty on the side of the road.

Everywhere there were people clambering onto boats pushing and shoving to be the first ones to get out. The Laidlaws waited and waited. It seemed as if they, too, would have to abandon their car as the line inched slowly forward.

French officials were making their way down checking off those who had bookings. Finally they arrived at the Chrysler and Robert greeted them with a hearty, "Laidlaw."

The official who did not speak a word of English looked down his list. A few moments lapsed.

"Non," he said shaking his head and began to move off.

"Can't be," thought Robert glancing over the man's shoulder as he went past.

"There you are," he said spotting a name beginning with L, "That's it, that's the one, cross that one off."

The bewildered official crossed the name off and Robert accelerated to the front of the queue and onto the boat. Two more cars followed, the doors were shut, and the last car ferry to leave French soil began its final trip over the English Channel.

At 11 am on Sunday, September 3, 1939, Britain declared war on Germany. As the family pondered their next move Robert took Lillian aside. He had regretted missing out on the opportunity of serving in the First World War, yet now aged 53 was too old to fight. Perhaps he could stay in England and work with one of the missions in some capacity. They had discussed this possibility briefly before and, praying, both felt a strong direction from God that it was the right thing to do. He should remain while Lillian and the family returned home to New Zealand.

It was a decision that did not come easily. Robert cancelled his return trip to New Zealand and booked the family's passage back home. On Monday morning he picked up the paper in the hotel. Across the front page were terrifying words, "Sinking of the Athenia." The British passenger liner had been torpedoed and sunk by a German U-Boat off the coast of Ireland, hundreds of civilian passengers had lost their lives.

Lillian, the boys and young Lillian were due to sail out the following morning. Robert's heart was torn between staying in England, or accompanying his family home. Just then Lillian entered the room after talking on the phone.

"Thomas Cook have just phoned," she said, "and the ship is not sailing now till Thursday morning."

She could see the worry on Robert's face.

"Lincoln and I are going for a cup of tea. Come with us and we can all talk it over together."

A strange sensation came over him. "No," he said, "You go on ahead. I'm going to stay here and pray."

Nodding in agreement, she left him alone and Robert got down on his knees.

"Oh God, here is an emergency. There is no time to wait patiently on you. It is imperative that you make clear to me what you want me to do. I don't know how you can. But I know you can. And if you will, I promise to accept your guidance."

There was a knock at the door. Robert got off the floor and opening it found himself looking into the eyes of the hotel messenger. With a slight bow the boy handed him an envelope. Tearing it open his eyes scanned the page. It was a cable from William Mackay at the Farmers.

"Do not hesitate to remain in England and engage in Christian war work. We will carry on. Mackay."

He leaned back against the wall and breathed a sigh of relief. A little voice inside him asked: "Is that plain enough?"

"Yes Lord," he said out loud, "I will with confidence entrust my wife and family to your care and will seek to serve you faithfully here in Britain."

Lillian and the children were scheduled to leave London by the 9 pm train on Wednesday which would get them into Liverpool to sail on Thursday morning. Robert had some business to attend to that day, so leaving the hotel he went out alone.

When he arrived back that evening he was handed a letter. This time it was from Lillian. She and the children had to leave early. Cooks had again rung and said that due to the threat of bombing the 9 pm train may not be running.

Picking up his bag he turned and dashed to the station. Thankfully there was no air raid that night and he arrived in Liverpool just after midnight. Sleeping briefly in a small bed and breakfast hotel he was on the wharf by 6 am looking for the family. After hounding some bleary faced officials, he found out they had been assigned to the *Newfoundland*, a small coastal steamer. The naval rating standing guard let him pass and to the wonderful surprise of everyone he arrived to share breakfast before they left. None of them knew when, or even if, they might see the other again.

Robert and Lillian on their wedding day Monday, July 26 1915.

'Norwood' the house in Argyle St, Herne Bay, that Robert and Lillian moved to in 1917.

The sunroom.

Farmers first free bus. The 'Traffic Truck' began its service grinding up and down between Hobson St and Queen Street in 1922. On Christmas Eve that year it carried 4000 shoppers to the store.

The free trolley bus, early 1960s.

Robert and family pose for a Christmas card just before the Second World War.

Robert in uniform during service
abroad with Army Scripture Readers.

A parade in the 1960s. Note the latest innovation: Santa standing 79 ft tall, complete with beckoning finger.

One of the many in-store attractions.

*Robert's 80th Birthday celebration
held at Farmers, September 8 1965.*

Robert being presented with his new Jaguar.

Robert and Lillian (front) with Sir William and Lady Mackay.

Robert, and Lillian with family at their golden wedding celebration in 1965.

Robert frying sausages on the shores of Lake Taupo.

Members present at the first annual meeting of the Farmers 20 Year Club, 15 March 1938

Farmers Trading Co. Board of Directors 1969.
L to R: Fulton, Kirkbride, Christian, Phillips, Laidlaw, Keak,
Busfield, Mackay, Robertson (secretary), Holder.

15

FOR KING AND COUNTRY

1939-1944

"Get the great principles of life fixed first, and then give attention to the details, and if you think constant reminders are not necessary, as a simple test start out tomorrow morning with the fixed determination to be cheerful all day long, in the home, in business, in street cars and if you don't need to remind yourself of that resolve several times during the day, congratulate yourself on having a naturally sunny disposition." [1]

Robert Laidlaw, 1925.

During the First World War Robert had supplied many copies of *The Reason Why* to his friend Ralph Norton, from the Alexander-Chapman mission, who was now working in Belgium. He had also supplied copies to the British-based Soldiers and Airmen's Christian Association and, having seen the family off, it was to the latter he now headed. The association had been founded in 1880, and a year earlier had joined up with a similar organisation, the Army Scripture Readers.

Arriving at their headquarters at 35 Catherine Place, Westminster, Robert was shown through to Captain Perry, the secretary of the organisation. Perry was thrilled, if not a little surprised, to have the writer of *The Reason Why* appear in person all the way from New Zealand offering his services. But it also presented him with a dilemma. He had recently appointed Montague Goodman, a well-known English Christian and retired lawyer, as field director and was unsure what to suggest to Robert. After a quick exchange it was agreed that Robert approach Goodman directly so he went immediately to his Oxford Street offices.

It was a meeting of like minds. Goodman, too, had never met him in person but Robert's reputation preceded him and Goodman at once asked him to join him as co-field director. He agreed and the two of them quickly formed not only a good working relationship but also a very firm friendship. The association they now headed had been set up to share the Gospel among the forces and had plentiful opportunity to do so.

Many soldiers were in training, others were on leave stationed all over England. Within a short time Montague and Robert had collected together a staff of 208 men and women, and set themselves to the work at hand. It was a large undertaking. The wages bill alone for such an effort came to £45,000 a year. It was not funded by the Government and every year they undertook the work solely on the basis of gifts from the British Christian community. With Robert controlling the expenses and overseeing operations it finished each year with a surplus.

He also took time out to write to the directors of the Farmers back in New Zealand. He had been receiving monthly reports on progress in the firm, and it looked as if William Mackay, the acting general manager, had everything under control. He was assured about the stability of the firm but there were other matters on his mind as he penned a thoughtful note from his London hotel.

"I thank you all most sincerely for your liberal action in

giving me leave on half salary. It is in keeping with the generous way in which you have always treated me and adds to my obligations to you, which I trust the future will enable me to discharge.

"I hope therefore you will not misunderstand what follows, or think it inconsistent with what I have just said. I would like you to cut out my salary altogether during my absence, and utilise the amount of £1000 you propose paying me, as under. £250 per annum to Mr Mackay, £100 per annum to Mr Crouch, and the remaining £650 per annum to be put into a special fund for the benefit of the staff, to assist during the readjustment period after the war when in all likelihood we will be reducing staff.

"Mr Mackay and Mr Crouch are obviously carrying more responsibility during my absence, and on the results are making a fine job of it. As regards the staff, when Britain ceases spending £6,000,000 per day on war, readjustments must take place that will have far-reaching effects. In the 1921 slump our company was in such a bad way financially that I was compelled to instruct managers to dismiss every man and girl possible to get our wage percentage right.

"This time our company is in a strong financial position, and I feel we should make provision now, so that we will be able to help our dismissed staff to the full extent allowed by the Unemployment Act, which I think is 20/- per week. If we have to dismiss even 10% or 150, this would cost us £7,500 per annum, and if 20%, £15,000 per annum.

"If all businesses would make provision in good times to ease unemployment and so maintain spending power in bad times, this in itself would tend to take the hump off the boom, by reserving money, and the hollow out of the depression by liberating money.

"There is a growing feeling here and in America among

thoughtful businessmen that if the capitalist system does not face its responsibility in some such way, the next world depression will result in Governments trying more and worse socialistic experiments in an effort to overcome a trouble we have failed to alleviate; so that I believe that to make provision is not only a moral obligation, but a long view economic safeguard.

"Please on no account allow my name to be mentioned outside the Board room in connection with this matter, as after all it is only seeking to use in the interests of the company what you so considerately propose to allow me from the funds of the company.

"Even the best-informed circles here seem to have no clear idea what turn the war is likely to take next, nor how long it may last. There is a complete absence of war enthusiasm, but nevertheless there is a very widespread determination to fight on till Hitlerism is so well out of the way that Europe will not need to live from one crisis to another.

"So far Mr Goodman and I have raised £14,000, although the heavy taxation is making it hard to get substantial sums from individuals. Our first hut has been opened at Blandford Camp, and we are hoping to obtain permission to start erecting in France in the New Year. In spite of being deeply interested in the work here, I cannot help on occasions longing for the time when the war will be over and I will be back at the Farmers again. With personal regards to you and every member of the Board."[2]

Before Christmas Robert had a large portable tent constructed capable of holding about 150 men. Made of timber with canvas sides it folded up into two Army trucks. Now complete with his own military convoy he was completely mobile and could hold a mission meeting just about anywhere.[3] Leaving Goodman in England, Robert joined the British

Expeditionary Force in France with his 'gospel tent.' However it wasn't a long stay. As the phony war drew to a close and Hitler's armies once again advanced, Robert was returned to England before the evacuation of Dunkirk.[4]

He set up base in Edgware, Middlesex, eight miles out of London, at the home of Ernest and Mabel Neale, cousins of Harry Ironside. Ernest had already sent his wife and son to Scotland for safety, so it was a pleasure to have Robert's company. Woodcroft Hall was the local church that Robert attended and by chance the same as English construction magnate John Laing. Laing and Robert struck up a firm friendship albeit on his brief visits as he was soon travelling all over Britain speaking at camps and local halls.

Throughout September the Battle of Britain waged fiercely and by November Hitler switched his activity to pounding Britain relentlessly with his bombers. Stringent blackout laws were enforced and the nights were long and frightening. Robert had returned to Edgware after a campaign in Wales at the Minster Hall in Cardiff, and he and Ernest were sitting talking in the dining room when suddenly their attention was fixed towards the ceiling. Through the thick noise of the Blitz they heard a faint scream. But it wasn't a human scream, it was a German bomb.

It got louder and louder. They turned to one another. In a split second they realised the inevitable and dived for cover as the bomb hit. A deafening explosion erupted and the little brick house was shaken to within an inch of its life. As the dust settled they stood groggily to their feet. Grabbing torches and helmets they went outside to see what had happened. Ernest's house hadn't been hit, but four houses down the scene was catastrophic.

Where a house had stood minutes earlier there was now nothing, just disintegrated remains up and down the street and a large crater about 10 ft deep and 20 ft wide. There was no hope of any survivors.

He and Ernest edged closer through the rubble, their torches flicking through the smoke. The house next door to the crater was also partially hit. One side had been completely blown off revealing its contents like a peeled back sardine can. What remained was leaning precariously on the house next door. Venturing between them they made their way to the back yard.

"Is anyone there?" yelled Robert. He listened and could hear faint voices.

"Yes, but we're trapped."

Inside the toppled house and stuck in a corner room the occupants were now imprisoned. He and Ernest clasped hold of a window and forced it open. Quickly they helped the man and his wife out and back to the safety of Ernest's house further down the street. No sooner had they got in the door than Robert, seeing the two were visibly shaken, announced they would kneel together and pray, thanking God for their miraculous deliverance. Together the four of them dropped to their knees.

Later, sipping a coffee the woman looked up at Robert.

"Is the hall of our house still standing?"

"Yes."

"Then," she said, almost in a dream, "my fur coat is hanging in the hall. Do you think you could get it for me."

Without so much as a hesitation he replied.

"Why certainly madam." And to his cousin's astonishment went out the front door and back to the scene of the blast.

By now the flames had a firm grip and the local fire volunteers had arrived to douse the blaze. Robert pushed through and made towards where the hall of the house might be.

A heavy hand grabbed him from behind and he spun

around. He found himself looking straight into the blackened face of the local fire chief.

"Can't go in there friend," he said.

Robert half in shock relayed his story. The chief sent him home and at 8 o'clock the next morning there was a knock at the door. It was the fire chief, and in his hand he held the lady's fur coat. Fortunately no one had been in the bombed house when it was wiped out. Like many, the man had sent his wife and family away, and he himself was on fire-fighting duty the night of the blast.

Over the next weeks and months Robert threw all his energies into the work of the Soldiers and Airmen's Christian Association. Reviving the disciplines he had followed all his life he drove himself from dawn to dusk every day. At many of the preaching centres in the camps and barracks across Britain he was the keynote speaker. Often in a week he would speak a dozen times or more going from one location to the next preaching and talking to the troops. With special passes from the Ministry of Defence he had the doors of every Army and Air Force base in the country thrown open to him.

The Christian Soldiers and Airmen's Association had 34 canteens, and men stationed at 150 different military camps over the British Isles. He visited them all, week after week, month after month, not only in England, but also Wales, Scotland and Ireland.

After one trip to Northern Ireland he was coming back from Larne across the Irish Sea when he struck up a conversation with a captain inside the darkened steamer. The captain saw that Robert wore a captain's uniform yet noticed ASR on his shoulders and wondered what he did. He told him of the work of the Army Scripture Readers and the Soldiers and Airmen's Christian Association and what he was doing among the troops. The officer took immediate offence and snapped at him vehemently.

"Don't speak to me about Christ," he said indignantly. "I am not interested."

Robert had obviously hit a raw nerve.

"Well," he replied a little taken aback at this outburst, "can you suggest a topic?"

"Yes," replied the Captain, "Which do you think influences a man's character the most, environment or heredity?"

Robert knew this one immediately, "Heredity," he said.

"Why?" asked the captain looking back with interest.

"Well," he said, "if you put a pig into a parlour, its heredity will soon turn its environment into a pigsty."

The Captain was not thrown off. "If that is so," he said, "what hope have we got against evil hereditary tendencies?"

"Not much, but God has a master solution although you said I mustn't discuss it with you."

"What is it?" said the Captain.

"A new heredity," he said, "which Christ expounded to Nicodemus in the third chapter of John's Gospel, when he told him of the new birth, of being born again of the Spirit of God. Which imparts a new power and a new life. The life of God himself."

"That's a new one on me," pondered the Captain. "Will you please let me think that one out for myself."

Robert agreed and the two went their separate ways.

The Soldiers and Airmen's Association also had a canteen at Odiham near Aldershot and Robert visited it on several occasions. On one particular visit a regiment of Canadian soldiers were encamped. He noticed that a corporal from the regiment had attended each of the meetings and paid close attention to everything he was saying, yet every time at the close of the meeting when an invitation was extended to come up the front, the corporal held his seat.

He was curious why one so attentive and interested could be so riveted. As the last meeting closed the corporal again did not join any of his colleagues up the front. Robert caught him before he left the hall and invited him to have a cup of coffee. The two found a quiet spot in the room and sat down. Instantly the corporal began to gush forward, almost relieved at the opportunity to speak.

"Six weeks ago," he said, "a lady asked me to her home and spoke to me earnestly about accepting Jesus Christ as my Lord. Since then she has written me a letter every week and says that she will continue to pray for me."

Robert looked at him, "Corporal, this dear soul has been praying for you and writing to you for six weeks, and you have listened to me for five nights and as I am leaving in the morning surely God is bringing His efforts on your behalf to a climax tonight. Will you accept Jesus Christ now?"

The corporal shook his head from side to side, "You don't understand," he pleaded, "I'm not as bad as you think I am."

Robert was unmoved and repeated his challenge, "Corporal, will you accept Christ now?"

The corporal moved uneasily in his chair and replied sympathetically to him, "I go to church pretty often."

Robert changed tack. "Corporal," he questioned, "are you a married man?

"No."

"Do you expect to get married some time in the future?"

"Yes," he said hopefully.

"Then the day will come when you will stand before a minister and he will ask, 'Will you have this woman to be your lawful wedded wife?' And you will say, 'I think she is a very nice girl.' The minister will repeat the question and say again, 'Will you have this woman to be your lawful wedded wife?' To which you will say,' I like her family and would be most happy to associate with them.' Is it not true that if you do not say 'I will' to the question she will never be your wife?"

"God asks you through me, 'will you have my Son, Jesus Christ to be your personal Saviour?' and you reply, 'I go to church quite often.' Corporal," Robert said with a quiet seriousness in his voice, "if you do not say 'I will' to God's question" – he paused – "Christ will never be yours."

The corporal's eyes flashed with new vigour as he rose to his feet. Extending his hand towards him he declared, "I will," with all the earnestness he had in him.

As the months stretched into years Robert had countless similar encounters with troops all over Britain each week, visiting a different camp or base and speaking at local churches wherever he went. Robert's little booklet, *The Reason Why*, was also producing astonishing results among the troops.

It was now one of the most widely used gospel tracts in the world, and more than six million copies in 27 languages were in circulation. Robert found himself meeting more and more people on his trips around Britain, who had already read it years earlier. At one Sunday night meeting a man came up to him after the service.

"Good evening" he said, "my name is Mackenzie Miller and I wrote to you 15 years ago about five youths who came to Christ through reading one copy of *The Reason Why* which they passed from one to another. Well," he said proudly, "they have all gone on splendidly. Three are most acceptable speakers and one is a prisoner of war."

Behind Miller another soldier was waiting to speak to Robert and came forward. In his outstretched hand he held a ragged copy of *The Reason Why*. He had no idea that he was now standing in front of the author.

"Four days ago," he said, "I signed this decision and I have come out to make public confession of my faith."

Robert greeted him warmly. *The Reason Why* the man held had been printed before the war. Someone in a soldiers canteen in Newport near Cardiff had handed it to him.

The month of July 1943 saw thousands of Christians from all parts of London and the neighbouring districts descend on St Paul's, Portman Square, London W.1. Combined meetings of different churches were an important feature in the calendar and by far the most significant was the Keswick convention held traditionally in the Lake District. Robert had spoken there with Harry Ironside in 1939, but because of travelling difficulties during wartime it had been held recently in London.

Last year Robert had joined the speakers' platform and from Bloomsbury Central Church gave two opening addresses.[5] Now a year later he stood in the lofty church with its white pillars and vaulted ceiling, accompanied by the choir who were in full voice. On the last night of the conference Friday, July 23, at 6 pm Robert took to the platform to address the congregation as he had done the year before.

"Do you know the greatest witness we Christian people could bear would be this: that if there were half a dozen Christian employees in your firm and the manager were asked to name the six most consistent, courteous and efficient members of his staff, he ought to name the six Christians, without knowing they are Christians at all? It is inconceivable that a Christian, rendering his service as unto Christ, would not give his Lord better service than an unconverted man would offer his earthly employer."

After Keswick he made two trips to the North of England and Scotland speaking at different canteens and meeting halls. In October he received an unexpected note from the directors of the New Zealand Bible Training Institute in Auckland. He had been a director since its inception in 1921 and had remained in frequent touch though he had not been there in person. The president of the institute and chairman of directors, R.L. Stewart, had recently died and the other directors sought to appoint Robert in his place. He was the obvious choice. Robert's contribution to the growth of the institute and his guidance, vision and business sense had strengthened it greatly. No one had been a more consistent and regular attender at board meetings throughout the years and no one had given like Robert in order to make the work a success. Robert immediately cabled the directors back.

"Humbly accept, and pray God's guidance and blessing."

Robert looked at his calendar. He had already been to Ireland in January and had spoken at 50 meetings in Belfast, Bangor, Dublin and Dungannon. Five years had passed since he had last seen his wife and family, and he now had accepted new responsibilities back in New Zealand at B.T.I.

16

D-Day

1944

"There is nothing remarkable about the capacity for work for which big men are noted. These men do not work any differently from any other sensible man. They simply formed the habit of making every moment count."[1]

Optimist, 1916.

Over the past few months, Robert had thought more and more about going home. He had witnessed the darkest times of the war in 1940 and 1941, but now there seemed to be more victories than defeats. Italy had been invaded in September 1943 and the Allies were now making slow progress up the peninsula. In Russia the German Armies were on the retreat and were being pushed further and further into Eastern Europe. The battle in North Africa had also been decisively won, and by 1944 it was clear that the tide of war had turned for the better. His son Lincoln, with the New Zealand Forces in Italy, was also concerned about the strain on his mother back home and had written on several occasions pleading with him to return.

It played on his mind. Almost overnight, however, the situation around him began to change. All around the British Isles, American, Canadian and British forces began to assemble in their thousands for an offensive into Europe, and in May a ban on all foreign travel outside of Britain was imposed. His prayers had seemingly been answered: obviously there was no way he could return home to New Zealand.

Early in the morning on June 6 1944, the Allies launched their offensive into Europe, landing on the beaches of Normandy on the coast of France. Suddenly London was buzzing with stories of the invasion. Operation Overlord had taken hold in Nazi-occupied France. May had been a busy month: he had been to Newport, a missionary conference at Bristol, Cheltenham, and again over to Cardiff in Wales. Already this year he had given over 150 addresses. His next scheduled speaking engagement was at the Christian convention in Port Stewart (Northern Ireland), the same one he had attended last year. In all he had been to Ireland seven times and felt sure he would be able to get across though the ban was in force. Clutching his papers he confidently ventured to the London passport office.

An hour later he emerged exhausted. All the persuasive powers he could muster had not been able to change the minds of the stern-faced officials. He had received an absolute refusal, several times over. He stood puzzled on the London pavement seemingly unaware of the activity around him. He felt sure he would get across to Ireland and now he had to write to the conference organisers and tell them he could not speak. What was going on? Closing his eyes he lifted his heart to God. "The door to New Zealand closed, Lord, the door to Ireland closed." Then a thought flashed across his mind: Europe.

Might not D-Day that had closed all these doors open the door into Europe? He was ministering to the troops: why could he not go where the troops had gone – to France? He rushed round to the ASR office a few streets away and laid out his plan with great gusto to Colonel Macaulay, the commanding officer. Macaulay sat in his chair almost dumbstruck.

"Why Robert," he said, "it is an answer to our prayers. The authorities have just given us permission to send 10 scripture readers to France, and we were praying only this morning that the Lord would provide someone able and willing to lead them."

With such a confirmation he eagerly readied himself for the trip, including getting 13 different inoculations against the many hazards associated with a war zone.[2] The small party was scheduled to leave for Normandy in early July but the huge troop movements into France, (over a million landed in the first three weeks), and a German counterattack, postponed their departure date. Robert filled in the time with more speaking engagements before bidding farewell to Ernest and the Edgware fellowship at Woodcroft Hall in early August.

He had been assigned 10 scripture readers and with the initial five he boarded a small naval transport headed for France. Slowly they made their way across the channel escorted by two old trawlers recently armed with cannons on their bows, not so much to ward off attack but to destroy mines which the Germans had been floating down into the shipping lanes. Three times they were put into action blowing them out of their path.

Several hours later he glimpsed the coast of France. Overhead a constant stream of Allied aircraft flew back and forth and before him a vast logistical panorama was unfolding. The small transport was dwarfed by hundreds of other vessels – landing craft, supply ships and troopships all packed into the artificial harbour (codenamed Mulberry) at Aramanche. The second of two large harbours created by the allied forces, it had been constructed by sinking dozens of old steamers to form a breakwater through which men, guns, tanks, troops and supplies were being ferried inland. It was a military operation on a scale never seen before.[3]

They were met at the docks by a friendly adjutant and Robert followed in his car to the Chief Chaplain's tent. For a war zone it seemed remarkably relaxed, but by now the supply operation was a finely tuned machine. More than anything else the noise was deafening as lines of American and British tanks churned their way past for the front. As they waited a young chaplain strode in and seeing 'Army Scripture Reader' on his shoulder, grabbed his hand and shook it warmly.

"Am I pleased to see you." he said eagerly. "We've been expecting you. The Army have given us the use of a small wooden inn not far from here," he said gesturing behind him, "and we're holding a Bible study there every Monday night. About six or seven come along, you must come."

With a sparkle in his eyes he added, "I had the joy of leading two men to Christ just last week and am about to post them this booklet," waving a copy of *The Reason Why* in front of Robert.

"Why," he said with a slight grin, "That's interesting, for I wrote that 30 years ago in New Zealand."

The chaplain's mouth dropped. "You don't mean that you're Robert Laidlaw the author?" Robert nodded with a smile.

"Oh I am so pleased to see you," said the chaplain, "for I have given away a great many of these."

After the welcome he and his party quickly settled into their new home. It was vastly different from the relative calm and safety of England. He was given a tent and a single bucket for his various ablutions. Nor was there anywhere to hold the kinds of meetings they had been running in England, and he began to wonder whether it had been such a good idea to come after all. That night he knelt in his tent and prayed.

"Oh God," he said quietly, "Give me a Philip experience Lord, as a confirmation that you have really brought me here."

He rose early the next morning and set out on foot to explore the countryside. Following the convoys inland he soon came across Bayeux about three miles down the road. The city had escaped too much devastation and the shopkeepers had already resumed trading. In some ways it was hard to believe there was a war on. For a few hours he wandered through the streets, then in the early afternoon began to make his way back to camp. On the road he overtook a British soldier and quickly they fell into conversation. Robert explained that he was in France with the Army Scripture Readers.

"That's interesting, "said the soldier, "for ever since I was 15 years of age I have studied comparative religions, and have at last decided that Christianity is the truest religion of all and have adopted it."

Robert looked across at his well-spoken companion.

"Well," he said, "that's a good start, but you know Christianity is not a creed to be adopted, or a philosophy to be argued, but a person to be accepted."

The soldier stopped walking. The remark had surprised him.

"For if Christianity," continued Robert, "is not Christ it is but one of many religions."

"That's a new thought to me," said the soldier inquiringly, "for I have often felt how formal our services seemed. I do really want to find God, and since I have been over here in France he has seemed even more real to me, but it's all a bit hazy and lacks definition."

Robert reached into his jacket and took out his Bible. As they continued down the road he opened the Scriptures to him and explained God's plan of salvation. Before they got back to camp the two of them knelt by the side of the road and as the war continued around them a young English soldier prayed, opened his heart, and received Jesus Christ as his saviour. God had given Robert his Philip experience and he was here to stay.

The next night a soldier invited him to attend a Bible study group that met once a week. When Robert arrived , there were seven young men in the room and one woman looking a little awkward in the company of the seven burly men. "Good evening," said Robert.

"Oh hello," she said, coming to life, "my name is Stella and you must be Mr Laidlaw I presume."

"Why" said Robert a little bemused, "how did you know that Stella?"

"Well, I heard you were coming. I am a sister of Corporal Beryl Morgan who gave her testimony at one of your meetings in the Royal Albert Hall."

"I shall never forget it," he said. "Your sister Beryl gave one of the finest testimonies I have ever heard from a young woman. She stood before that great audience of many thousands as composed as if she were addressing a few friends, and then held them spellbound as she told of how she'd come to Christ and in the Army."

Stella nodded agreeably as the chairman for the night's meeting motioned it was time to begin.

"The topic for tonight" he announced, "is the advantages of being brought up in a Christian home."

One by one each of the men in the room, including Robert, related their experience and spoke at length of the advantages they had received. As the last one finished Stella asked the chairman if she might speak. After a quick nod she began.

"I thank God I was not brought up in a Christian home."

All eyes, including Robert's, turned to see what she might say next.

"All the young women in the Army who profess to be Christians, and were reared in Christian homes, seemed to me have grown into their faith and it doesn't seem to mean very much to some of them. I was brought up in a godless, worldly home and I lived a very worldly life, until one wonderful night I turned from darkness to light as I discovered what Christ had done for me. He came to mean not something, but everything, to me. I love him so much I would do anything for Christ because of the greatness of my obligation to Him."

Robert looked at her glowing face and listened to the thrill in her voice. He couldn't help but think that the curse of the Church was that it was filled with so many 50-pence debtors, and so few truly grateful 500-pence debtors like Stella.

A few days later back in camp the Jewish rabbi came and knocked on the side of his tent.

"Come in," beckoned Robert.

"What can I do for you rabbi?"

"I have been assigned a gentleman from the Jewish Welfare Committee in London who have gifted six mobile canteens to the YMCA. The RAF have flown him over especially so he can see first-hand the good use being made of them. Unfortunately I don't have a car, and this man has promised some friends whose son was killed at D-Day that he'd try and find the boy's grave on the top of the cliffs overlooking Mulberry."

"I'd be only too happy to take him. You go and bring him here."

As the rabbi went off Robert knelt in prayer.

"Lord," he said quietly, "give me wisdom and spiritual power to speak to this man about the Lord Jesus Christ, and help us in all this desolation to find the grave."

Robert and the visitor clambered into his car and set off for the coast. As they drove down the road Robert turned to his passenger.

"I want to tell you," he said above the noise of the engine as they bumped along, "that I am a pro-Semite."

His Jewish companion looked across at him.

Robert smiled. "May I tell you why?" he asked.

"Certainly," replied his passenger more than a little interested to hear what his driver was going to say next.

"Well, it may surprise you to know that I am pro-Semite because I am a Christian. You think that the British are a Christian nation, but that is not so. Only a small proportion are true Christians when tested by the Bible. You see true Christians who believe in Jesus Christ believe in your Scriptures equally as we believe in the New Testament Scriptures. And as you well know in your Scriptures God promised a curse on those who curse Abraham or Jacob and their seed, and a blessing on those who bless them. As every true Christian wants the blessing of God we must therefore of necessity be pro-Semites."

Robert swerved to miss a shell hole.

"That's very interesting," said the Jew.

"Now may I tell you," he continued, "as courteously as I can, why I believe you made a mistake in rejecting Jesus of Nazareth as your Messiah?"

His Jewish companion was not put off but found this Gentile an interesting mix. "You may," he said.

"Well," continued Robert, "many of your prophets foretold both a suffering and a reigning Messiah. Take, for instance, the greatest of your writing prophets, Isaiah. In chapter 9, verses 6 and 7, he speaks of a reigning triumphant Messiah sitting on the throne of David, but in his 52nd and 53rd chapters he speaks most vividly of a suffering Messiah."

"That is true," added the Jew. This Gentile obviously read his Scriptures.

"And because you could not reconcile these two lines of prophecy," continued Robert, "which seemed to contradict each other you applied the suffering to your nation and the reigning to your Messiah. It did not occur to you that both could be easily reconciled by his coming twice – first as a suffering substitute for your nation's sins, and for the sins of the whole world, and the second time as your King, and as the mighty Monarch of the universe, King of Kings and Lord of Lords for us Gentiles as well."

The Jew was fascinated.

"We Christians, that is true Christians not nominal ones, sincerely believe that all your prophets have written about the glories of your Messiah will literally be fulfilled."

They continued in conversation until they reached the sea. Robert drove as far as he could into the maze of craters that lined the coast overlooking Port en Bassen where the troops had landed two months ago. A white tape across the makeshift road brought them to a halt. The area had not yet been cleared of mines and they could go no further. They got out of the car and carefully proceeded on foot through the shell holes and smashed concrete gun emplacements that had stood so resolutely before the invaders.

"There is the grave," said his companion, pointing, and he was right. A hundred yards away was a single cross with a six-pointed Star of David.

As they got closer they saw the boy's name inscribed on the cross. Some French peasants had put a few flowers in an old jar and half the soldier's cap hung weakly on the cross. At its base was a tobacco tin. The Jew bent down and picked it up. Inside were some papers, a prayer in Hebrew and a poem. He passed the poem to Robert. It was a solemn moment and standing on the windswept cliff top he read the crumpled script.

"Thou hast given us home and freedom, Mother England,
Thou hast let us live again free and fearless, midst thy
free and fearless children,

265

Sharing with them as one people grief and gladness, joy
and pain,
For the Jew has heart and hand, Mother England
And they both are thine today;
Thine for life and thine for death, yea thine for ever –
Wilt thou take them as we give them, freely, gladly,
England say."

Several hours later when they pulled back into camp the
Jew took his hand. "My friend," he said, "this has been the
greatest day in my life. I thank you." Robert was almost
brought to tears, it had touched them both.

Meanwhile life in camp got busier and busier and his tent
soon became a gathering point for men of all walks of life. A
few days after his Jewish visit he was called on by the resident
Church of England vicar. The man looked anxious and came
straight to the point.

"I have been given the use of a local church this Sunday
evening, and I was wondering if you would come and take the
service?

"But why?" inquired Robert, wondering what would induce
the vicar not to speak at such an opportunity.

"I am a high churchman, Mr Laidlaw, and these men are off
to the front. I have nothing to offer them and they need nothing
less than conversion. Would you bring them a message?"

Robert could hardly believe the words he was hearing and
was angered by the clergyman's cowardice. Somewhat
reluctantly he agreed to take the service. That Sunday night
he drove to the church, and as the sun went down about 90
soldiers filed into the pews in the little Caen chapel. Robert
sat at the front with the vicar and watched as his opposite lit
the candles and performed the service. Soon it came his turn
and he crossed to the pulpit.

Both preacher and congregation knew that possible death

was merely a few miles up the road and as best he could Robert laid out the gospel to them. Half an hour later as he closed the service he extended an invitation to those present to make a stand for Christ and accept Him as their personal Saviour. Thirty-three soldiers rose to their feet and walked to the front. A tear came to his eye. He looked down into their faces and saw men hungry for more.

"God has rebuked my lack of faith," he said soberly, "for I have brought only 25 copies of *The Reason Why* with me tonight."

For some there would be no more tonights and he knew it.

"But," he said, "I will have all the others at the canteen tomorrow night for those of you who don't get one."

After two weeks in camp the second batch of five Army Scripture Readers arrived from England with another two cars. This greatly increased their mobility but negotiating the roads proved no easy task. In the wet they turned to thick mud, and in the midday sun a dust storm rose as 500 tanks and trucks passed every hour. By the end of September the Allied advance had steadied and the Army Scripture Readers under Robert's command followed the victorious allies through France into Belgium. The roads were strewn with overturned German tanks, trucks and guns. The further East they travelled the warmer the welcome became. Everyone smiled as they drove along the streets, little children ran up to shake their hands and welcome banners hung from all the buildings.

Arriving in Brussels the second day after it was liberated, Robert went straight round to the headquarters of the Belgian Gospel Mission to see if they could assist him in his work. He was met by Dr Vansteenberghe, director of the mission and after introducing himself made his request.

"Why," said Vansteenberghe, "my brother, this is the answer to our prayers. Ever since the Allies arrived we have been praying that some way might be found to use this fine building to reach the soldiers with the gospel. God has surely sent you here today."

If it was an answer to Dr Vansteenberghe's prayers, it certainly was an answer to his, too. The mission provided him with a room and a bed as well as bathroom, a large step up from the canvas and mud of the past six weeks. At the first Gospel meeting he addressed in Brussels, a Belgian came up to him at the end of the meeting. The man seemed overjoyed to be standing in his presence and in broken English recounted his story.

"I am one of the mission's first converts, from 1918 when it was started," he said. "Mr Norton gave me a John's Gospel and *The Reason Why* and I read them both right through and signed the decision page," he said pulling out a ragged booklet from his jacket. "Here," he said. "Look.... and the Lord has kept me faithful to Him for these 26 years." Robert looked into his kindly eyes. He lent forward and the two of them met in a warm embrace. It was a unique encounter.

Fighting was still going on in the outskirts of Antwerp, and as he had a suitable car the three officers with whom he was billeted asked him to take them to the front. They loaded into the car then stopped briefly at the Canadian headquarters before proceeding up to the front line. The officer in charge came out of the headquarters shaking his head. He could see exactly where the three officers and the 59-year-old scripture reader were headed and wanted no part of it.

"There are all kinds of fools," he said, "but it's not my funeral. If you really want to go there is a convoy leaving in 15 minutes. You can have a place in that."

They drove with the convoy for about seven miles before stopping at sundown. Robert went to the lead vehicle and asked if they might press on alone.

The major in charge of the convoy looked surprised but agreed: "I'm sending a bren gun carrier up ahead with a despatch to the front. You can follow that."

As they sped forward people came out of their houses throwing flowers and cheering. They had been liberated only a day earlier. Finally they reached the last village. The Canadian Army had taken it two hours earlier and as dusk was falling all firing had stopped and the wounded were being ferried to the Red Cross station.

Robert dropped the officers off and began to head back. Two miles down the road a youth and his elderly mother waved down the car.

"Will you please take us to Antwerp?" asked the youth in fairly good English.

Robert gave the official reply.

"This is a military car," he said, "and we are forbidden to carry civilians."

"I am a Jew," replied the boy. "My mother and I have been hiding in that farmhouse for two long years and not once dare I venture outside lest someone see me and inform the Germans. But this afternoon your troops drove the Germans out and now we are free." He rose his hands in the air. "Penniless and with nothing, but I am free, mother and I are free."

He looked at them. He had not been so close to someone so ravaged by the scars of war. His mind thought of the millions who had not successfully hidden, who had been tortured and killed. He thought, too, of the cliffs overlooking Mulberry and the precious moments he had shared there with the Jew from London.

"Climb into the back seat," he said and ushered them in. The Jewish youth burst forth in conversation. At last he could speak without fear of being heard.

"My mother and I escaped two years ago from Antwerp

when all the Jews were being sent to Germany to concentration camps and to death. We escaped with nothing but this little bag and the clothes we are wearing."

"You speak good English," Robert commended.

"I knew no English then," said the boy, "but I have learned it listening to BBC London from 6 am every morning to 10 pm every night."

Robert's headlights picked up a checkpoint ahead and he was waved down by the guards.

As he coasted to a halt, the sentry saw his uniform and motioned them on. His companion on the other side of the car flashed his torch into the back seat and picked out the two Jews huddled together.

"Stop," he barked.

"What's the matter sergeant?" asked Robert.

"You cannot proceed any further carrying these civilians," he said.

Robert explained the situation but the guard would not be persuaded.

"Is there an interrogation officer present at this station?" asked Robert.

"No," replied the soldier, "but if you go back about half a mile and turn off to your left you'll come to a bridge and there's one there."

Robert swung the car around and drove off full speed into the night. He carried out the directions but when he arrived at the bridge it was empty and so he continued on into the heart of Antwerp where the couple assured him they still had friends they could contact. As they got out of the car Robert reached behind the seat and pulled out a copy of *The Reason Why*. He handed it to his young passenger. The young man was overcome with gratitude and said he would read every word. Robert sat in the car and watched as they disappeared into the night as quickly as they had come out of it.

Returning to Brussels he continued his speaking work among the troops and towards the end of October received a letter from New Zealand. It was from a close friend who was concerned about Lillian. For some time the friend had watched her trying to handle the strain of running a large house, and urged him to return to New Zealand as soon as possible. He had ignored his son's similar requests on previous occasions but this time something stirred inside him and he acted. Catching an Army transport he flew to London to see a friend, the High Commissioner for New Zealand, Sir William Jordan, who arranged a passage back to New Zealand.

Robert then flew back to Brussels to work for another month before returning to London again in late November. After holding a farewell meeting at Woodcroft hall in Edgware he said his goodbyes to Cousin Ernest, John Laing and Montague Goodman, then travelled up to Malvern in Scotland where he spent Christmas with friends before boarding a ship at Liverpool bound for New Zealand. It was an uneventful voyage and the convoy came as far as Sydney, where a week later he boarded a flying boat making the Tasman run.

17

HOME AGAIN

1945-1953

"In every walk of life, every blessing has attached to it, whether expressed or not, a condition which is the very foundation on which it rests. If we try to tear it away from its firm base, phantom-like it vanishes in the process or turns into a curse and smites us for our folly. For instance there is no true happiness that is selfish; so if we are looking for a truly Merry Christmas and a Happy New Year, let us look for the hidden condition – we'll find it in some unselfish or even self-sacrificing act, which done in the interests of someone else's happiness, boomerang-like, will come back in multiplied joy to us." [1]

Robert Laidlaw, 1918

On February 8 1945, the large sea-plane touched down in Mechanics Bay, Auckland, and a wall of spray erupted from the blue waters as she slowly planed to a halt. Opening up the throttle the pilot manoeuvred into position and drew alongside the makeshift jetty. A small party of friends and relatives had been waiting expectantly for the arrival of the plane's only passenger.

They were a mixture, some family, some friends, some from the church, some from the Farmers Trading Company, and foremost among them the two Lillians, mother and daughter. Robert had seen neither of them for five and a half years and

273

although Lillian had sent him photos, when he farewelled his daughter in 1939 she was a bubbly 13-year-old. Now she was a fully grown woman.

The door of the plane swung open and he came into view. Immaculately attired as always he had changed little. His hair was now more silvery grey and had thinned slightly. It was cropped in a short military style and if anything he had lost weight, yet his beaming eyes and trademark smile remained. He made straight for Lillian and his daughter and the three held each other tightly. Once again, the man of the house was back on New Zealand soil.

Six days later he once again entered his old haunt, the Farmers Trading Company building in Hobson Street. Its many attractions remained the same. The children's playground, the end of year Christmas parade, the prize competitions and free bus were now something of a tradition. War had again taken its toll among the staff yet many of the faces were still familiar. Arriving on the second floor he headed to his large office before meeting the directors. Since he started the journey home he had been thinking about what he would do once he returned. The only possible answer was now very clear in his mind and he made his way to the fifth floor boardroom.

The mood in the boardroom changed dramatically when he entered. It was a meeting of old friends and some time passed before they finally sat down and the night's proceedings got under way.

"I would like to express, "said the chairman, "the great pleasure of the board in the safe return of Mr Laidlaw and in such fine health." The table resounded with a hearty "hear, hear," from the rest of the board.

"It is a great joy to us," said the chairman, "that he is once again going to be closely associated with the Farmers Trading Company."

Robert smiled gratefully and hoped that what he was about to say would not be too alarming.

"Thank you, Mr Chairman, for your warm welcome. It is indeed a great joy for me to be back in New Zealand and I have been especially pleased with the outstanding success of the assistant general manager Mr Mackay in my absence, and extend my congratulations to him in the manner in which he has handled this responsible position."

There was another round of agreeable murmurs in the room and he paused before continuing.

"But as Mr Mackay has managed the business so successfully in my absence and I am now in my 60th year, I feel he should continue in control which in turn will leave me free to devote more of my time to Christian work."

The faces round the table looked back somewhat uneasily, yet the news had not come as a complete surprise. Robert had been given leave of absence throughout the war years for three months at a time. The original request had been extended and extended and it was obvious where his heart and energies were now being diverted. Accepting his resignation with regret the board's reply was to make him an 'appointee director.' It was a new position that had not been used before, and meant that they could keep the benefit of his watchful oversight without direct responsibility. They recommended a salary of £2000 a year (the same as the assistant general manager), with the use of a company car, office, secretary and garage.

Robert graciously accepted and soon settled into a new, smaller office on the fourth floor, the same as the furniture department. His secretary was in an adjacent room. The room was about 12ft square with a commanding view of the harbour and dockyards looking across to the North Shore and Takapuna. The walls were panelled in walnut and a pull switch for the light overhung his desk by the window.

At the far end of the room was a wardrobe with shelves for his books. The second floor manager's offices were only a quick descent via the nearby stairwell, so he had instant access to the 10 am managers' meeting every morning where the various problems besetting the company were discussed over morning tea. He was a regular attender.

From this new base he then renewed his friendships with many of the organisations he had been so actively involved with before leaving New Zealand. His home church received back its valued elder and brother in the faith. At the Bible Training Institute the directors welcomed back their new president and chairman. Rotary welcomed its Auckland founder and one of its most energetic supporters. Yet all found Robert with a new energy and a new focus.

Before the war he had spoken a dozen or more times each year at different church and business gatherings. There were the odd campaigns like in Australia in 1935, or Dunedin and Invercargill in 1937, but nothing like the fervour he now displayed. In February and March he spoke six times at his own church as well as the ABC bible class quarterly, a Brethren conference, the Bible Training Institute annual meeting, the Christian Business Men's Association and the Junior Chamber of Commerce.

In April and May there were more conferences, a broadcast service on National Radio, then he followed international evangelist Lionel Fletcher down to Christchurch where they held a campaign together. It was only the beginning. From there he then went on to be the keynote speaker at Eastern Beach winter house party, meetings in Rotorua and Wellington and more radio broadcasts.

Before the year was out he had given over 90 addresses. He was now doing in New Zealand, exactly what he had been doing so fervently in England. The response was the same, too, and hundreds came forward to accept Christianity.

On top of this there were also his commitments at the Farmers Trading Company where he attended the monthly directors' meetings, managers' meetings as well as the different staff social events during the year. One such occasion was the 20-year-club which had been launched by some of the longer-serving members in the firm. Each year at an annual dinner new members who had completed 20 years of service were received into the club.

It was no small gathering. The club had more than 200 members, more than 50 had faithfully served Robert for over 30 years, nine for over 40 years. This particular night one of the staff from the despatch department was being welcomed into this prestigious group and during the evening the man directly approached Robert, who greeted him in his characteristically warm fashion.

"You know," said the despatch man, "There is one thing I would like to ask you about. Something has puzzled me for several years now and perhaps you might be able to answer my question."

"Ask away my friend," replied Robert.

"When I came here 20 years ago and started work in the despatch department there were one hundred and fifty men working there. Yet immediately I was impressed by the absence of swearing. I have often wondered why that was."

Robert looked thoughtfully for a moment at the man in front of him. He knew the answer to his question intimately and beckoned him closer.

"Let me tell you," he said, "of an incident that occurred in the early days of our firm when our staff was quite small. I was going through the packing and despatch department which was then under the charge of my brother Jack when I heard one of the packers swear at another. Immediately I called together the 16 men employed on the floor and said. 'I happened to hear Bill swear at Harry. Now I want to tell you that I will not allow any one above you to swear at any of you men, under any circumstances whatever. And I put it to you that," he said, recounting the words as if it were yesterday, 'if no department manager is allowed to curse you, that you should not be allowed to curse each other. Is that fair?' And all the men agreed, and that was the end of it."

The despatch man in front of him nodded knowingly: the effects of that piece of wisdom were still being felt 40 years later.[2]

Other events at the Farmers also received his special attention. The arrival of Santa at the Auckland store which had begun so spectacularly before the war had continued and got even bigger. In 1948, 15,000 people lined the route to see the festivities. At the head was a pipe band and a team of Farmers marching girls.

Santa in all his glory was high on a beautiful float surrounded by pretty fairies, clowns and Disney characters. Following the procession were several busloads of children from city orphanages and blind homes. When Santa reached his destination at the Hobson Street store 1000 balloons were released from the roof all with a free ticket to the Christmas attraction that year in the children's playground on the roof – 'Cinderella in the Magic Cave.'

The crowds who had watched his arrival now surged en masse into the store to watch Santa on the fifth floor unlock the padlock to the door of the cave, and declare the year's Christmas attraction open. The orphans were then led through the cave by Santa and the fairies, and each received a gift before refreshments were served for them in the dining room accompanied by the clowns. It was the same year after year and the numbers turning out each year to witness the festivities grew. Robert's 1934 innovation had turned into a city tradition.

Since arriving back home it had become clear that his large three-storey house at 73 Argyle Street was just too big for the family's needs. Only two of the children now remained at home. John, the eldest, had married and during the war Lillian and Lincoln had both shifted down from their top floor bedrooms onto the second floor to minimise the upkeep of the home. Gone, too, were the four servants. While Robert was away Lillian had employed just one live-in help and she alone remained. With a new stage in life opening up, the time seemed right to scale down.

It was to his daughter Lillian that Robert raised the idea of designing them a new home on part of the existing property. In 1937, he had bought the adjacent block to his house in Argyle Street and demolished its house creating even larger grounds. It was this section and closer to the clifftop overlooking the harbour that he settled on as the site for their new home. Lillian had recently qualified as an architect and was thrilled to have such a job to cut her teeth on.

Due to restrictions still in place in the aftermath of the war, homes were limited in size to 1200 sq ft per family. While he wanted a smaller house there was no way Robert could see himself living in that amount of space, so he went to see the city engineer. It was a short but effective meeting. The engineer in his usual manner outlined the various restrictions and regulations with which Robert would have to comply. He listened carefully then replied with characteristic insight.

"If I build two flats," he said, " and chose to live in both of them at the same time would that be permitted."

"Well, er yes," replied the engineer helplessly. He had been completely outmanoeuvred.

And so work began. Throughout 1948 Lillian designed the home, and the following year the Auckland building firm which had done Robert's work at the Farmers for years and built Monte Vista, built the new home.

The new two-storey home was built ostensibly as two flats but without a door between them. Both "flats" were 1200 sq ft with the top storey at right angles to the bottom and projecting over a large carport. The front door was on the lower level underneath the carport and opened into a small entry hall. Straight ahead was the kitchen and one bedroom while to the left was the living room. It was encased by two walls of picture windows and itself opened onto the dining room.

A staircase wound up to the upper floor and here were four bedrooms in a row all facing north with three opening onto a deck on the roof of the living room below. Robert and Lillian took the extreme north-west room and next to this Robert set up his new study. Lillian and Lincoln for the time being moved into the remaining two bedrooms.

The house was a reduction in many ways and Robert auctioned off much of the large ornate carved furniture that filled the old home. To replace it he had Lillian design all the furniture for the new home, which was then built by the Farmers' furniture factory. Gone was the black oak dining table and in its place a new kauri one. The big house was then sold.

In 1950 he went to Australia for three months to conduct a series of mission meetings.[3] When he returned home it was to fulfil an appointment with the Board of Trade. He had been appointed to the Government Import Advisory committee which advised the Minister of Customs on import controls.

The committee worked on schedules for New Zealand import licensing, and while he found the work interesting it took him away from many of the pursuits which were now his first call. The Bible Training Institute, of which he was still president, did not see him at their board meetings throughout this time. At the end of nine months he stood down from the government position and resumed his normal duties.

In November 1950 he and Lillian welcomed her half-brother, Dr Harry Ironside, now 74, and his wife on what was his first visit to New Zealand. It was a long-overdue trip and while they had been to Chicago on numerous occasions, this was the first time Harry had come to New Zealand.

Nor did Robert waste the opportunity and booked the world-renowned Bible teacher into a string of engagements in the new year beginning on February 1 in Hawera and culminating in the annual Ngaruawahia Easter Convention March 22-26. Dr Ironside was well known in Christian circles having published over 100 books and was pastor at one of the most famous churches in America, Moody Memorial in Chicago.

Together they went to the annual camp at Eastern Beach where Robert had organised Harry as the guest speaker. After the camp, as was now tradition, they all headed south for Taupo and the light relief of 'Monte Vista' and 'Piri Pono.' Several days after arriving, Harry developed chest pains. These were soon diagnosed as bronchitis but when they continued Robert decided it best to seek a second opinion and drove him over to Rotorua on Saturday January 13.

On Sunday morning they attended the local Brethren assembly in the city but by the afternoon Harry's condition had worsened, and he was admitted into Rotorua Hospital where it became clear he was suffering from a heart condition. After bidding his fellow travellers goodnight he went to sleep but did not wake again, dying in the early hours of Sunday morning. It was a blow for the church, even more so for Lillian who lost the man who had raised her like a father. He was buried near the Laidlaw plot at Purewa Cemetery in Auckland. That year Robert continued to speak at gatherings up and down the country.[4]

In 1952 he and Lillian left for another overseas tour, travelling again to America and Europe. Where beforhand he would have filled such a trip mostly with business engagements, now he filled it with gospel meetings. In England they went up to the Keswick conference where he had spoken so powerfully during the war. After touring Europe they flew to New York where, after a short stay, Robert headed for Detroit and straight for a Billy Graham gospel meeting. From there Robert and Lillian continued across America.[5]

In November they finished their tour in San Francisco, and on the 16th returned to New Zealand by BCPA airliner. While it had been predominantly a preaching trip, Robert still had a keen eye for developments in the business world and picked up on events that were to prove completely accurate. In Europe he was especially taken with how strong the West German and Japanese economies had grown and expressed his fears of trade competition.

"With low wages," he said, "seven and a half pence an hour compared to two shillings seven pence an hour in Britain, and brand new equipment in the textile trade, Japanese competition is only getting underway. Much of Britain's equipment was out of date. "West Germany," he added, "is getting into its stride in one of the most spectacular recoveries of all time, especially in the engineering and metal trades. Last year its exports were nearly double those of 1950, and in Bonn it is hoped that this year there will be a proportionate increase. Thus British engineering can look for similar competition to that which affected her textile trade."[6]

Back in New Zealand he resumed his yearly commitments. He had started a charitable trust in 1946 named Bethesda, meaning House of Mercy. Establishing its capital with Farmers shares, he used it for supporting Christian and charitable work in New Zealand. Before the war he had been giving 50% of his income away. He had now increased this to 90%.

As much as he was concerned with preaching, he was also concerned with the practical ramifications of undertaking Christian work. He purchased a fleet of half a dozen small cars for missionaries who came home to Auckland on furlough. He had them serviced at the Farmers garage and they soon proved so popular he found they didn't need garaging because they were always on the road. Meanwhile *The Reason Why* had been translated into 30 different languages and was being used all over the world. Over 16 million copies had gone out and there was a regular stream of correspondence from friend and stranger alike.

18

MANAGEMENT AND MEN

1953-1960

"Any business is, in large measure, the elongated shadow of one man. In a small business the contact is immediate. In a large one it must be through delegated authority. But the impetus to success never rises up from the bottom; it trickles down from the top. It's here that some quite able men fail."[1]

Robert Laidlaw, 1955.

As a keen Rotarian Robert had been occupied for many years in different civic projects. In 1953 he gifted a large floral clock 18ft wide to Auckland City, in honour of the Queen's impending visit in December that year. He had it manufactured in London and shipped out where it was installed in the Albert Park opposite Auckland University.

In August that year he was invited by the New Zealand Institute of Management to speak at a management conference being held at Auckland University. The Institute was only eight years old, but had already attracted large numbers of executives as the topic of 'management' increased in popularity all over the industrial world. It had been close to Robert's heart for decades, and when he arrived the lecture hall was packed with hundreds of businessmen waiting anxiously to hear what this master business builder would tell them. After a short introduction he walked briskly to the lectern and placed his notes in front of him.

"Mr chairman, gentlemen," he said looking round the room, "When I received Mr Don's letter asking me to speak at this conference, all the world was agog over Hillary and Tensing's conquest of Everest, but as the tumult and the shouting died down, it became evident from Sir Edmund's own statements, and from the many thoughtful articles which appeared, that behind it all lay competent management. From the selection of the men and equipment in London, to the click of the camera on the summit, the most efficient management characterised the whole expedition and crowned its efforts with success."

He then recounted his own recollections of Everest: "Some years ago," he said, "while visiting Darjeeling, 8000ft up the Himalayas, I rose at midnight and rode to the top of Tiger Hill to see the sun rise on Everest. And that impressed on my mind an account I read of the 1924 expedition in which Mallory and Irvine lost their lives in the final dash. One of the members, on returning to London, was giving a lecture on his experiences. Behind him on the stage was a huge picture of Everest, and as he reached his peroration he turned, and apostrophising the mountain said, 'We tried to climb you once, you defeated us. We have made a second attempt; again you are the victor; but we shall yet defeat you, because you cannot grow bigger, but we can.'

"And that is why," continued Robert, " the whole world has been thrilled by Hillary's triumph over insuperable difficulties. Let us draw inspiration from his accomplishment as we consider the growing problems that confront management in these times of political, economic and international chaos, and remind ourselves that 'Easy Street' never yet produced a really competent businessman. It takes storm and calm, shadow and sunshine, winter and summer, to produce an oak with roots deep set, and knarled trunk, a noble tree – a work of God.

"Let us now turn to the consideration of the three basic links between nature's bounty and the consuming public, primary production, secondary industry and distribution. While it is obvious that the primary producer would pile up supplies if there was no manufacturer, and the manufacturer would do the same if there were no means of distribution to the consumer; and while in an inverse ratio, the distributor would be helpless without the manufacturer, and the manufacturer without the primary producer, yet, strangely enough each of the three tends to look upon the others as competitors, rather than cooperators.

"Why is this? Well, all three are dependent on the same spending power of the consumer, and they feel they are not getting their full share of what the consumer finally pays for the finished product. For instance, the sheep farmer gets five shillings per pound for his wool, and three pounds goes into a finished suit, plus three pounds lost in scouring and processing. Say £6 altogether at five shillings each making 30 shillings. Yet the retailer demands from £15 to £20 for a suit, and the consumer generally takes his stand with the primary producer, and looks on both manufacturer and distributor as a species of parasite.

"And the manufacturer who makes 30 shillings worth of wool into three yards of worsted at 50 shillings per yard, £7/10, feels the same about the retailer who makes up the material and sells the finished suit for £20. Now the test, as to whether the manufacturer, and retailer, are an economic advantage to the consumer or not, can be readily applied. Supposing the consumer spun the wool, wove his cloth and made up his own suit, and did the same with all his other requirements, would his standard of living be lifted or lowered?

"The question need only be asked to be answered. Eliminate the manufacturer and distributor, and the great majority of the goods we are familiar with such as sewing machines, cycles, watches, refrigerators, motor cars, household furnishing, kitchen gadgets etc. would disappear completely. So, we can fairly claim that modern industry and commerce, are an economic advantage to consumers, supplying them with quantity, quality, variety and value, infinitely greater than they could obtain by the use of their own individual time and talent, expended on the raw material.

"But as the consumers are also the producers, for everyone gainfully occupied is producing goods and services in the final analysis, all that is available to anyone to consume, is exactly the total that everyone produces, no more, no less. How is it then, that if we work for everybody else, we can all have more goods than if we each worked exclusively for ourselves? The answer is simple.

"Specialisation makes possible mass production. For instance, thousands of men specialising in the production of motor cars can work together in a suitably constructed building, equipped with highly technical machinery, with many horsepower per man available. And it is right here that management comes into the picture. The more the men and the bigger the factory, without direction the greater the chaos, but with efficient management the greater the quality and quantity of output.

"I was reading in a recent issue of Fortune the biography of Walter P. Chrysler, which gave an account of the difficulties the Maxwell Motor Car Co. got into through bad management. The Directors offered the management to Chrysler, and he accepted on condition that they paid him a salary of $1,000,000 per annum, which equals £360,000 sterling. They agreed, and with the same factory, workmen and machinery he had the company on its feet in a year or so. This proves by the way that a good manager earns more than he gets, because on him depends the company's capacity to pay wages to its staff, and dividends to its shareholders as well as a salary to himself.

"Moreover, the need for efficient management will become increasingly urgent, as a simple analysis of present trends clearly shows. The *Intelligence Digest* of November last year gives the world's daily births as 233,000; deaths as 170,000; leaving an increase of 63,000. Which works out as an annual increase in population of 22,950,000.

"This means that the population of the United States, 160 million is being added to the world every seven years. If this multitude was segregated in one country, it would astound us that such a vast population had to be fed, housed and supplied with goods every seven years. Or, view it from another angle: this 1% increase per annum in population compounded, means that the world's population will double in the next 70 years.

"Instead of 2.3 billion, we shall have 4.6 billion, and it will only be by efficient management of soil, of industry, and of commerce and by the altruistic management of the wealth of the richest nations that so many people can possibly be fed and supplied with the necessities of life, on the available cultivated land, and from the estimated raw materials known to exist.

"So you see, scientific management has literally got to make two blades of grass grow where one grew before. But there is another complication I want to call your attention to. The rising cost of goods and services, or viewed from another angle, the steady depreciation of our money. Recently Mr R.A. Butler, the Chancellor of the Exchequer, put figures before the House of Commons showing that since 1938, taking the pound sterling as worth 20 shillings at that date, it had steadily declined in value each year so that at the end of 1952, that is in 14 years, it was worth only eight shillings.

"Feeling that probably the younger men here don't realise how rapid the rise in prices has been, I have taken a few items from our sixth catalogue issued in 1915. Garden rakes cost 11 pence, lawn mowers – 18/11, Swiss watches – 2/11, a tent six by eight – 12/3; three piece suits – 23/7, and lastly everything to build a four-roomed house, timber plumbing, roofing iron, range, tanks, paint, everything except labour, total cost £135/15/8.

"In those days Britain had a worldwide reputation for price and quality, but note the problem rising costs are creating today for the Motherland, on which we are so dependent for our prosperity. Shortly after I arrived in Britain in May last year, the Incorporated Sales Managers Association held its annual conference, and some straight things were said by these men who mean so much to the export business of the UK.

"During the discussion on rising costs Mr Cyril Osborne MP asked: 'How can we expect the natives of West Africa to pay 6/4 per yard for textiles made in the UK, when comparable materials from Japan can be purchased for 1/9 per yard. On what basis could the African be expected to depress his already low standard of living to support a high standard in Britain?'

"The average textile wage in the UK is 2/7 per hour, in Japan it is seven and a half pence, and Japanese competition is only starting as only six million spindles were operating last year as against 13 million pre-war. And all Japanese equipment is brand new, whereas much of ours is ancient. In fact 95% of our looms are not automatic, but in USA the direct reverse is the case, 95% of theirs are.

"In England, welfare is based on redistribution of wealth, earned in the past, while America's high standard of living is based on increased production per man hour, and that is made possible by management's willingness to supply new capital equipment, and foster a desire on the part of the men to run it at full capacity. General Motors Corporation, the largest motor car manufacturer in the world have so consistently maintained a 2½% increase in productivity per annum per man hour that they have signed an agreement with their workers unions to advance all wages by this amount annually.

"Two and a half per cent per annum compounded, will double wages in 28 years, yet the wages cost of their product will remain stationary, and if all the ancillary manufacturers supplying the steel, glass and upholstery etc. would do the same, the total cost of their cars would remain unchanged, while wages doubled.

"This surely is a tribute to General Motors' management of its manpower, its capital resources, and its technical skill, and sets a standard that all competent management may well emulate – increasing wages, therefore increasing the purchasing power of the community, without increasing the price of the product to the community, and so ensuring a steady rise in the standard of living, instead of allowing wages and the cost of living to chase each other round in an ever rising spiral.

"I know how easy it is to make excuses," he said kindly. "I'm an expert myself. We say we haven't got the capital for better equipment, or the space for improved layout, or our men would not respond, but the truth is we can too easily take care of rising costs by increasing our prices and still sell our output, so why should we take our problems home on Saturdays and week nights, and keep a torch and notebook by our bedside to jot down ideas that come to us at 2 am which past experience proves will elude us, if we leave them till the morning?

"I devote quite a deal of time to religious work, and know there is a vast difference between preaching as a profession and preaching as a passion, and there is a similar difference between management that is a profession, and management into which the whole personality is thrown with enthusiasm. Don't think it means sacrifice to take one's executive duties seriously; the thrill of accomplishment is multiplied compensation.

"Professor William James, the greatest of our early psychologists, after investigation made an estimate that has never been seriously challenged, that the average man uses 10% of his mental capacity. I suppose executives use 15%, and that is why they are managers." There was a murmur of laughter from the audience as some wondered which of their colleagues used 15%.

"Supposing," continued Robert, "of that 85% lying dormant, we used 35% and so brought 50% of our personal powers to bear on our jobs, what transformations," he exclaimed, "would begin to take place in our factories and businesses, for remember gentlemen, esprit de corps does not bubble up from the bottom, it filters down from the top.

"But let me give you a practical example of what can be done when a competent executive sets out to do it. Thirty-five years ago we were paying 18/6 per dozen to have denim trousers made up. The manager of our own clothing factory who had, before coming to us, been in charge of a large wholesale clothing factory, suggested that we have our denims made outside as on his previous experience they did not pay at 18/6 per dozen.

"Knowing that we wished to use denims as a featured low price line, the manager of our tent and raincoat factory suggested that he experiment with denims. He put two girls to work, explained what he was after , won their cooperation, studied every motion, and at the end of the week he reported that he could substantially reduce the price, and at the end of three weeks he undertook to make up denims at 12/6 per dozen for our clothing department and continued doing so for several years, showing a 10% manufacturing profit for his factory. Here was a 33% cut in manufacturing costs on the standard price changed by all clothing factories in Auckland. I can only assume they didn't know their real costs, or our manager cut out waste motions, or probably the reduction was partly due to both.

"Let us turn for a moment to the two great enemies of efficient management, the cartel, which the Oxford dictionary defines as a manufacturers union to keep up prices, and the monopoly, which in the end yields similar results. Lord Acton says rightly, 'All power corrupts; absolute power corrupts absolutely.' We humans with self-interest so deep seated at the very core of our beings, cannot be entrusted with too much power, whether it be a dictatorship of the right or the left in politics, or of the cartel or monopoly in business.

"For instance, when a cartel is formed, generally speaking, the costs of the most inefficient manufacturers in the group are taken as a basis, and a selling price is fixed so that they can make a profit. And thus the more efficient lie back with so much profit assured that they begin to squander it lest the government investigates the cartel's fixed price.

"A monopoly results in exactly the same thing. Having crushed its competitors, or made sure their raw materials cost so much that their competition is harmless, it either deliberately increases prices to make more profit, or having lost the incentive to reduce costs, it has to raise prices to take care of its decreasing efficiency in management.

"Gentlemen, the basic justification for the capitalist system is competition. I am not speaking of competition from other countries with a much lower standard of living, but of competition inside any given country. Destroy good honest, straightforward competition based on efficient management and we are asking for state control, and the eventual destruction of the very system on which, in my opinion, our own, and the prosperity of the whole community depends.

"Now while it is commonly admitted the manufacturer adds to the value of the raw material he uses, I have heard it said that the distributor adds nothing to the value of the goods he handles. But is this true – take for instance a pound of tea in Ceylon. It is of the same intrinsic value there as a pound of tea in Auckland, yet a pound of tea in Ceylon is of no practical value to a New Zealand housewife who wants to make tea for her family. The primary producer adds to its practical value by picking it, the factory in Auckland by packing it, and the distributor adds to its practical value in exactly the same way by delivering it to Mrs Smith of Mission Bay.

"We have endeavoured to show previously, that an efficiently run merchandising business is not an economic parasite, but an economic necessity, just as essential and valuable a link in the chain as the primary producer and the manufacturer, so it devolves upon the distributor, as well as on the manufacturer by good management, to make his contribution also towards a reduction in the rising cost of living.

"May I define," he said, "an efficiently organised distributing business thus. One that buys quality merchandise keenly, and sells it competitively, and between these two points is so well managed that it pays satisfactory wages to its employees, and reasonable dividends to its shareholders, and yet builds up sufficient reserves to ensure stability and growth; that begets loyalty in its staff, and goodwill among its customers, and functions as a vital organism rather than an organisation. Now there has been a tendency on the part of some distributors to add to their costs a substantial amount of unnecessary expense, costly buildings, luxury fittings, valuable selling space occupied by displays etc., such as one meets within many

American department stores whose working expenses commonly run around 33⅓% with gross profit at 37½%, showing a little over 4% net. These actual figures were given to me by a world-famous department store which I visited in the States last year.

"Compare this with the Farmer's Trading Company's costs of distribution. Last year our gross profit was 20.8%, working expenses were 16.6% and net profit 4.2%. Our American friends could hardly believe it even when I explained that our low-cost buildings were in the cheap land area, our fittings were of the plainest, every foot of floor space was used for intensive selling rather than display, and that our prices were so attractive that we did not need high-priced super sales staff, and that our business was still growing rapidly, and so keeping volume always a jump ahead of expenses. Sales last year were £7,200,000 which represented an increase over the previous year of £900,000.

"The idea that everything must be bigger, better, faster and more luxurious," he said forcefully, "is outstripping the capacity, and the willingness of the public to pay, and leaving a wide-open field for men of courage and imagination. For instance, tourist air travel is rapidly gaining in popularity in America, with no meals or amenities aloft, more crowded seating, and substantially lower fares.

"When the liner *United States*, costing over six million dollars, America's finest ship, with its greater speed and luxury than the *Queen Mary*, entered the Atlantic trade, some said Britain must eclipse it, but Commander King Hall offers an infinitely wiser suggestion. Build he says, a fleet of 20,000 ton 15 knot steamers, (15 knots being the most economical speed), carrying passengers all one class with no meals served, but snack bars at which cheap food may be obtained, and cut luxury liner fares in half, thus tapping the enormous field of potential travellers in the USA who have their roots in Europe, but could never afford to visit their homelands at present excessive prices.

"The ordinary service grocery store has been completely replaced in the USA, by self-service, resulting in a 40% increase in sales from the same floor space. Forceful, and imaginative thinking on the part of management is needed to cut costs by new methods.

"But," he said with a smile, "I can tell you of a way in which costs can be cut, at least in merchandising, without the introduction of any new radical changes, and I have seen it work many times. With 74 branch stores, our half-yearly balance usually shows one in the red, and if this occurs twice a change is made in the management, often with astonishing results. Our store supervisor puts a young man with plenty of enthusiasm in charge. Remember the location is the same, the stock the same, and the same staff, and the cost and selling prices are fixed by head office, and yet sales jump as much as 33⅓%, the store is cleaner, the windows better dressed, the staff is on its toes, the service is quicker and more polite, and in the first year a loss has been turned into a substantial profit.

"Although I would prefer both, if I had to choose between enthusiasm and experience in an executive, I would choose enthusiasm. A man with his experience behind him, and lacking in zeal, can see too many reasons why a thing cannot be done, whereas a younger man with less experience bites off more than he can chew, and chews it successfully and gains quite a lot of experience in the process.

"If every man here," he said pointing to the audience, "returned to his job without having learned anything new, but with 25% more enthusiasm, every subordinate would sense it in 24 hours, and within a week most of the staff would have caught the infection and things would begin to happen. Men don't like dictatorship, but they quickly respond to leadership, which induces me to say, men are much more important in business than merchandise."

Now he got to the heart of what all his experience had taught him over the years. "I was reading recently, "he said, " the story of the J.C. Penny Company of the USA with 1600 drapery stores, and sales of over $1000,000,000. Some years ago Mr Penny wished to raise a considerable sum of money for extension purposes and went direct to the president of one of the large financial institutions, who asked him the usual relevant questions about his real estate, stocks, reserves, sales, net profits etc., and having made careful notes said – 'I will discuss it with my colleagues and give you an answer in 48 hours.'

" 'But,' said Mr Penny,' you have not mentioned our greatest asset of all, our 1600 store managers and their executives. You could burn every Penny store down in a night, but if you left our staff intact we would rise phoenix-like from the ashes, but if you destroyed our staff in a night as well as our stores, J.C. Penny would be destroyed.

"Surely," declared Robert, "the man is more important than the merchandise, not only because he is the greater factor in the economic structure of manufacturing and merchandising, but because he is a man. One hundred years ago, when a ship was lost it was posted at Lloyd's thus – 'The good ship Kent has founded in the Bay of Biscay with 260 souls on board,'" he said emphasising 'souls.'

"But we don't refer to men like that anymore. Today a factory employs so many hundred hands; our only interest seems to centre in what a man can produce of a material nature, not in what he is. An executive who treats his men as he does his machines, on a mechanical instead of a psychological and spiritual basis can never be a really great manager. Forty-two years ago when we had a quite small staff, nine young men were put in charge of various departments, and every Monday morning at 8 am they met in my office, where we openly discussed not only our business policies, but the detailed expenses of every department.

"Every manager, even in those remote days came to see his department as an integral part of a composite whole, which saved them from becoming insular in their thinking, and all through the years, has kept them in the closest touch, with what all the other departments were accomplishing, so that instead of being only department managers, they became merchants with a comprehensive view of the overall problems, and earnestly cooperated to make their full contribution to the success of the whole.

"At the end of every month each manager knew how many weeks stock he had on hand, his wage percentage, his sales quota for the next month, and was urged to make decisions without reference to the General Manager, except in the most important matters, so the growth of our executives kept pace with the growth of our business and vice versa.

"There is no better example of this than Mr Calder Mackay, our general manager, who started with us 43 years ago when he arrived as a lad from Scotland. First of all he was the product of the business, but as I have said, the man is more important than the merchandise, and now the business has become the product of his ability and enthusiasm.

"You may be interested in the objective we had before us in those early days as published in our catalogue three years after we started:

"Our aim, to build the greatest business in New Zealand; to serve the farmers in the best possible manner, with the best possible merchandise; to simplify every detail of every transaction; to absolutely satisfy every customer with every purchase; to eliminate all delays; to sell only goods it will pay our customers to buy; to treat our comrades with kindness, and our competitors with respect; to work as a cooperative whole because all at it, always at it, wins success.

"And at the same time we issued our guarantee which we have honestly endeavoured to live up to through all the intervening years:

"We guarantee absolute satisfaction to every customer in every transaction, no exceptions.

"Most of you I take it, are industrialists, and therefore know how deadly friction can be to a machine. We employ a staff of some 2,150 and know how important harmony is, and that friction can be more destructive among human beings than in machine bearings. However important it may be to eliminate friction lower down, it is imperative that top management maintain harmony of a high order among executives.

"Sir Winston Churchill gives an excellent example in his book, *My Contemporaries*. Writing of Lloyd George, Prime Minister during the First World War he says: 'He did not shine on the public platform; he did not shine on the floor of the House, when compared with the lustre with which he shone in Cabinet meetings. I have seen him handle a war Cabinet when half the members were opposed to his proposition and at the end of forty minutes get a unanimous vote in favour of it with each one feeling he had made a considerable contribution towards it being carried.'

"'Lloyd George,' says Mr Churchill, 'was never interested in the effect of what he said on himself, but only in the effect of what he said on the man to whom he said it. He never tried to make a point, at the expense of the man whose support he was trying to win.' In this surely is a lesson for all of us. It is that same rare ability which General Eisenhower had of welding into the army, the air force, and the navy of both Britain and the USA during the war, and later the self-interested members of NATO, that has put him at the head of the most powerful nation in the world today. It is obvious that to be able to harmonise a board of directors, an executive meeting, or an employer-employee relationship, is one of the most valuable qualities a manager can possess or cultivate."

As he reached the end of his speech he drew things to a close, "Let me conclude on the same note on which we commenced – Everest cannot grow bigger, but we can. Never," he said thoughtfully, "shall I forget the dark days we experienced in Britain after Dunkirk, when we had 12 tanks, 50 guns and not enough rifles to arm one division.

"When we were advised to fill beer bottles with benzine and throw them at German tanks if a landing was effected; when we were bombed in London 90 nights out of 92 from September to December 1940, when our men were drilling with broom sticks and later on with 4ft lengths of steel tube with an 8 inch dirk welded on to one end; when we lived in nightly expectation of an attempted invasion; there stood out a man who couldn't get out of third form at Harrow, who failed twice to pass a simple entrance exam to Sandhurst, but who thereafter never ceased to grow, and at the age of 64, in Britain's greatest crisis, inspired 50 million people to stand resolute against the armed might of the Axis powers, and led them through to final victory. Winston Churchill, all through those terrible years, was the living embodiment of Browning's lines:

'One who never turned his back,
But marched breast forward;
Never doubted clouds would break,
Never dreamed though right were worsted,
Wrong would triumph;
Held we fall to rise,
Are baffled to fight better,
Sleep to wake.'

"He proved himself the hero of dauntless faith. And what was equally important, he transmitted that faith to the whole nation. Yet I doubt there is a man in this building who was so backward in his youth as Sir Winston. What possibilities, therefore, lie before everyone here, of completely eclipsing his business stature of the past, and fitting himself to face successfully whatever crises the future holds, for the call is still –

'Give us men to match the mountains
Who have risen from the plains
Men with empire in their purpose,
Men of throbbing, conquering brains.'"

With that he closed and the hall broke into spontaneous applause as row after row of men rose to their feet. The atmosphere was electric – all around the room men's hearts had been lifted and their gratitude was deafening. The conference had heard nothing like it. Robert calmly bundled his papers and walked back to his seat.[2]

In January 1955, his work for public welfare was given official recognition when he was awarded the C.B.E. in the New Year's honours for his contributions to the public welfare and philanthropic work. In March of 1946, nine years previously, he had been awarded the M.B.E. for his work in England among the troops. In the rush of life he also found time for more relaxing pursuits and played the occasional round of golf with his son Lincoln. He had taken it up in the war in England and it, too, was not removed from his eye for precision. While his son could drive the ball further, Robert could hit it straighter.

Packing the car up in the May school holidays that year Robert and Lillian made the traditional pilgrimage to Monte Vista at Taupo. As the house could sleep 16, once again they invited a large group of friends from different parts in the country to join them at the lake. Robert's boat excursions and picnics were always a highlight and Piri Pono with the advantage of size could pack in about 20 passengers.

On Saturday afternoon, although a brisk winter's day the lake was relatively calm and Robert decided to take his party of guests on a trip to a secluded bay past Acacia Point. It would only be a short jaunt but he was eager as always to be at the helm of Piri Pono. The big launch roared mightily as he put his hand to the throttle and warmed her up for the trip.

During the Second World War the Air Force had commandeered her and replaced the boat's original engine with a Chrysler, but Robert found it disappointingly slow. He had had it pulled out and had two GM motors fitted. Now, with double the horsepower, he intended to give his guests a taste of what it felt like to be in a very fast boat. Eventually 23 passengers were squeezed on board and Robert gunned Piri Pono into life racing out of Two Mile Bay. She bounced obediently over the surface with spray billowing out from the hull.

Those fortunate to be huddled close to the captain remained dry, those enjoying the views from the stern received a drenching. Within a short time the bay came into view. He had been here many times before, a favourite trip for quick outings in the boat. There was a large rocky outcrop in the middle of the bay and he often scooted Piri Pono between this and the shoreline at speed. It was a great thrill. Lining her up for the approach he accelerated towards the gap. He edged closer and closer and then, crash. The boat shook with a tremendous thud and wheeled around on its nose. Bits of wood and propeller flew out behind in the wake.

Robert looked around at his shocked guests. This was not part of the show. He did his best to calm everyone down but it was obviously only a matter of time before Piri Pono sank. The bottom of her hull had been torn out. To make it worse the average age of his assembled company was like his own ... almost 70, and many of the women were in fur coats. They would certainly suffer hypothermia if in the water for any length of time.

Taking immediate charge he fearlessly pushed his housekeeper and a schoolboy into the icy water with the anchor rope and orders to swim. The pair reached the shoreline about 30 metres away and slowly pulled the listing boat over. All the party managed to scramble safely ashore just as the bow of Piri Pono disappeared beneath the surface to the bottom of the lake. Fortunately a passing launch had seen their plight and they were soon rescued and ferried back to Monte Vista.

Robert quickly swung a salvage operation into action and two local launches were organised to go out and refloat Piri Pono and bring her back to the boat harbour. There was only one hitch in the plan. The only time the local launchmen could go to rescue the boat was the next morning. Robert agreed owing to the expediency of the situation but as it was Sunday and it would clash with the local church service he could not see his way clear to go. The next morning as the Laidlaws went to church the salvage crews headed off. All through church Robert's mind wandered. What was happening to his boat?

As soon as the closing hymn was over the family were bundled in the car with unusual urgency and sped back home to Monte Vista. He screeched to a halt outside the house.

"Goodbye everyone," he yelled as he hurried to the boat shed. Within a few seconds the familiar "put put" of a Seagull motor was heard and Robert emerged into view waving to the party as he went by in his eight-foot dinghy. Further across the lake the salvage operation had gone well and Piri Pono was strapped between the two launches as the crews made the slow trip home. The captain at the helm of one of the launches looked up. There, in his path was a small boat bearing down on them. He wiped the screen of the cabin to get a better look. He had never seen anything like it. An elderly gentleman wearing a hat and a dark three piece suit was excitedly waving them down. Moments later a very pleased Robert was aboard and again reunited with his beloved boat.[3]

Since returning to New Zealand, of all the activities he was involved in the dearest to his heart was the Bible Training Institute. He had seen it grow year after year since those fledgling beginnings in 1921. Recently demand for courses had been increasing steadily and a new property was sought that might be able to house 150-200 students with at least 15 acres of land and room for tennis courts, fruit trees, and playing fields.

Very quickly Robert was out on the road with other directors of the institute looking for suitable sites. Several possible properties were turned down simply because, after questioning the owners, Robert felt that they were not decisive enough. Finally they found a suitable location and on October 9 1957, Robert and a group of directors assembled on an elevated 19 and a half acre site in Henderson on the outskirts of the city of Auckland, 11 miles from the CPO. The land, an orchard, had been purchased for £8000 including tractor and implements, and 411 Queen Street was then sold to the Salvation Army which already had a lease on an existing building over the road, using it for cheap accommodation.[4]

The agreement with the Salvation Army had been quite amicable. A mutually agreed price was accepted, and BTI was allowed the use of its premises until it had built its new building in Henderson. It would be a large undertaking and the cost of the new buildings was estimated at £160,000. The sale of the Queen Street property brought in just over one third of the total cost so the Institute was looking expectantly for donations to make up the balance. Robert got the project off to an impressive start giving £10,000 and paying the architect's fees (another £5000). After a year of planning, building began on January 12 1959.

In December that year the Principal of Bible Training Institute, John Deane, with whom Robert had worked closely since his appointment in 1946, left Auckland with his family. He, his wife, daughter and two grandsons went by car to deliver Christmas presents to family in Te Awamutu before John was scheduled to fly out to Australia for a conference. Leaving just before noon the party got as far as Huntly when their vehicle slammed head on into a parked truck. Help soon arrived at the crash scene and the casualties were taken to Waikato Hospital. Grace, John Deane's daughter died shortly after arrival and John Deane himself a few hours later. Neither had recovered consciousness. His wife and one grandson, David, remained in a critical condition.

Family rushed to the hospital from various parts of the North Island, but throughout the next two days Mrs Deane and David showed little sign of improvement. The funeral for John Deane and his daughter was scheduled for Wednesday in Auckland and in the morning the family left for the trip back. Only a few minutes after they left, little David died. In Auckland the mourners had already begun to gather when an official from the church stood up and announced that word had come through from Hamilton that David had died and the service would be delayed. Those sitting in the pews were almost too stunned to react.

Half an hour later the men who were to lead the service came forward and stepped up to the platform. Robert was among them. A local minister and friend of the Deane family opened the service. After he had spoken there was a pause, and from the back of the church the undertaker and his pallbearers moved forward, gently cradling a small white coffin. Slowly they made their way toward the front as friends and family wept openly. Robert was the next scheduled speaker on the programme to speak on behalf of the Institute. He moved to the pulpit and looked down at the three caskets that now lay before him. A hush came over the congregation. Many wondered what words he could possibly say. Without a tear in his eye he lifted his voice to the church.

"Our God is not on trial here today ...   he was tried two thousand years ago and proved that he was love, love that was prepared to sacrifice. We are on trial today and our devotion and trust in the face of this inexplicable thing are being tested."

19

ONWARDS

1960-1971

"A man assumes importance and becomes a power in the world just as soon as it is found that he stands for something; that he is not for sale; that he will not lease his manhood for salary, for any amount of money or for any influence or position; that he will not lend his name to anything which he cannot endorse. The trouble with so many men today is that they do not stand for anything outside their vocation. They may be well educated, well up in their specialties, may have a lot of expert knowledge, but they cannot be depended upon. There is some flaw in them which takes the edge off their virtue. They may be fairly honest, but you cannot bank on them."[1]

Robert Laidlaw, 1969.

1960 was a festive year in more than one way. On Guy Fawkes night Saturday, November 5, emergency services in the city had been particularly busy. The fire department received 47 callouts as homes, garages and acres of bush were all set alight. Robert, as he often did, staged a large fireworks display for friends and family on the lawn outside their Argyle Street home.

The show increased in size dramatically, however, when a party of revellers on the beach set fire to the bank leading up to the house and within minutes the dry grass was a sizeable

307

fire. When the fire crews arrived on the scene the irrepressible Robert quickly had the operation under control, barking out orders to the fire crews and chief on how to best attack the blaze and where to put the hoses. All obeyed without question.

Over the weekend workers had also been busy at the Hobson Street store. From Auckland's Epsom Showgrounds a convoy of trucks brought the most intriguing and largest Santa the country had even seen to the Auckland store. Constructed in fibreglass and weighing over two tons, he stood 79 ft tall. In every way he was a lifelike image of Father Christmas even down to his portly tummy which measured 90 ft around its girth.

It had been a massive operation and Santa was put together in six sections, his finger beckoning shoppers to the country's biggest store. The following weekend the traditional Farmers Christmas parade swung into action with nearly two miles of decorated floats, clowns, storybook characters, accompanied by 16 marching teams and 10 pipe and brass bands. As always there was free parking in the Farmers carpark.

February 18 the following year was the scheduled public opening of the BTI. Over 1700 cars carrying 5000 to 6000 people came from all over. The Transport Department provided five traffic officers to direct traffic, and for an hour and a half before to the proceedings started people poured in to the central courtyard and buildings of the BTI.

Just after 2.15 pm Robert got up on the main platform at the south end of the main lecture room, surrounded by 50 special guests, to begin the meeting. This was a special landmark for him. He had been behind this project since its inception and here he was, 40 years later at the launch of a new era.

In November a sudden temporary occlusion of blood deprived him of the sight of one eye. His body was struggling to keep up with his enthusiasm but not to be held back he continued his usual activities with characteristic fortitude without apparent handicap.[2]

In May 1962, at the age of 77, almost 10 years after he addressed the NZIM management conference he was inv to be the guest speaker at their graduation ceremony at ...e Auckland Town Hall. He encouraged the young management hopefuls by emphasising a number of points which he saw as vitally important in business and was just as magnetic, still as incisive.

"Honesty," he said, "is not the best policy. Honesty is not a policy at all. It is a principle on which the basis of a good life is founded. The next point, is to develop skill in the handling of men, a skill which is the opposite of throwing one's weight around.

"A manager does not need to draw an imaginary line between himself and his men if a real one exists, and woe betide him if he does. The manager who has his department so well organised and his staff so well trained that he can step out of it at any time, and tell his general manager so, is heading for advancement.

"It is a manager's duty," he continued, "to ensure that his merchandise makes a profit and that a satisfactory price is obtained. Profit is the acid test of management. It is because of shallow thinking that the idea has been accepted that a company which makes a good profit must be fleecing the public. A company making poor profits, even losses, is jeopardising the interests of its staff, its suppliers, its shareholders and the state.

"A company that can pay 10 shillings in the pound to the state, have sufficient left to pay a good dividend to its shareholders and still have sufficient to carry forward to ensure future progress is working in the interests of the community in general and the staff and shareholders in particular. Flashes of brilliance," he concluded, "are not a substitute for good, honest, earnest, conscientious attention to the task in hand."[3]

The next month on June 1 1962, Robert and Lillian left Auckland by aircraft on their fifth overseas tour together.[4] As was his usual practice, Robert engaged travel guides at all the new cities they entered and in Moscow he had several interesting discussions with his different guides. Suited western businessmen were not a common sight and while walking round the city his guide who could contain his interest no longer, asked the obvious.

"Are you a capitalist?" he said intrigued to see what this aged business man would say.

"Yes I am," replied Robert.

"Then you must dislike me very much," replied the guide.

"If a capitalist dislikes a man," said Robert, "it is not because of his politics or economics but because of his personality."

"Do you mean to say that I could have a capitalist friend in New Zealand?" inquired the guide.

"Yes," said Robert his face beaming, "and I hope to have a Communist friend in Russia.

"But let me tell you," said Robert, "why I think capitalism is superior to Communism. Butter which costs you 8s a pound cost New Zealanders 2s, and milk, which is 10s a gallon here, is 3s 4d in New Zealand. I am a capitalist because I believe it is better for the working man.

"When my company," he added, "put out a balance sheet the Government took half of the profits for redistribution for the welfare of the people. We divided the remaining half of the profits in half again and one quarter was paid to the shareholders from whom, if they received enough, the Government took 7s in the pound. That left a quarter of the profits to be ploughed back into the business to create more jobs for the workers."

The guide had no response. Here was a man who knew his facts. They arrived back in New Zealand on October 12.

Meanwhile the Institute had opened its own bookroom in Queen Street and purchased a printing firm. As chairman of the Institute Printing and Publishing Society, Robert arranged for the institute press and the BTI Bookroom to to take over the printing and distribution of *The Reason Why*. Until 1961 it had been printed by the Farmers printing department.

One afternoon while at a meeting at the bookroom with two young executives he unexpectedly began to speak about the importance of guidance, and the discussion took a sober turn.

"I want to tell you," he said and paused for a moment, "the tremendous pressure I was put under during the First World War over the ownership of my business Laidlaw Leeds."

It had been a long time since he had told anyone of these events, and the men to whom he was talking had not even been born when they had taken place. The story he recounted of the degree of public criticism he endured and the allegations that his money had saved him going to war, was still painful to him.

He told them of the *Truth* newspaper campaign to find a buyer for his business and turn it into a public company. He told them of the eventual sale to the Farmers Union, and the sudden death of his brother Arthur.

"You know," he said as tears started to come to his eyes, "the sale of my business was the greatest mistake I ever made."

The room was silent.

"I prayed to God and said 'Lord, if you don't show me by Friday afternoon I'm going to sell Laidlaw Leeds to the Farmers.' I now realise the mistake I made. I asked God to guide me by a negative rather than a positive action. My prayer should have been 'God unless you show me by Friday, I'm not going to do it.'"

His eyes met those of his two young friends.

"I deeply regret the decision I made that day," he said shaking his head, "when I think of the amount of money that could have been made available to Christian ministries and missions if I hadn't sold out. It is vital to hear from God in making life's major decisions, and I never heard from Him to sell my company."

In July 1965 a large gathering of family and friends packed into Howe Street Chapel for Robert and Lillian's golden wedding. Towards the end of the night's entertainment Robert got up to address the group:

"Well my dear friends," he said, "though my wife has sought to thank you I want to add a word of thanks too. We thank all those who have contributed to tonight's programme and for the kind things, undeserved, they have said."

He then traced his birth in Scotland and how the family came to New Zealand. Eventually he got to the subject of his engagement to Lillian:

"When my mother was in England, I had the job of opening her mail. And one day I happened to open this letter from Lillian in America, so I wrote back telling her my mother was in England and that I would send the letter on. Well," said Robert shrugging his shoulders, "that started a correspondence, and we wrote to each other for four years.

"And I was desperately anxious to know," he said pacing himself, "if she had any boyfriends. So I tried in subtle and devious ways to say things that might make her tell me, but she never let on whether she was, or wasn't interested in anybody.

"But there was an Exhibition coming on in San Francisco – a world fair. And Lillian sent me some pictures and pamphlets put out about it – I suppose hoping that I might be thinking of coming over. It was 1915, and World War One had been running a year, and I don't know whether it was war worries or not but I got shingles and went to see my doctor. 'Oh,' he says, 'you need a sea voyage.' So there you are I thought – a sea voyage, see Lillian and see the world fair. What more guidance could I want!'"

The room broke into bouts of laughter. Lillian couldn't conceal her smile.

"So I went to San Francisco," continued Robert, "And on the fourteenth night after arriving she said to me, 'what about going for a walk in the park?' And quite close to where she lived was a beautiful park.

"And it was," said Robert screwing up his face mischievously, "a combination of adverse circumstances. It was a full moon, a balmy Californian evening, perfectly still and quiet. There wasn't another soul in the park as far as I was concerned. And we sat down on a seat in the centre of the park next to a sundial.

"Now I don't know what I said," said Robert shaking his head, " but she said, 'certainly, I do, but you'll have to get my brother's permission first!' "

Robert held the room in hysterics as he recounted the rest of the tale.

"And now 50 years have passed," he reflected, "And what variety of warp and woof the master weaver has woven into the fabric of our lives. He has given us a delightful daughter and two fine sons. I rejoice tonight that we are a loving, integrated, understanding family in sweet blessed fellowship with each other.

"I can only say that God has filled our cup to overflowing and I bless Him for it. Unfortunately at our Silver Wedding we were separated. I was in London for five and a half years and it was impossible for us to celebrate this occasion. So we are doubly grateful to the Lord that we are able to celebrate our Golden Wedding.

"And I was wondering," he said reaching into his jacket pocket, "how in some simple and yet sincere form I could express my gratitude to her and mark this important occasion, this golden wedding? And I thought now when anyone does a courageous or a meritorious act, what do you give him? Well we present them with a gold medal, so I had Charlie Morris, manager of our jewellery department, take me to the best medal maker in Auckland, and I had him fashion a gold medal and this is what is on it."

Opening the little box the hall lights caught the sparkle of solid gold.

"Golden Wedding Medal," he read putting his glasses on, "awarded to LVL in acknowledgment of 50 years loving and gracious care of RAL 26/7/15 to 26/7/65. Now," concluded Robert, "if she would like to step up I'll pin the medal on her."

Lillian came forward to a hearty round of applause and RAL pinned it on his gracious wife and kissed her.

"It's all right for the bridegroom to kiss the bride on a wedding day," he whispered.

A few days later he was admitted to hospital for major surgery suffering from a lower aortic aneurism. It was caught before it ruptured but he was in hospital for several weeks and a plastic tube was inserted in the artery. The heart trouble he had suffered in 1925 had never left him. He had never been able to undertake strenuous exercise, but now this was more serious.

A month later, in September, he celebrated his 80th birthday and the Farmers wanted to mark the occasion with a special gift to their founder. Bill Mackay, who had carried on as general manager since the war, contacted Lincoln, Robert's son. They wanted to buy him a car and Mackay made it clear that they would get him whatever he wanted. A very fast Jaguar was felt most characteristic.

On Wednesday night, September 8 1965, he was brought down to the Farmers. Escorted up to the second floor, he was guided by management and friends over the sky bridge connecting the main building and the carpark. As he walked into the darkness of the carpark, suddenly brilliant lighting flooded the floor and there in front of him was a shiny black Mark 10, 4.2 litre automatic Jaguar.

Robert was speechless. It was a complete surprise and a cheer erupted from over 100 former staff and senior management waiting in the shadows. Many had served him faithfully for decades and his delight was obvious as he slid into the leather upholstery, gripping the wheel firmly. There was a round of speeches and, as usual, he still managed a suitable impromptu reply.

In 1968 he celebrated his 83rd birthday, yet since his operation he had made fewer and fewer public addresses.[5] He gave his final radio broadcast on February 25, and in April at a luncheon gave what was his last address to his beloved Bible Training Institute; in 1965 he had stepped down as president.

His health could no longer sustain the demands of public life. He and Lillian still entertained visitors in the home, and Robert went for daily walks around the neighbourhood with his new companion, a walking stick. Under pressure from some of his friends he put pen to paper and in 1969 produced a short autobiography, *The Story of The Reason Why*.

Professor Blaiklock read the draft and wrote the foreword. He had been instrumental in getting Robert to undertake the task, and had finally convinced him despite his reluctance to put his own name forward. He also officially retired as a director of the Farmers at the October meeting in 1969. In response the board granted him the title 'Founder Director' and he was free to attend any of the meetings. But it was the last time he went.

All through 1970 he grew more and more unwell. He suffered several strokes and his condition deteriorated, largely restricting him to bed. He attended his last elders' meeting at church on Saturday, April 4, 1970, and during the year sold the family holiday home 'Monte Vista' at Taupo and distributed the proceeds among the family. He was no longer able to make the trip and his beloved Piri Pono had been sitting idle for some time in the boatshed waiting for her master to return. Her brightly polished hull was now covered with a fine sprinkling of dust.

In the afternoon on Friday, July 10, 1970, Lincoln picked him up from Argyle Street and together they went to Hobson Street. The Farmers Trading Company was to buy his South Island department chain, Calder Mackay Company, and although bedridden he was the largest shareholder in Calder Mackay and wanted to make it clear he was of sound mind and body when the decisions were made.

He and Lincoln pulled up outside the despatch department at the rear of the Farmers building. Together they took the lift to the boardroom on the top floor. It had been nine months since his fellow directors had seen him, and a handful were there as well as his faithful solicitor, Joe Johnston, and Bill Mackay. After a brief greeting, he bent down and signed the sale documents. The Farmers was now the biggest department store chain in the country. Lincoln drove him home.

The last of his official commitments he had held tenaciously was the BTI. He was no longer the president of the Institute but still attended both the board meetings of his beloved Bible College, and its associated Institute Printing and Publishing Society. He attended his last meeting on the December 9, 1970, but could no longer find the strength to continue. Sadly he wrote to them both indicating that he would not be able to attend any further meetings of the board.

On Saturday, March 6, 1971, three months later, his church held its annual Sunday School picnic at Wenderholm Park north of Auckland. Though Robert was physically weak he convinced Lillian and the nurses that he be allowed to go.

As they got his things ready he turned towards his helpers.

"I wonder if you would take a letter for me?"

"Certainly Mr Laidlaw," replied the nurse and got a pen and paper.

The Bible Training Institute on receiving his letter of resignation had written back releasing him from all business matters but would remember him as President Emeritus. They had written in some detail expressing their gratitude and appreciation of all his efforts. He held their letter in his hand.

"It's to the Board of Directors, BTI."

He spoke slowly but thoughtfully.

" ... I look back," he said, "with deep gratitude to God for all He has wrought through BTI and my earnest prayer is that He will bless it in the future as He has done over the last 50 years.

"With my warmest Christian regards to the Board and Staff,

His assistant typed up the letter and brought it over for him to sign as the nurses finished getting him dressed.

Robert slowly picked up a pen and brought it to the paper. He went to make the movements but they wouldn't come. His signature was barely legible and the pen slipped over the page. Robert sensed their embarrassment.

"You know," he said with a schoolboy grin on his face, "I'm always speaking to everybody else about death and dying, but I never seem to have time to get around to it myself." His quip broke the tension.

His eldest son John drove him out to the picnic and as soon as he arrived a large company of admirers crowded round the gleaming black Jaguar, eager to see him. Sitting in the car he joined in the conversation though his voice laboured. The heat was intense and he gratefully accepted an icecream. Not long afterwards, feeling unwell, he turned to John.

"Let's go home," he said. Bidding goodbye to the revellers they left and headed back to Auckland. As the Auckland Harbour Bridge approached Robert looked across to the city. There on the skyline was his Hobson Street store. On the rooftop its bold red neon sign flashed like a beacon over the city.

The plastered walls held a lifetime of memories. As the car pulled off the bridge and headed up towards Argyle Street it slipped silently from view and Robert went home to bed. Over the next week he deteriorated further and lapsed in and out of consciousness. Bronchial pneumonia set in and at times he required oxygen. Many of his old friends from the Farmers and BTI came in to see him, but largely he was too weak to respond. His eye movements gave out what interest he could muster.

The Institute was now in its jubilee year, and had just published its history. Robert was the only original director who lived to see it. Every day the housekeeper went into his room, and even if he wasn't conscious she sat by his bed and read him portions from the Bible. Friday dawned and the family came in and out all day. Late in the afternoon the nurse standing next to him reached down and felt his wrist for a pulse. It was faint, then without warning stopped. Robert was gone.

The funeral was held a few days later at Mt Albert War Memorial Hall. One thousand two hundred people filled the building and spilled out onto the hastily erected overflow seating outside. Mourners stood looking in through the large plateglass windows. His old BTI colleague and friend Professor Blaiklock, walked across the platform past the rows and rows of flowers that filled the stage, and stood behind the microphone. He had known Robert since 1927 when he first began giving lectures at the BTI, and had worked with him as a fellow director since 1938. Blaiklock spoke at length about his friend and then concluded:

"Since the day in Dunedin, nearly 70 years ago, when Robert Laidlaw became a Christian, he never failed to demonstrate in his life the faith he never feared to avow. As few other men, he devoted his life to making known to others the truth that he had discovered. He made it known with infectious ardour. His *Reason Why* in which he set out with logic and a businessman's precision his strong convictions, is the best-known of all tracts. It exists in 16 million copies. It is in 30 languages. I have it in half a dozen languages – 'Le Porquoi, Der Grand Weshalb,' Blaiklock stopped himself.

"But I am in danger of exceeding any mandate our friend might give me. Death has done to him all that death can do. It has silenced an eager voice; it has removed a loved familiar presence. We are left a little the less for his passing, perhaps feeling the press of the battle a little more heavy on our shields, but he would not have it thus. He would not wish us to grieve unduly. He would, I am sure, quote a mystic word of Christ's: 'Unless a corn of wheat fall into the ground and die it abides alone, but if it die it brings forth much fruit.'

"In the bush behind my own house is a fallen tree. It is a puriri which fell when the pioneers ravaged the hills for timber a century ago. It fell but poured its life into every branch which stood skywards out of the prostrate trunk, and several puriris reach with vigour to the light. That is what he would wish, that his death should have significance, as his life always had, significance in new life rising from his.

"Your very presence here is a demonstration of your regard, a strong tribute to the Christian man we knew. If he could dictate my last words I know what he would bid me say. He would commend his Lord and beg those who paid him the honour of their last respects look to the meaning which he so richly found in life, and to the Person who so dominated his mind, and heart, his speech, his conduct."

The overflowing crowd listened attentively to the Professor's eloquent tribute. Then one of Robert's colleagues got up to pray, and some were moved to tears. One friend had appealed to the intellect, the other had touched the heart. Robert had been doing both all his life.

In 1913, with business prospering and his staff growing, Robert Laidlaw wrote a small booklet in which he set out to explain to his employees his reasons for being a Christian. Printed in 1914, this clear, no-nonsense account of his faith quickly found a greater audience and Laidlaw had more copies printed in response to many requests.

The word kept spreading and, by the middle of the 20th century his little booklet had become the best-known and most widely read gospel tract in the world. At the time of his death in 1971, more than 16 million copies had been printed in 30 languages; by 1987, this figure had grown to well over 33 million. It is still being printed today in the hundreds of thousands. Here, unedited, is what he wrote.

The Reason Why

By
Robert A. Laidlaw

Written by a Christian businessman to the members of his staff ...

Suppose that a young man sent his fiance a diamond ring costing him $1000, placing it in a little case which the jeweller threw in for nothing. How disappointed he would be, if upon meeting her a few days later, she would say, "Sweetheart, that was a lovely little box you sent me. To take special care of it, I promise to keep it wrapped up in a safe place so that no harm shall come to it."

Rather ridiculous, isn't it? Yet it is just as foolish for men and women to be spending all their time and thought on their bodies, which are only cases containing the real self, the soul, which, the Bible tells us, will persist long after our bodies have crumbled to dust. The soul is of infinite value. Longfellow expressed it this way:

Tell me not in mournful numbers,
Life is but an empty dream,
For the soul is dead that slumbers,
And things are not what they seem.
Life is real, life is earnest,
and the grave is not its goal.
Dust thou art, to dust returnest,
Was not spoken of the soul.

Indeed this statement was not made of the soul, for in Mark 8:36 our Lord Himself asks, "What shall it profit a man if he gain the whole world and lose his own soul?" So, in Christ's estimate, man's soul is something incomparably more valuable than the whole world.

I would like to discuss with you some of the basic things that relate to your most valuable possession, your soul. For instance:—

Is there a God?
Is the Bible true?
Is man accountable?
Is there divine forgiveness?

These are some of the problems which most perplex those who think seriously about the future.

How may I know there is a God?

I have an innate conviction that God exists. No matter how my intellect has tried, in the past, to produce reasons proving He was not, or how much I have wanted to believe that there was no God, that "still, small voice" came to me again and again, just as it has come to you, in the quiet of life's more sober moments. Yes, I knew that at least for me there was a God. And as I looked at others I realised how many were looking for God, seeking in "religion" to silence that same voice that spoke within me.

True there are some men who don't believe in God. But to me the problems of unbelief in God are greater than the problems of belief. To believe that unaided dead matter produced mind, that mind produced conscience, and that the chaos of chance produced the cosmos of order as we see it in nature, seems to call not for faith but for credulity.

The president of the New York Scientific Society once gave eight reasons why he believed there was a God. The first was this: Take ten identical coins and mark them one to ten. Place them in your pocket.

Now take one out. There is one chance in ten that you will get number one. Now replace it, and the chances that number two will follow number one are not one in ten, but one in one hundred. With each new coin taken out, the risk will be multiplied by ten, so that the chance of ten following nine, is one in 10,000,000,000 (ten billion). It seemed so unbelievable to me that I immediately took pencil and paper and very quickly discovered he was right. Try it yourself.

That is why George Gallup, the American statistician says: "I could prove God statistically. Take the human body alone—the chance that all its functions would just happen is a statistical monstrosity."

Surely no thoughtful persons would wish to base their eternal future on a "statistical monstrosity." Perhaps that is why the Bible says in Psalm 14:1 "The fool hath said in his heart there is no God." But let us consider the problem from another viewpoint.

Suppose we are standing at an airport watching a big jet come in for a landing. I say to you, "A lot of people think that plane is the result of someone's carefully designed plans, but I know better. There was really no intelligence at work on it at all. In some strange way the metal just came out of the ground, and fashioned itself into flat sheets. And then these metal sheets slowly began to grow together and formed the body and wings and tail. Then after a long while the engines slowly grew in place, and one day some people came along and discovered the plane, all finished and ready to fly."

You would probably consider me a lunatic and move further into the crowd to escape my senseless chatter. Why? You know that where there is a design there must be a designer, and having seen other productions of the human mind just like the plane in question, you are positive that it was planned by human intelligence and built by human skill.

Yet there are highly educated, professional men who tell us that the entire universe came into being by chance, that there was really no higher intelligence at work on it. They claim to know no God but nature.

On the other hand there are many thoughtful men who believe that God is transcendent: that is, while He reveals Himself in nature (in that its laws and principles are expressions of His power and wisdom), He Himself is greater than the universe. But all that atheists can offer us is the riddle of design without a designer, of creation without a Creator, of effect without cause.

Every thoughtful person believes in a series of causes and effects in nature, each effect becoming the cause of some other effect.

The acceptance of this as fact logically compels one to admit that there must be a beginning to any series. There could never have been a first effect if there had not been a First Cause. This First Cause to me is Deity.

Although man has discovered many of the laws that govern electricity, the greatest scientists cannot really define it. Then why do we believe it exists? Because we see the manifestation of its existence in our homes and industries and streets. Though I do not know where God came from, I must believe He exists, because I see the manifestations of Him everywhere around me.

Dr. Werner Von Braun, director of NASA research, and developer of the rocket which put America's first space satellite into orbit says: "In our modern world, many people seem to feel that our rapid advances in the field of science render such things as religious belief untimely or old-fashioned. They wonder why we should be satisfied in 'believing' something when science tells us that we 'know' so many things. The simple answer to this contention is that we are confronted with many more mysteries of nature today than when the age of scientific enlightenment began. With every new answer unfolded, science has consistently discovered at least three new questions.

"The answers indicate that everything as well ordered and perfectly created as is our earth and universe must have a Maker, a Master Designer. Anything so orderly, so perfect, so precisely balanced, so majestic as this creation can only be the product of a Divine idea."

The late professor Edwin Conklin, a noted biologist, very aptly said: "The probability of life originating from accident is comparable to the probability of an Unabridged Dictionary resulting from an explosion in a printing shop."

God exists whether or not men may choose to believe in Him. The reason why many people do not believe in God is not so much that it is intellectually impossible to believe in God but because belief in God forces the thoughtful person to face the fact that he is accountable to such a God. Many people are unwilling to do this. Most of those who take refuge in atheism or agnosticism do so because it is a convenient "escape" from the stern reality that man is accountable to his Creator. It is usually not so much a case of "I cannot believe" as it is a case of "I do not want to believe."

I know only two ways by which God's purpose and God's person may be known. First there is the process of reason. As a good detective can, for example, tell you many things about my skills, habits and character just by examining something I may have made or handled, so much can be learned about God by a careful examination of the universe, the work of His hands.

But the detective who examines only what I make can never say that he knows *me*. He may know some things about me, but before he can say that he knows me, there must be a process of revelation: I must communicate with him. I must tell him what I think, how I feel and what I want to do. This self-revelation may be in conversation, in writing, or in some other way. Only then does it become possible for him to know me. Just so, if God is ever to be known and His thoughts, desires and purposes perceived, He must take the initiative and make at least a partial revelation of Himself to men.

Of all the many books this world contains there is one only that claims to be a direct revelation from God, telling us of Himself and His purposes for us. That book is the Bible.

The Bible is a book of such importance that it is surely worthy of thoughtful investigation. So, with the advice of Francis Bacon neither to accept nor reject, but to weigh and consider, let us approach this book with its unusual claims.

To be fair to ourselves and to the Bible, we should read it through. As a judge must not make his decision when the case is half heard, neither must we. Rather, like the judge, we should compare the evidence of the witnesses, and weigh and consider every work, seeking for its deepest significance rather than accepting its surface meaning.

Surely the importance of its claims justifies spending the necessary time, on the study of its sixty-six books, written by at least forty different writers (some well educated, some barely educated, some kings, some peasants) over a period of 1600 years in places as far apart as Babylon in Asia and Rome in Europe. With such authorship one would expect to find a miscellaneous collection of contradictory statements. Its unity is therefore especially striking, for each contribution is the complement of the others.

In my considerations of this whole matter, slowly the truth of 2 Peter 1:21 became certain to me. There was no other reasonable explanation. "Holy men of God spoke as they were moved by the Holy Ghost." This belief was confirmed as I read prophecy after prophecy in the Old Testament which found its fulfilment, even to the letter, hundreds of years later.

For instance, Isaiah 53 foretold the death of Christ with minute accuracy more than 700 years before His crucifixion. Yes, the difficulties in the way of doubting the Book seemed to me greater than those in the way of believing it. I had to be honest with myself and admit that the problems were all on the side of unbelief. I even went further and said: "I believe the Bible to be the word of the living God. I can account for it in no other way."

Such an admission brought me face to face with a serious difficulty, however, for the Bible set a standard of righteousness that I had not attained. It pronounced that anything short of its standard was sin. Remembering that God knows your every secret thought, just measure

326

yourself alongside the standard: "Thou shalt love the Lord thy God with *all* thy heart, and with *all* thy soul, and with *all* thy mind. This is the first and great commandment." (Matthew 22:37,38).

Confronted with such a statement, can you claim to have lived up to it throughout your life? Have you put God first in everything? No man can honestly claim such perfection. Every honest heart echoes Romans 3:10 and 23 "There is none righteous, no, not one ... All have sinned, and come short of the glory of God." All have failed to reach God's standard.

A young man once asked me, "Do you think it fair of God to set the standard of holiness so high that we cannot reach it, and then judge us for falling short?"

I replied, "God has not set an arbitrary standard of holiness as an official sets an arbitrary standard of height for his bodyguards. In such a case, a man may have all the other qualifications, but if he is an inch too short he is disqualified.

"God has not really set a standard at all: He is the standard. He is absolute holiness, and to preserve His own character He must remain absolutely holy in all of His dealings with man, maintaining that standard irrespective of the tremendous implications which it may hold for both Him and us."

My conscience and my common sense compelled me to admit I had fallen short of God's standard of absolute holiness and, therefore, I was a sinner in His sight.

On my admission of having sinned came God's condemnation in Ezekiel 18:4: "The soul that sinneth, it shall die."

It appealed to me like this: The law in Great Britain says that all drivers must keep to the left side of the street, while in New York the rule of the road demands that a driver keep to the right side. Now, suppose I go driving in London and keep to the right side. On being brought before the judge, I say, "This is

ridiculous. In the United States we are allowed to drive on the right side."

"You are not being judged by the laws of America," he replies. "It does not matter what the laws of other lands may be, you should have concerned yourself only with the laws which judge you here, where you are."

In the same way as far as God's standard was concerned, I was lost, because God's standard was the only one by which I was to be judged in eternity. I was hopelessly lost. I began to see that it didn't matter at all what I thought, or what my friends told me. The judgment would be on what God has said, not what my friends say. Moreover, because in God's judgment we had all sinned, there was no use in looking to other men for help, for they were under the same condemnation as I.

But this same Bible, which told me of my sin, told me also of Jesus Christ, who claimed to be the Son of God.

It is the clear teaching of the Bible that this person, Jesus Christ, is God the Son. He saw that men were lost and that they had forfeited their lives to sin. His life was not forfeited. It was sinless and spotless. This pure life of His He was willing to give in place of man's sinful life that we might go free.

He Himself tells us in John 3:16 that "God so loved the world, that he gave his only begotten Son, that whosoever believeth in him should not perish, but have everlasting life."

If Jesus Christ is the Son of God, then we may indeed be sure of salvation; but the difficulty faces us: Is Jesus Christ really the Son of God? He could only be one of three— the Son of God, or a deceiver, or an honest man Himself under a hallucination. But we find Him meeting some of the cleverest men of His day, who were purposely sent to catch Him in His words and He so silenced them that they did not dare ask Him any more questions (Matthew 22:46). And when we ourselves consider the wisdom of His statements from an intellectual standpoint, we see plainly that He was under no hallucination as to Himself.

Then was His wisdom so great that He was using it to deceive the people? Have you ever heard of a young man associating with swindlers and rogues and because of that association becoming ennobled, pure and honest? No! You admit you have not heard of such a case; but I know a young man who by the reception of Christ into his life has been lifted from the basest desires to the noblest manhood. I simply cannot believe that the reception of a deceiver into one's life could transform it for good.

The other day I heard a man say, "I owe it to Jesus Christ that I can walk down the street with my head held erect and my shoulders squared to the world. I owe it to Him that I can look a pure woman in the face and grip an honest man by the hand."

I call to witness the opinion of the whole civilised world that Jesus Christ was at least a good man. If so, then an honest man, and if honest He must have been what He claimed to be, the Son of God, sent to lay down His sinless life in place of your sinful life and mine. Leaders from several professions have this to say about Jesus Christ:

United States Senator Mark O. Hatfield, testifies: "I saw that for 31 years I had lived for self and decided I wanted to live the rest of my life only for Jesus Christ. I asked God to forgive my self-centred life and to make my life His own. Following Jesus Christ has been an experience of increasing challenge, adventure and happiness. Living a committed Christian life is truly satisfying because it has given me true purpose and direction by serving not myself but Jesus Christ."

Robert E. (Bob) Richards, former Olympic track star, said: "My only reason for being in sports is to give my testimony to youth of all the world that Jesus Christ can save from sin, and that one can be a Christian and still excel in good, creative things. Young people need to realise that God unleashed a tremendous spiritual power when Jesus Christ died on Calvary."

Lt. Gen. William K. Harrison (Ret.) former Senior Delegate of the United Nations Command Truce Team in Korea and later Commander-in-Chief of the Caribbean Command, wrote: "It is wonderful to believe in the Lord Jesus Christ and I am exceedingly thankful that God has graciously led me to saving faith in Christ. God gives us who believe in Christ a daily, personal experience which is convincing evidence of the reality of the new life in Christ."

Convinced that the Scripture is true, and that Jesus Christ is the Son of God, believing that He willingly came, that God so loved me that He has willingly sent Him to suffer the full penalty of my sins that I might go free, if I would retain my self-respect as an intelligent being, I must accept the Lord Jesus Christ as my Saviour.

But I do not ask you to accept Him as yours, for you may have an objection: although it is plausible that the Bible is true, are not alternate views also plausible? Why not be reasonable and submit them to a fair test as well?

On telling my conviction to a friend, he replied, "You are all right, but so am I, although I don't see things as you do. It seems to me that it doesn't matter so much what a man believes, so long as he is sincere in his belief."

Let us test that statement. One fine Sunday morning a neighbour of mine said to his wife and family, "Let us take the car and go for a picnic." Travelling north, he came to a railway crossing and, sincerely believing there would be no trains on a Sunday morning, attempted to drive across. He was killed on the spot, one son had an arm broken and his little daughter was in a cast for months. Did his sincere belief that all was clear save him? No, it did not.

I know a nurse who, on night duty, sincerely believed she held the right medicine in her hand, but she was wrong, and in twenty minutes her patient was dead in spite of frantic efforts to save him.

Of course we need sincerity, but we must sincerely believe truth, not error. In fact, having sincere belief in error can be the very means of deceiving and finally destroying us. The Bible leaves no room for doubt. In John 14:6 Christ says: "I am the way, the truth and the life: no man cometh unto the Father but by me." Acts 4:12 states: "There is no other name under heaven given among men whereby we must be saved." If you can get to heaven any other way you will be witness throughout eternity to the fact that Jesus Christ spoke falsely when he said there was no other way. But, since He gives full evidence of being the Son of God, claims to be God's appointed way?

The real reason we want some other way is because the way of the cross is a humbling way and we are proud at heart. But let us remember the way of the cross was a humbling way for Christ also, as we read in Philippians 2:5-8

> Have this attitude in yourselves which was also in Christ Jesus, Who, although He existed in the form of God, did not regard equality with God a thing to be grasped, But emptied Himself, taking the form of a bondservant and being made in the likeness of men. And being found in appearance as a man, He humbled Himself by becoming obedient to the point of death, even death on a cross.

Some people have suggested that all a person needs to do is sincerely reform, do better in the future, and thus live down past short-comings. This is supposed to make one fit for heaven. Will this work?

Let us assume that the manager of a business goes to his accountant and finds that his company owes $50,000 to manufacturers and other merchants. He says, "Write letters to all those people and tell them that we are not going to trouble about the past, that we have turned over new pages in our ledger, but we promise to pay 100 cents on the dollar in all future business, and from now on live up to the highest standard of business integrity." The accountant would think his employer had gone mad, and would refuse to put such a proposition to the creditors.

Yet thousands of otherwise sensible people are trying to get to heaven by just such a proposal, offering to meet their obligations toward God for the future, but refusing to worry about the past at all. Yet in Ecclesiastes 3:15 we read, "God will call the past to account." Even if we assume that we can somehow begin to live an absolutely perfect life—which is no better than we ought to do, but which is certainly impossible for us—we are still sinners.

God's righteousness demands that no past account shall be considered settled till it has been paid to the last penny and every claim of justice met. The murderer may cover his sin and live the life of a model citizen for ten years after his crime, but when he is discovered, man's law condemns him to death. Though he has murdered no-one for ten long years—it judges him still a murderer.

To hide past sin, either *thoughts, words or deeds*, by what seems to be an absolutely perfect life, still leaves us sinners in the sight of Him to whom the past and future are as open as the present. According to God's standards of holiness, we all have sinned, and we must bring that sin out into the open and have it dealt with righteously.

We each need someone who can clear the books. The Bible declares that Jesus Christ is the only One who could pay this penalty. "We are reconciled to God by the death of his Son" (Romans 5:10). Yes, the Lord Jesus Christ gave up His life in place of ours that we might go free. Our past sin is paid for, and God, against whom we had sinned, has given us His receipt showing His satisfaction with the completed work of Christ on the cross in that He raised Him from the dead. Christ once crucified is now our living Saviour. He died to save us from the penalty of sin and now He lives to deliver us from the power of sin.

But why did Christ need to die?

Could He not have saved us without that? Man had broken God's law and the penalty was death. How could Christ righteously deliver us without meeting our full penalty? Do you not see that if He paid anything less than the full price there would still be judgment for us to meet? But it is evident that because He died, the law we had broken can judge us no more. The Bible says in Romans 8:1 "There is therefore now no condemnation to them which are in Christ Jesus."

On one occasion an unfinished court case extended to a second day and as is the usual practice, so that no outside influence could be brought to bear on the jurymen, they were kept in custody overnight. On entering the court the next morning the Judge, addressing the jury, said: "Gentlemen, the case is dismissed: the prisoner has been called to a higher court." The accused had died in his cell during the night and there was no use going on with the case, since the law cannot judge a dead man.

Again, if a man should murder one person he is put to death, but if he should murder six people he is still just put to death, because this is the utmost penalty of the law. No matter what a man's sins may be, the law knows no greater penalty than to take his life.

Therefore it matters not though there are sins in my life that I have long since forgotten. I fear none of them, for I have this confidence that the Lord Jesus Christ, my Substitute, suffered the utmost penalty of the law on my account, freeing me absolutely from all its claims against me, both great and small.

On the basis of the greatness of Jesus Christ's sacrifice, some have suggested that if Christ died for all, we must all be saved. But God does not say so. He says there is salvation for all, not that all are saved.

Here is an illustration. It is a bitterly cold winter and unemployment is rife in one of our great cities with many in dire need. The municipal authorities provide free meals. You meet a poor fellow on the street who says he is starving. Naturally you ask if he does not believe the notices that are up all over the city, that there is enough food for all provided free.

"Yes," he replies, "I believe that is true in a general sort of way, but I am still hungry."

You tell him that he is likely to remain hungry in spite of the provisions unless he eats and drinks personally of what is provided for all.

Just so, although the death of Christ provides salvation for whosoever will, only those are saved who personally accept Christ and believe that He died in their place. I must take Christ as *my* Saviour, or His death will avail me nothing just as a man could die of thirst beside a spring of water if he refused to make its life-giving stream his own by drinking of it for himself. There are some people who still pose the question: How could the Lord Jesus Christ's one life be considered the substitute for the lives of so many, so that God offers salvation to whosoever places their faith in Christ?

That seems a fair question—a problem in arithmetic that can be demonstrated on paper. Christ was God manifest in the flesh—Divinity in humanity—so that the Life He gave was an infinite life, which can meet the needs of any number of finite lives. Get a sheet of paper and write down all the big figures you can think of—millions or more—add them up. Now you have a big number, then multiply it by 10— 100—by a million if you like cover sheets of paper and after all you still have a finite number —a number that has bounds set about it—a beginning and an end, however far it may extend. No, by adding finite things together no man has ever been able to make that which is infinite. The *infinite life* of Christ given for sinners is more than sufficient to save all who accept Him as the One who died for them.

But how could Christ suffer for my sins when they were committed 2000 years after He died?

At first this seems a problem to a thoughtful person, but the more thoughtful you are, the more readily you will see the solution. God is omniscient (that is, He knows all things), and God is eternal. In Exodus 3:14 God calls himself "I AM" (present tense), and Christ says in John 8:58 "Before Abraham was, I AM" (present tense). In other words, to one who knows all things and is eternal, there is, as it were, neither past nor future, but one eternal present. Events yet to take place 2000 years ahead must be as clear to Him as events which happened 200 years ago, and both must of necessity be just as clear to God as events happening now.

But why did not God make man incapable of disobeying His will and therefore incapable of sinning?

Such a question is like asking why does not God draw a crooked straight line or a round square, or make an object black all over and white all over at one and the same time. Man is a creature with the power of intelligent choice, so that the question really is: Why didn't God make a creature with the power of intelligent choice and yet without the power of intelligent choice at one and the same time?

If I had the power of hypnotism, I would be able to put my two sons into an hypnotic state, thus robbing them of the power of intelligent choice, and then say, "Sit on those chairs till I return"—"Get up and eat"—"Stop eating"— "Kiss me goodnight," and unfeeling arms would go around my neck, and unresponsive lips would be pressed to mine. I

would have prompt and perfect obedience to my every command, but would I find satisfaction in it? No!

I want boys with free wills who are capable of disobeying me, but who willingly choose to carry out my instructions, which are the outcome of my love for them and are given for their own good. I cannot conceive of God, who put these desires in my heart and yours, being satisfied with anything less Himself.

God does not want puppets who jump in a given direction according to the wire that is pulled nor does He want robots in the form of "men" who mechanically and absolutely obey His will as do the planets that whirl through space. God can find satisfaction in nothing less than the spontaneous love of our hearts and our free-will decisions to walk in paths that please and honour Him if we so choose.

Man is truly a magnificent creature, far above the animal creation around him. There is no "missing link." But a great gulf is fixed between the highest beast and man, for God has given man the awesome power of being able to say no to God as well as an effective yes. In your own interests, may I ask which you are saying to God now as you read this booklet?

What does God care about this little world of ours compared with the vastness of the mighty universe?

Think of our own solar system, with the planet Neptune thirty times as far away from the sun as our earth, so that it takes 164 of our years to make one of Neptune's, and beyond this, suns with planets revolving around them as our solar system revolves around the sun! Of what importance can our earth be to God, and of how much less importance can man be?

So said the astronomer as the faith of his youth fled—this is what the telescope had done for him. The vastness of the heavens had robbed him of faith in his mother's God, for how could God trouble Himself about man, who is less than a grain of sand in comparison?

331

But his thirst for knowledge would not let him rest. The heavens were available for study only at night; how should the free hours of the day be spent? Why not a microscope? And lo! worlds were opened at his feet—worlds as wonderful as those above, and slowly his faith came back.

Yes, the God who could attend to such minute details as to make a drop of ditch water throb with miniature life was sure to be interested in man, the highest form of His creation. The man found balance instead of bias, and balance brought him back to God. John 3:16 was true after all.

But is faith logical?

Yes, it is logical. It is a mistake to think that faith is opposed to reason. Faith and reason go when reason can go no farther. Reason, to a great extent, is dependent on faith, for without knowledge it is impossible to reason, and knowledge is very largely a matter of faith in human testimony.

For instance, I believe strychnine administered in a large enough dose will poison a human being, but I have never seen the experiment performed. Yet I have such faith in the written testimony of men that I would not take a large dose of strychnine for anything.

If you check up carefully, you will find that nine-tenths of the things you "know" are a matter of faith in human testimony, written or spoken, for you have not verified them for yourself. Then, having accepted the testimony of men on other matters, will you not accept the testimony of thousands of Christians when they affirm that they have verified the things written in God's Word and have proved them to be true?

But why should God judge my sins as worthy of death?

I cannot answer that, but I would suggest that because of His infinite holiness no sin could exist in His presence. In some primitive cultures a native chief may club his wife to death on slight provocation without falling in the slightest degree in the estimation of his people. The same act in our land would have to be paid for by the life of the murderer.

The act is the same in both lands, but in one instance no judgment; in the other, quick retribution. The difference is simply the result of our enlightenment. If a sin, which in a primitive culture is considered as nothing, would cause a man to lose his life in our land, think, if you can, what some other sin, which appears to us as nothing, must look like to an infinitely Holy God—"For God is light, and in Him is no darkness at all" (1 John 1:5).

It may be just, but is it merciful of God to refuse to take us all to heaven even if we reject Christ as our sinbearer?

Yes, both just and merciful. Would it be kindness to transfer a poor ragged beggar into the glare of a beautiful ballroom? Would he not be more conscious of his rags and dirt? Would he not do his best to escape to the darkness of the street? He would be infinitely happier there. Would it be kindness and mercy on God's part to bring a man in his sins into the holy light of Heaven if that man had rejected God's offer of the only cleansing power there is? If you and I would not wish our friends to see inside our minds now and read all the thoughts that have ever been there (and our friends' standards are perhaps not any higher than our own), what would it be like to stand before God, whose absolute holiness would reveal our sin in all its awfulness?

Revelation 6:16 tells us of the feelings of those who refuse to accept Jesus Christ as their Saviour and persist in going to eternity in their sins. They call on the mountains and the rocks to fall on them and hide them from the face of Him that sitteth on the throne. Yet it is the presence of this same Christ that will make Heaven for those who have accepted Him as Saviour and Lord.

You see the absurdity of talking about God taking us all to heaven—heaven is a condition as well as a place. The presence of the Lord Jesus Christ will constitute heaven to those who are cleansed from their sins, while that same presence would make a hell of remorse in the hearts of any who, still in their sins, should stand in the infinite light of his holiness. Let us be quite reasonable—could you really be happy in the presence of One whose love you had rejected, and whose great sacrifice you had not counted worthy of your acceptance?

Salvation by Substitution

or

THE INNOCENT BEARING THE PENALTY FOR THE GUILTY

We have considered reasonable evidence that God does exist and that He has revealed in the Bible His holy claims on men and women. We have been shown that "all have sinned, and come short of the glory of God" (Romans 3:23). We have been faced with Jesus Christ, God's Son, who came to this earth to die for the sin of man. We have also considered numerous objections raised by people who have other ideas about God's plan of salvation. Now we are going to think through the wisdom and the wonder of God's plan of salvation for sinful people. In a word, it is salvation by substitution.

God's love would have forgiven the sinner, but God's righteousness prevented the forgiveness. God's righteousness would have judged the sinner, but God's love restrained the judgment. How to reconcile His inherent righteousness with His character of essential

love was a problem that no human philosopher could have solved, but divine wisdom and mercy find their highest expression in the solution—the various suffering and death of God the Son.

"But," one may object, "does not Christianity fail at its very foundation by basing everything on substitution?" Substitution will not stand thoughtful investigation. It makes Christ, the Innocent, bear the penalty for the guilty and thus lets the guilty go free. It is diametrically opposed to our every idea of justice, for we believe that justice should protect the innocent and bring the full penalty upon the guilty.

But see God's perfect justice and perfect mercy revealed at the cross. He does not there take the innocent and compel him to bear the penalty of the guilty. God acts like the judge in this story:—It is on record that of two young men who studied law together, one rose to a seat on the bench, while the other took to drink and wasted his life. On one occasion this poor fellow was brought before his old companion, charged with crime, and the lawyers present wondered what kind of justice would be administered by the judge under such trying circumstances. To their surprise, he sentenced his one-time companion to the heaviest penalty the law allowed, and then paid the fine himself and set his old friend free.

God, against whom we had sinned, in justice sat upon His judgment throne and passed the heaviest penalty He could—the sentence of death upon the sinner. Then, in mercy, He stepped down from His throne and in the person of His Son took the sinner's place, bearing the full penalty Himself, for 2 Corinthians 5:19 tell us "that God was *in* Christ," not *through* Christ, but *in* Christ, "reconciling the world unto himself."

God the Father, God the Son, and God the Holy Spirit are one God. The same God against whom we had sinned passed the judgment, paid the penalty, and now offers us full and free pardon, based upon absolute righteousness. That is why the Apostle Paul writes in Romans 1: 16,17 "I am not ashamed of the gospel of Christ, for it is the power of God unto salvation to everyone that believeth ... for therein is the righteousness of God revealed ..." I, too, can say I am not ashamed of the Gospel of Christ, for no man can honestly find a flaw in the righteousness offered by God to man. That is the righteousness you may possess now, at this very moment, if you will accept it.

But is the acceptance of Christ as my Saviour *all* that is necessary to save me for all eternity? Yes. I admit the very simplicity of it seems to make it hard to grasp. But if I owe $500 and have nothing with which to pay, and a friend pays the debt for me and gives me the receipt, I don't worry about it anymore. I can look my creditor straight in the face, for I hold his signed receipt. As Jesus Christ gave His life in place of mine, He said: "It is finished," meaning that the work of atonement was completed, and God gave me His receipt. The assurance that He was satisfied with Christ's finished work is that He (God) raised Christ from the dead on the third day.

"But I can't see it, " said a certain cabinet-maker, as a friend tried to explain this to him. At last an idea came to his friend, who, lifting a plane, made as though he would plane the top of a beautifully polished table that stood near.

"Stop!" cried the cabinetmaker. "Don't you see that's finished? You'll simply ruin it if you use that plane on it."

"Why," replied his friend, "that's just what I have been trying to show you about Christ's work of redemption. It was finished when He gave His life for you, and if you try to add to that finished work you can only spoil it. Just accept it as it stands—His life for yours, and you go free." Like a flash the cabinetmaker saw it and received Jesus Christ into his life as his Saviour.

"But," says someone,"there is one more problem that puzzles me. I know a polished gentleman who is not a Christian and states so quite definitely, and I know a rather crude uncultured man who is a Christian and who shows his genuine belief in many ways. Do you mean to tell me God prefers the uncultured man simply because he had accepted and acknowledged Christ as his Saviour?"

This question arises from a confusion of ideas. A Christian is not different in degree from a non-Christian, he is different in *kind*, just as the difference between a diamond and a cabbage is not one of degree, but of kind. The one is polished, and the other is crude, but the one is dead while the other is alive, therefore the one has what the other had not in any degree whatever, *life*—and such is the difference God sees between a Christian and a non-Christian.

Here is one of many such statements He makes in His Word. 1 John 5:11,12 "And this is the record, that God has given to us eternal life, and this life is in his Son. He that hath the Son hath life; and he that hath not the Son of God hath not life." So that the vital and all important question for every one of us becomes not am I cultured or uncouth, but am I alive or dead towards God? Have I received God's risen Son who brings me life from above, the life of God, called in the Bible eternal life? Or have I not received Him and am I therefore classed by God as among those who "Have not life?"

But how may I receive the Lord Jesus Christ as my Saviour?

If I know that, according to Ephesians 2:1, I am "dead in trespasses and sins," as regards my relationship with God; if I believe Jesus Christ gave His life in place of mine, and that now by the receiving of Him as my Saviour I may have eternal salvation, will perceiving these facts in a cold mechanical way give me everlasting life? Most certainly not!

334

A wealthy man loses all his money, and rather than sacrifice his social position, he agrees to give the hand of his daughter to a rich man whom she despises. At first she refuses point-blank, but when her father shows her the expediency of the marriage, that it is his only hope of being saved from utter want, she consents, and goes through the marriage ceremony, and becomes, according to the law of the land, the rich man's wife. But is her heart really his? Surely not!

You see it now, don't you. When a man and a woman would be truly one, they must love with such a love as to receive each other into those innermost recesses of their hearts in such a deep, true way that they cannot fully express in words all that they feel.

We all have the innermost recess of our beings, which is sacred to us, where emotions stir that no one else could possibly understand. Jesus Christ, God's Son, because of His love for us, claims the right to enter there. He will take no other place in our lives. The love He has shown for us entitles Him to that place. Will I withhold it?

When I think that Christ's love for me was so great that He left His Father's glory and came to earth, becoming truly human that He might suffer and die in my place to give me eternal life, my heart softens toward Him.

If, when I lay sick and helpless in a burning building, a friend had rushed in to save me, and wrapping the blankets about me that I might receive no harm, had himself been critically scarred and burned about the face and arms, would not my heart go out to him? God knows it would.

And now I am face to face with my Saviour. I see Him suffering in the Garden of Gethsemane in anticipation of His death on the cross for me. I see Him in Pilate's Judgment Hall; the soldiers have been striking Him in the face, saying, "Prophesy, who struck you?" I see them crowning Him with a crown of thorns. They have taken Him bleeding and bruised from judgment to Calvary where they are driving spikes through His hands and His feet.

As He is then lifted up to die between two thieves, the people gather around to mock and revile Him, though He is pouring out His life to redeem them. Then I begin to understand what self-sacrificing love really means as I hear Him cry: "Father, forgive them, for they know not what they do."

But even if we could enter sympathetically into the physical sufferings of Christ until tears streamed down our cheeks, and that was all, we should have failed miserably to comprehend the true significance of the cross.

We read in 2 Corinthians 5:21 that "He (God) hath made him (Christ) to be sin for us, who knew no sin." Come with me, I plead with you, with bowed head and humbled heart, and let us, if we may, enter into the soul-sufferings of Christ the Son, and of God the Father, as that Holy One, who loathed sin as we would loathe leprosy, is "made sin for us."

If the higher the development of the physical organism the greater the capacity for pain, then the higher the development of the moral character, the greater the capacity for soul-suffering.

Have you ever heard of a venerable old gentleman, justly proud of his honoured name—a man who would sooner lose his right hand than use it to do a dishonourable deed? His son and heir goes astray from the paths of virtue and in a drunken brawl murders someone. And the old man walks no more erect, his head is bowed in shame, and soon his soul-suffering brings his gray hairs in sorrow to the grave.

If that be possible (and it is possible even for us to feel the disgrace of a greater sin than we are used to), think what *sin* must be like in all its awfulness to an absolutely holy God! Now we understand why, in the Garden of

335

Gethsemane Christ turns in loathing from sin and cries in agony of soul: "My Father, if it is possible, may this cup be taken from me, yet not as I will, but as you will." (Matthew 26:39). Yet in spite of that agonised cry from Gethsemane, "God so loved the world that he gave his only begotten Son" to be "made sin" for us, "that whosoever believeth in him should not perish, but have everlasting life" (John 3:16; 1 Corinthians 5:21).

Now do you understand why I said that if I would retain any ideal of manhood, or any nobleness of character, I dare not reject One who has endured so much for me? My intellect has reasoned it all out; my emotions have been deeply stirred; and now they both appeal to my will for a decision. To be true to my God and myself and my eternal future I have only one course open, and I must take it. Today Jesus Christ is my personal Saviour and my Lord.

Because of His love to me, because of the way He has blessed me here, and because of my assurance of a glorious hereafter, my heart's desire is that you might share in the blessings I enjoy. Christ has done all. I say it reverently. He can do no more. He has borne the penalty of your sin; He has been raised by the power of God; now He presents Himself to you. Will you accept Him as Saviour and Lord?

You are saying: "It seems so mysterious; the mystery of it all baffles me." "I do not ask you to understand the mystery of it. I cannot understand its mystery myself, nor can any Christian in this life. I am asking you to rejoice in its fact.

Electricity remains a mystery. We have discovered many of the laws which govern it, but we cannot tell what it really is. You and I do not worry about the mystery of electricity as we make use of its benefits. You must have known men who accepted Jesus Christ as their Saviour and were so changed as to be actually new men in Christ. Will you not let these facts that you have seen for yourself influence you?

Yes, it is just as simple as switching on an electric light.

Come, saying: "Oh, God, I cannot understand the mystery of it all. I cannot understand why you cared enough for me to send Jesus Christ to bear the penalty of my sins. But with all my lack of understanding I am willing and I do yield to you; absolutely. I trust in the fact of His death for me and the promise that You have made in John 3:16, "that whosoever believes in him shall not perish, but have everlasting life."

Just as you leave the mystery of the electric current with the engineer and take the benefits of the light for yourself, so leave the mystery of salvation with God and take the infinite benefits of a personal Saviour to yourself. Yield to Him now—He wants to come into your life. Say and mean it: "I am Yours, Lord Jesus, yielded to you, body, soul and spirit and you are mine." Then clinch it by signing the following declaration form.

MY DECISION

Before God, who knows the innermost secrets of my soul, I accept Jesus Christ into my life as my Saviour and Lord. I yield absolutely to Him. I know, on the authority of His own written Word in John 5:24, that I have everlasting life, for there He says, "I tell you the truth, whoever hears my word and believes him who sent me has eternal life and will not be condemned; he has crossed over from death to life."

Signed _____

Address _____

_____

_____

Date _____

A Further Word

Perhaps you have not yet made a decision to place your faith in Jesus Christ. Then consider the following:

Someone says, "I am one of those individuals who most emphatically resents being brought to a definite decision on any important subject. It is not that I have no willpower. In fact, I am so strong-willed that I am determined neither to pull up against the current nor pull down with it. I am determined to do nothing but just drift, slowly drift, down the stream of time.

"But I hate to think about it! True believers in Jesus Christ look forward to eternity with joy. But I— why am I not honest enough to admit to myself that my resentment at the question is only because I do not want to decide in the way I know I ought to. Yet I must face it some day. Then why not now?"

Now that you have done so, read this little book again. It will seem so much clearer. Then read the entire gospel of John in the New Testament.

Now for the last point, a most important one. If you open your Bible at Romans 10:9–11 you will read: "That if you confess with your mouth that 'Jesus is Lord', and believe in your heart that God raised him from the dead, you shall be saved. For it is with your heart that you believe and are justified, and it is with your mouth that you confess and are saved. As the Scripture says, 'Whoever believes in him will not be disappointed.'"

You say you have accepted Christ—go and tell some one—do not be ashamed to confess Him. Why should you be? Suppose I had fallen off the wharf, injuring myself so that I could not swim, and a labourer working on a coal barge had plunged in and saved me. If a month Later you saw me walking down Main Street and the same labourer, all begrimed with coal dust, coming up from the opposite direction, and you saw that I noticed him first and deliberately turned to look into a store window so that I would not have to stop and greet him because I was ashamed to be seen talking to him, what would you think of me?

You have declared that you believe the Lord Jesus Christ has given His life to save you. Occasions will arise when you will meet Him face to face in the presence of those who despise Him. Will you be ashamed and look the other way, or will you honour Him in both word and deed as your Lord and Saviour? Having really accepted Him, you must and you will acknowledge Him.

I make no apology for the truth which underlies these pages. I have sought to write what I believe God would have me write in the discharge of my duty to Him and to you. I follow this booklet with the earnest prayer that God will bless it to your eternal welfare.

The Soldier's Choice

I was seeking to lead a young soldier to accept the Lord Jesus Christ, but, like most men, he tried to evade the essential issue with the promise, "I'll think it over."

"Harry," I said, "let me illustrate. You are out with the boys some night scouting an enemy post. And on the way back you get hit hard. Another soldier stops long enough to pick you up and carry you back to your own lines, and for his trouble gets two bullets in the back. You are both taken to the hospital and by tender care are won back from the very jaws of death.

"Two months later the doctor brings in a poor fellow who limps badly and moves with evident pain. They stop at your bedside, and the doctor says, 'Harry, I want to introduce you to Bill Smith, the man who risked his life to save you.' You fold your arms and say, 'I'm not sure I want to meet him. I'll think it over.' You wouldn't say that, would you? You would grasp him by the hand and try to tell him something of the gratitude you felt.

"I want to introduce you to the Lord Jesus Christ, the Man who not only risked His life, but sacrificed it, to save you. And you propose to turn your back on Him and say you'll think it over?"

"No," he said, "I'll accept Him." Together we knelt while he told the Lord that he, at that moment, accepted Him as his personal Saviour. Are you "thinking it over," or have you faced the issue squarely and decided aright?

AUTHOR'S NOTES

Chapter 1

[1] *Optimist* Dec 1915, p.15.

[2] The Laidlaws lived in Hawick about 90 miles inland. Dalry was the town where they were married on December 24 1883. They holidayed there and were at the coast for the birth of Robert.

[3] Their departure may well have been a hurried affair as up to September 9, they were not yet booked to travel. A passenger list of those booked up to that date appears in the *Otago Daily Times* Oct 30, p.2.

[4] The Laidlaws are not mentioned in the passenger list published in the *Otago Daily Times* on Friday, Dec 3, 1886, p.2. However, the list only contains the names of about 280 passengers, whereas 305 are said to have been on board.

[5] Electric lighting was installed at Mosgiel Woollen Mills in 1885. Other notable businesses were also launching out or expanding at this time including Donaghys, Hallensteins and Shacklocks.

[6] *Treasury* June 1899, p.95. Later worshipped at Gospel Hall, Moray Place. Exact date of change is unknown. Some time between 1899 and 1906.

[7] Story recounted in Robert's own file of illustrations. Says he never forgot the feeling of terror that it was too late - that he had not become a Christian and now only judgment awaited him.

[8] The young inventor was Richard Pearse who went on to fly a powered craft, possibly before the Wright Brothers. Pearse really remained an unknown until after his death. Ironically neither did Robert know who he was cycling with. He recounted this incident on various occasions in his life, never knowing that it was the now famous Pearse he was riding with. As for the timing of the bicycle story, Pearse patented his vertically pedalling bicycle in 1902 but rode it before this time. He did not live in Dunedin but in Waitohi, just outside Timaru in the South Island. Cycling clubs were common and it is possible that on a journey to Dunedin or Timaru that Robert met Pearse and rode his bike.

Chapter 2

[1]   RW Emerson, *Optimist*, Jan 1915, Back Cover.

[2]   The date of this event does differ but the strongest evidence is found in an article 'Industry and Commerce' and *The Story of The Reason Why* which confirm taking up the position of junior clerk after his 16th birthday rather than 1902.

[3]   *Treasury* Aug 1902, pp.205-208.

[4]   *Otago Daily Times* Monday, 22 Sept, p.5.

[5]   *Otago Daily Times* Fri, Sept 26, 1902.

[6]   This notebook is no longer around but Robert kept it, possibly even until he died, making reference to it in *The Story of The Reason Why* published just before he died.

[7]   Robert learnt to drive while 18 which would have put this event around Christmas 1903-1904. Robert's father brought further motor cars in quick succession and also in 1904 brought a 8 Hp. Darracq. Obviously still a novelty, there was an early Dunedin post card printed with Robert at the wheel driving the family.

[8]   One account says that Robert's father sold his business in 1899. However Robert says it occurred when he was 19, in *The Story of The Reason Why* (p.7). He turned 19 in 1904. This is a far better fit as we know Mr Gray promoted him when his father was away, at which stage he was 19 and a half (see *Optimist* 21st Birthday Souvenir).

[9]   The extent of this trip is difficult to place. Lillian Watson, Robert's future wife, would later report that she was visited by Mr and Mrs Laidlaw senior in America in 1906. We know from the account *Treasury* May 1905, p.61. that Mr and Mrs Laidlaw went away together in approximately March/April 1905 and stayed away at least until the beginning of 1906. Although the actual amount of money paid for the business is not known there are several things that point to it being a large sum. Firstly, Robert's father left for a trip to England the continent and the USA. Secondly, he retired on the proceeds from the sale of the business still a relatively young man(44).

[10]   Robert's father had been a commercial traveller before, and knew how wayward life on the road could be.

[11]   Isaiah chapter 45 verse 2.

[12]   This is a very difficult event to place exactly. Robert picked up these magazines while a commercial traveller which means that the events could not have

happened before 1905. However, he also refers to *System* being in its first year of publication. This was clearly impossible as *System* began in Dec 1900. However it had recently greatly expanded its format and size and Robert may have thought then that it was new when it was just its new format. The best account of this event is in the 21st Birthday Souvenir published in 1930. It is also worth noting that none of the issues up to Dec 1905 contain articles on Sears Roebuck or Montgomery Ward and only two have short articles slightly related to mail order businesses. Therefore, two things stand out: one, the influence of Montgomery Ward and Sears Roebuck came in later editions of the magazine and two, the first real account of a mail order business that Robert read, was in the December 1905 issue as is mentioned here. The 12 back numbers he mentions sending for would just have been 12 previous issues, and not the first year's issues. *System* also by 1905 had offices in Australia and it is possible that December issues could have made it to NZ shores relatively quickly.

[13] The actual sequence of these two important events is difficult to place. They are reported in different orders in different accounts. The Robertson thesis puts the Mont. Ward catalogue in 1905 but doesn't tie *System* down to a date. Here I have used the sequence that Robert himself pens in the closest account, that of the *Optimist* 21st Birthday Souvenir published in 1930, where *System* occurs first followed by the Mont. Ward catalogue.

[14] *Principles of the Mail Order Business*, by Arthur E. Swett was obviously a popular book and advertisements for it can be found in *System* as early as January 1905 when it was already in its third edition.

[15] Up until World War I, an accountant might be retained on the good wage of £2 per week (£104 per annum). Houses at the time in Ponsonby could be purchased for £75, better class dwellings in Epsom or Mt Eden for between £450-£650.

Chapter 3

[1] *System*, December 1905.

[2] Even in 1930, £4 per week was considered a good weekly wage for a married man - and this was after the very inflationary period of WWI.

[3] Their 1895 catalogue and Robert's first catalogue are similar in layout and style.

[4] 1910 Laidlaw Leeds Catalogue, p.1.

[5] 1910 Laidlaw Leeds Catalogue p.1.

[6]   1910 Laidlaw Leeds Catalogue p.4.

[7]   1910 Laidlaw Leeds Catalogue p.28.

[8]   The actual date that Robert and Jack moved into Fort Street is unknown although there are several clues. We do know it was before September as Robert comments later that both he and Jack scanned North Island postal directories before mailing out the first catalogues and these were sent out in September 1909. In the *Optimist* 21st Birthday Souvenir, Robert also says that Jack joined him at the small Fort Street premises as the work was nearing completion, referring to finishing the catalogue. This puts it then, at the latest, August, if not slightly earlier.

[9]   For confirmation of this see, *Adventure in Merchandising*, unpublished Thesis by G.D. Robertson p.4. (University of Auckland).

Chapter 4

[1]   *Optimist* April 1912, pp.3-6.

[2]   Robert's records, in analysis of future accounts, that for several years the average order size at Laidlaw Leeds was around the £2 mark. From this we can estimate the average number of orders he did at this stage. It should also be realised that an order of £2 was actually quite a large order and would likely be made up of many different goods and lines.

[3]   Something of Robert's card index systems is recorded in *System* August 1917 by Elmer Murphey. He picked up the various ways these could be used in business from *System* as early as 1905. (From *System*s launch in 1900 it discusses such methods.)

[4]   This advertisement appears on page 1 of the *New Zealand Herald* Thursday, November 11, 1909. The next advertisement appears on Friday, November 26, and reads, 'Wanted First Class Assistant used to packing - apply 62 Fort Street.'

[5]   Some accounts of the first five months of trading say that Robert had lost his £240 capital with the exception of £16 (see *Inside Story* p.16). This is an inaccurate description. Robert had not 'lost' any capital, it had been turned into catalogues, and substantially larger premises - instead of taking the profits that he was realising he was investing them back in the business. In fact, early profits must have been good to enable such a move of premises early on.

[6]   These figures are from an 'Sales Analysis Book' that the family still have to this

day. In it are daily sales figures almost from the start of Laidlaw Leeds right through to 1918, and monthly expenses and monthly analysis of all sales as well as monitoring of expenses as % of sales. Many of these figures are also reproduced in Robertson's Thesis, *Adventure in Merchandising*. Robert gave Robertson access to his own private records and so other important trading information is also recorded in the thesis.

[7] The net profit figures for the first three years of trading are never given exactly but are recorded in Robertson's Thesis where, from Robert Laidlaw's own private records, his net profit in later years is expressed as a percentage of sales and as an average is consistently around 6%. It should also be remembered that Robert likely reinvested this in the business in these early years with so many shifts in premises and such big increases in stock holdings.

[8] Laidlaw Leeds catalogue 1911, foreword.

[9] Laidlaw Leeds catalogue 1911, p.1.

[10] These figures and the dates recorded here are given at the start of the 1912 catalogue.

[11] The only other person who possibly comes near is Henry Shacklock who, too, was something of a pioneer. He built, and installed various labour saving machines as well as designed products that would be easier and faster to manufacture in his Dunedin ironworks in the 1880's, but did not apply such concepts business wide as Robert did.

[12] See *Optimist* December 1912, p.4.

[13] *Optimist* April 1912, p.6.

[14] See article by American journalist Elmer Murphey, *System*, August 1917, pp.198-200.

[15] *Optimist* April 1912, p.6.

Chapter 5

[1] *Optimist* April 1912, p.13.

[2] Laidlaw Leeds catalogue number 3, 1912, p.3.

[3] Laidlaw Leeds catalogue number 3, 1912, p.17.

[4] Until March 1929.

[5] The first 4 months of *The Optimist* were not printed but rather typed entirely by hand. No copies remain in existence today. Following editions were all printed

and at least two full sets survive.
6   The Bible, 2 Corinthians 9:6.
7   The Bible, Galatians 6:7.
8   *Optimist* Vol 1, No 4, p.3.
9   See *Optimist* February 1912, p.4.
10 *Optimist* Vol 1, No 4, p.11.
11 Began running in Jan 1912
12 *Optimist* Vol 1, No 4, p.15.
13 Laidlaw Leeds *Optimist* March 1912, Cover. Robert was the first businessman in New Zealand to print such a statement.
14 Catalogue number 3, p. 2.
15 While matching developments in the continent and USA as regards motion study because of his reading of business journals, Robert was 40 years ahead of business in NZ adopting such practices. It would be after WWII before other firms in New Zealand took up such things as motion study.
16 *Optimist* April 1912, p.7.
17 See *Optimist* August 1912.
18 See *Optimist* May 1912, p.7. (Robert matched them pound for pound to take the £2 course.)
19 *Optimist* Dec 1912, p.4.
20 *Optimist* Jan 1913, pp.2-3.
21 *Optimist* November 1912, p.4.
22 *The Story of The Reason Why*, p.22.
23 This of course would free up money in the business for building, that no longer had to be invested in stocks. Robert's father at this time had £14,000 invested in his son's business. This possibly went as high as £20,000 - the additional £6,000 may have been contributed to the building project.
24 See *The Story of The Reason Why*, p.25.
25 *Optimist* June 1913, p.10.
26 The timing of these events is confirmed in *The Story of The Reason Why*. See pp.22-23.

Chapter 6

[1] *Optimist* December 1913, p.4.

[2] The actual cause of the blaze remained a mystery for some time and is still problematic. It was eventually presumed that the fire had started in the lift motor set on top of the warehouse. It had then spread down into the fourth floor where it took hold in the bedding and furniture department. Flaming debris then dropped down the elevator shaft and started another fire in the ground floor. There are several problems with this theory and arson must also be considered a possibility. The night watchman did not start until 9 pm and so the building was vacant when the fire started. There were also thousands of people in Queen Street that night and if the fire had started in the top of the building it would have been quickly visible. Also problematic is the pile of soft goods and rubbish alight at the bottom of the elevator shaft. It is clear Robert ran a very meticulous operation and it is difficult to conceive that there was a pile of softgoods littered at the bottom of the lift shaft. Even if this was so, where was the lift – it wasn't on the ground floor? Any dropping debris would have had to burn through a large cargo lift and then fall to the bottom and then spread sufficiently to do serious fire damage to both ground and first floors before the brigade arrived.

[3] Robert leased two-storey premises in Customs Street to store his large stocks of iron and wire. See 1913 catalogue. In addition Robert rented temporary space in Commerce Street to house his later fire sale.

[4] *New Zealand Herald* Mon ,June 2, 1913,

[5] *Optimist* Jan 1913, p.2.

[6] There are conflicting accounts on how this building was financed. We know that a figure of around £17,000 came in through the lawyer. It is not clear whether this was to be in the form of a mortgage or not. Robertson's thesis says Robert had to make a £22,000 cash payment and had obtained £16,000 by way of mortgage. It is probably likely that these figures are most correct and in fact the £17,000 promised from the lawyer (*Story of The Reason Why*), in the finish was £16,000 and came in the form of a first mortgage over the property. The figure of £22,000 seems to suggest that this was the money owed to Julian which would have put the final building price at £32,000 and the land at £6,000. These figures seem reasonable enough.

[7] *Optimist* June 1913, p.15.

[8] *New Zealand Herald* Sat, June 7, 1913, p.13.

[9] This figure is established in several accounts and from Robert's own records.

[10] *Optimist* March 1914, pp.4-5.

[11] At the time of writing, early versions of *The Reason Why* were unable to be located. I went through several versions where the language was updated and the earliest revised edition found was printed by the Farmers Trading Co. Ltd. This puts it, at the earliest, in the late 1920's after the FUTC name change. Robert's initials (R.A.L) are given as the author in this version. Later versions in the 1960's printed by the Institute Press carried his full name.

[12] *Optimist* April 1914, pp.1-2.

[13] Laidlaw Leeds catalogue, released Oct 1913, p.3.

[14] See *Optimist* December 1914, p.2.

[15] *Optimist* December 1914, p.2.

Chapter 7

[1] *Optimist* January 1926, p.3.

[2] *Optimist* May 1915, p.2.

[3] All accounts put this departure as April. This is generally assumed from readings in *The Optimist* but actual date of departure is Friday, March 26, 1915. See shipping section *NZ Herald* Sat, March 27, 1915.

[4] Robert writes later, that of all the firms he visited in every case but one he met the top executive in the firm he visited. It is possible that he met Henry Ford.

[5] *Optimist* Jan 1916, 'Motoring to Success', pp.1-4.

[6] *Optimist* October 1915, p.14.

[7] He had read in the English papers that the Overseas Club was raising money to present four planes to the newly formed Royal Navy Flying Corps.

[8] 'Robert Laidlaw', by Elmer Murphey in *System* August 1917, p.199.

[9] 'Robert Laidlaw', by Elmer Murphey in *System* August 1917, p.199.

[10] *Optimist* July 1917, pp.1-3.

[11] Noted in Robert's own cash book.

Chapter 8

1 *Optimist* April 1912, p.11.
2 *Auckland Star* Thursday, Feb 7, 1918, p.2.
3 *Auckland Star* February 19.
4 *Optimist* March 1918, pp.4-6.
5 The evidence suggests that Robert was not approached by Boddie until after the appeal. This is supported by the timing of Boddie's announcement in the Directors' minutes not until March, and also most strongly by Robert's own account of the flow of proceedings in the July 1918 *Optimist*, where he says he was approached after the appeal.
6 Some Brethren from the Assemblies had already been incarcerated as conscientious objectors.
7 It is not known whether this was anyone associated with the FUTC or not. Certainly, it is not for at least another week that Boddie even tells the other Directors of his talks with Robert. The most likely explanation seems that it was perhaps a competitor's store.
8 He preached with a number of prominent Brethren evangelists. About 750 from all denominations attended each meeting over the Easter period, March 29 to April 1. *Treasury* May 1918, pp.77-78.
9 *Auckland Star* April 12, 1918, reprinted in *Optimist* May 1918, p.2.
10 *Optimist* May 1918, p.3.
11 Auckland *Truth* Newspaper Saturday, April 20, 1918, p.6.
12 Directors' minutes FUTC April 30, 1918.
13 See table at end of book for a breakdown of settlement.

Chapter 9

1 Originally published in one of the four original hand typed editions of *Optimist* Nov 1911 - Jan 1912. Which one is not known as none could be found. Appears reprinted in May edition of *Optimist* 1914, pp.1-3.
2 Directors' Report and Balance Sheet March 31 1919.
3 Neither did Robert's preference shares give him the same voting rights as ordinary shareholders, unless a decision went to poll. Polls could be taken only on very major issues, or if it appeared the capital base of the company

might be in danger. At a poll, each of Robert's fully paid shares would give him one vote. The directors knew that, had Robert wanted to, he could have forced the issue and outvoted the other shareholders at any time if he felt it necessary.

4   It was only later on that Robert had many of the rights and conditions attached to his shares changed, as he himself became involved deeper and deeper in the future of this company and its financial well being.

5   Shares not allotted until July 28 1918, the same Directors meeting Robert renegotiated his terms.

6   Many years later one commentator would remark, "If ever there was a reverse takeover then this was it. When considering the purchase of Laidlaw Leeds the Chairman had quoted Shakespeare, 'There is a tide in the affairs of men, which if taken at the flood, leads on to fortune.' The tide was flooding alright but I suppose one could say that instead of commanding their new ship they found themselves taken off the bridge and politely confined to the saloon." From Robertson, Gordon D. (An address given in the 1970's entitled Company History 1909-1929 Auckland Institute and Museum Library. MS 1707. (88/116) p.4.

7   Laidlaw Leeds *Optimist* Dec 1918, p. 2.

8   Laidlaw Leeds *Optimist* Jan 1919, p.2.

9   Laidlaw Leeds *Optimist* July 1918, p.2.

10 Laidlaw Leeds *Optimist* August 1918, p.2.

11 In England, chain stores were called multiple shops. See July *Optimist* 1919 for facts and figures on overseas operations.

12 In November they were 425, by May 1920, there were 857.

13 *Optimist* November 1919, p.2. For three days in May 1920, the firm held its second branch management conference. To coordinate all their various activities this was now a necessity. The firm had grown immensely in size with branches as far away as Wellington at the bottom of the North Island.

14 From Robert's book of illustrations, no. 220.

15 Incident recounted by Robert in December *Optimist*, 1920, pp.9-10. Their flight was so new that it even made the pages of the *New Zealand Herald* in October. See November *Optimist* 1920, p.11.

16 See *Inside Story of Farmers* p.157.

17 In a letter to David Robertson, Robert noted that he was particularly impressed

with what Cadbury had done for his workers at Bournville. See *Optimist* Dec 1920, p.11.

[18] *Optimist* August 1921, p.3.

[19] Even with 29 branches the Hobson Street store alone contributed at least 70% of all these trading figures. In August, Hobson Street did £51,193 while the total business was £71,194. In September, Hobson Street. did £63,168 with total sales of £71,408 and October £51,444 compared with £72,079. Note all sales figures by month here are from Monthly Managers' Reports. All reports were month previous - so the September Managers' Report contains the trading figures of August etc.

[20] In a later speech, G.D. Robertson notes that "Many economies were achieved because of this but also some problems - our structure was dominated by this development for many years."(See speech p.6.)

Chapter 10

[1] *Optimist* April 1921, p.1.

[2] *Optimist* June 1921, p.1.

[3] Figures taken from 1921 and 1922 balance sheets.

[4] *Optimist* April 1921, pp.3-4.

[5] Within 9 months, nearly the entire £250,000 would be taken up. Robert's bonds offered a higher security than shares at a guaranteed rate of interest free of income tax. They were of varying amounts, £25, £50 and £100. Customers could select repayment dates either in 4 or 8 years time and most selected 4.

[6] *Optimist* June 1921, p.2.

[7] *Optimist* July 1921, pp.1-2. Lord Jellicoe, the Governor General also officially opened the new building on Thursday, July 16, 1921. Robert presented him with an illuminated address of welcome.

[8] *Optimist* August 1921, p.15.

[9] Taken from 'Review of Farmers Union Trading Co's Balance Sheet' by 'Cambist' of the *Truth*. The FUTC reprinted and circulated it circa March 1922.

[10] Before he writes down the value of stocks at the end of the current financial year they still tally £421,458 - a fall of only 63,000 on previous year. The fall needed to be more than double that.

[11] In *Inside Story* commented on p.171 that he mentioned this idea at a managers' meeting in Nov 1921.

[12] *Inside Story* says nearly 4000, 1926 catalogue p.22 says over 3800.

[13] The sales for the 1922-23 year were £1,153,000. This is an estimated sales figure taken from Robertson's thesis. The company did not publish sales figures for the years 1923-1925 inclusive. Robertson was able to reconstruct these from monthly sales records but some of the managers' reports for months in these years are now missing from archives, and so it was not possible to verify Robertson's estimations.

[14] From the *Radiator* April 1923, pp.8-9. The *Radiator* was a small booklet put out in place of *The Optimist* and issued amongst the staff.

[15] Speech given in Wellington. Recorded in *Optimist* November 1924, pp.1-4.

[16] Most months the trade out of Hobson Street was just over half the total done by the entire business.

[17] Letter to Directors dated September 12 1923.

[18] Robertson's estimation was £1,183,000 but Robert in the August 1924 *Optimist* quotes a past sales figure for the year of £1,168,000. Given the tenor of his discussion I am inclined to use this figure as the accurate one for the year.

[19] At the AGM Robert explained to the ordinary shareholders that as the company stood at the moment if they liquidated it then the A Preference shareholders (who also had prior claim to the distribution) would get about 10 shillings in the pound and the B and ordinary shareholders would get nothing. See *Herald* Wednesday, June 25, 1924.

[20] On June 24, there was a extraordinary general meeting and the A preference shareholders, who previously had the right to ask the Court to liquidate the company on their dividend becoming 30 days overdue, waived the right.

[21] *Optimist* August 1924, p.1.

Chapter 11

[1] Laidlaw Leeds Company Magazine The '*Optimist*' May 1914, pp.10-11.

[2] *Optimist* February 1925, pp.1-2.

[3] *Optimist* August 1925, p.2.

[4] Andrew Laidlaw. Died on August 14 1923, 33 hours old.

[5] Letter to the Editor *New Zealand Herald* June 22, 1927.

6 Excerpts from a letter written by Robert, presumably to *New Zealand Herald*, reproduced in *Inside Story of Farmers*, M. Kay, pp.188-189.

7 In 1931 the Farmers held a promotion, and part of the giveaway were Waiheke Island Palm Beach sections then valued at £50-60.

8 Robert's Letter to the Board dated May 2 1927.

9 Letter to the Board from Robert dated Oct 17 1927.

10 Letter to the Board by Robert dated August 18 1926.

11 Opened some time after the 1928 June AGM. Robert originally floated the idea at a Directors' meeting in 1926.

Chapter 12

1 *Optimist*, 21st Birthday Souvenir, p.4.

2 Speech recorded in *Auckland Chamber of Commerce Journal*, July 1 1930, pp.23-24.

3 Reproduced in part in *Inside Story*, pp.210-211. Posted to shareholders on March 26, 1930.

4 *Optimist* March 1931, pp.10-11.

5 Letter to the Board dated February 10 1931

6 *Optimist* April 1931, p.3.

7 Adapted from *Optimist* August 1931, pp.5-6.

8 *Optimist* February 1932, p.4.

9 *Optimist* Feb 1932, p.3.

10 For list of countries visited in order see *NZ Herald*, January 27 1932, 'Rapid World Tour.'

Chapter 13

1 *Optimist* March 1912, p.4.

2 Sections were worth between £40-£50.

3 *Optimist* February 1932, p.1.'

4 *Auckland Star* Wednesday, May 22, 1935.

5 Farmers *Store News* Friday, May 17, 1935, p.1.

6 *New Zealand Herald* September 18 1935.

[7]   Adapted from *New Zealand Herald*, September 18 1935.

[8]   Gilbert Hicks.

[9]   On July 20 1938, he was granted leave of absence to go abroad during 1939 on half-salary with an additional £1,150 for expenses.

Chapter 14

[1]   *Optimist* February 1932, p.1.

[2]   Directors' meeting Sept 16 1936. Robert had delayed commencing work on the new building on account of the possibility of an early war in Europe. In the end he decided to go ahead.

[3]   While in San Francisco he gave 11 messages, including one on a local radio station and another to the local Christian Businessmen's Association. In Los Angeles he spoke five times, and he also spoke at Austin, Texas. While in Chicago he spoke three times at the Moody Memorial Church and later also in New York.

Chapter 15

[1]   *Optimist* February 1925, p.1.

[2]   Excerpts from letter dated December 15 1939.

[3]   This tent was Robert's inspiration and was drawn up by Tom Haughey, the same architect who had designed Eastern Beach Camp for him. Haughey, with his wife, was in England at the same time as the Laidlaws on a working holiday.

[4]   The date of this French trip is difficult to place although there are many references to it actually occurring. Robert's previous letter to the Farmers suggests it was in the new year. This is consistent with Tom Haughey's own recollections. Robert's speech diary however suggests that when he went he was only absent for a few weeks as he is recorded at other places during this time. In January 1940, he had headed up to Scotland for a conference and spoke 16 times. In February and March he went to Northern Ireland for similar engagements and then back to Edgware before travelling to Oxford in April, and Purley in May. Dunkirk evacuations occurred between May 26 and June 2.

[5]   Tues, July 12, 1942.

Chapter 16

1   *Optimist*, 1916.
2   The *Treasury* Aug 1 1944, p.127.
3   Ironically all the ships that Robert had ever sailed on were at D-Day in various capacities.

Chapter 17

1   Robert Laidlaw, *Optimist*, January 1918, p.2.
2   Recounted in speech to NZIM, August 1953. Adapted from speech notes.
3   He was in Melbourne from March 22 to April 4, then over to Sydney from April 15 to 29 and, finally, up to Brisbane from May 6 to 21. Over the three months he gave 70 different addresses.
4   Robert spoke 86 times. Everywhere from camps at Hastings, Thames and the Winter Eastern Beach House Party, to his normal engagements at the Bible Training Institute and the radio broadcast services from Howe Street Assembly.
5   He spoke at Baptist, Presbyterian and Methodist churches in the South, and in October spoke in Manhattan and Kansas City Missouri to the Christian Business Men's Association (CBMA). In Los Angeles he spoke to another chapter of the CBMA and at the Fuller Seminary. In San Francisco, at the conclusion of the trip, he gave 18 addresses.
6   *New Zealand Herald* November 17 1952, entitled 'German and Japanese Competition - Aucklander's Fears.'

Chapter 18

1   Robert in an interview with *Management* magazine, April 1955, pp.21-27.
2   From Robert's speech notes entitled 'Management and its implication.' Delivered to the NZIM Management conference, August 1953, University of Auckland.
3   While this incident was often recounted with some hilarity, at later times the near tragedy of the situation was also realised. Robert presented the young man who had swum to the rock, David Liddle, with a gold watch for his part in getting everyone to safety.

4   The Methodist Trust Board who owned the building the Salvation Army were using as the Peoples Palace extended the terms of their lease so that the Salvation Army could extend the lease on the BTI, and allow everyone to move once the buildings in Henderson were finished in 1960. See Principal's page August 1959 *Reaper*.

Chapter 19

1   *Optimist* August 1913, p.1.

2   *Reaper* Dec 1961, pp.366-367. On December 4, 1961, he chaired the first BTI luncheon in the new buildings and the evening graduation service again at the Town Hall. Later, in December, he also attended the dedication service of the old BTI building in Queen Street on behalf of the Institute. The Salvation Army had remarkably renovated the building, and there was no one more suitable than Robert to be there as it embarked on its new mission.

3   Adapted from NZIM Notes, *Management*, June 1962, pp.61-63.

4   They were now seasoned travellers and intended to venture to Sydney, Tokyo, Hong Kong, Bangkok, New Delhi, Moscow, Athens, Jerusalem and Britain.

5   In 1966, he and Lillian left the country for another tour. Flying out in late September, they visited South America calling on missionaries and in 1967 he went to Sydney in May.

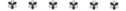